HERE IS ONE of the most notable literary achievements to emerge from the Arthurian legend, along with a very modern and popular treatment of the centuries-old tale. Both Tennyson's IDYLLS OF THE KING and Lerner and Loewe's CAMELOT, a musical based on T. H. White's THE ONCE AND FUTURE KING, tell the exciting story of King Arthur, Guinevere and the Knights of the Round Table—but in very different fashions.

ALLAN KNEE has taught English at the Bentley School and served as American and English literature editor for the Columbia Encyclopedia. His plays and stories have appeared in various magazines.

THE LAUREL-LEAF LIBRARY brings together under a single imprint outstanding works of fiction and non-fiction particularly suitable for young adult readers, both in and out of the classroom. This series is under the editorship of M. Jerry Weiss, Distinguished Professor of Communications, Jersey City State College; Charles F. Reasoner, Professor of Elementary Education, New York University; and Carolyn W. Carmichael, Associate Professor, Department of Communication Sciences, Kean College of New Jersey.

ALFRED LORD TENNYSON

IDYLLS of the KING
(*selections*)

CAMELOT

Book and Lyrics by ALAN JAY LERNER

Music by FREDERICK LOEWE

(Based on *The Once and Future King* by T. H. White)

EDITED, WITH AN INTRODUCTION AND NOTES, BY
ALLAN KNEE

Published by Dell Publishing Co., Inc.
1 Dag Hammarskjold Plaza, New York, N.Y. 10017
Copyright © 1967 by Dell Publishing Co., Inc.

Reprinted by permission of Random House, Inc.
Laurel-Leaf Library ® TM 766374, Dell Publishing Co., Inc.
All rights reserved
First printing—February, 1967
Second printing—February, 1968
Third printing—October, 1968
Fourth printing— November, 1968
Fifth printing—October, 1969
Sixth printing—December, 1970
Seventh printing—September, 1972
Eighth printing—July, 1973
Ninth printing—July, 1974
Tenth printing—February, 1975

Printed in the U.S.A.

Contents

Introduction

THE ARTHURIAN LEGEND has been one of the most popular and enduring legends of Western literature. Growing out of Celtic folklore and myth and embodying the medieval ideals of love, friendship and chivalry, the legend has been a source of inspiration to numerous writers since it was first fashioned into stories by European poets and minstrels in the eleventh and twelfth centuries. Malory, Chaucer, Spenser, Walter Scott, Matthew Arnold and Mark Twain are but a few of the great men of letters who found material in this famous cycle of stories. Two of the most notable achievements to emerge from this legend are Alfred Tennyson's *Idylls of the King,* a series of loosely connected stories united by a single theme, and T. H. White's *The Once and Future King,* the book upon which the musical play *Camelot* is based.

Who was King Arthur? When and where did he live? Was he real or legendary? Was he human or divine?

Even though the stories centering about King Arthur and his knights are so fused with mythology, folklore and mysticism, it is generally agreed that Arthur actually did exist. He was a sixth-century Welsh chieftain, a warrior of exceptional ability and ambition, a defender and supporter of Christianity. One of the great leaders of the Britons against their foes, Arthur beat back the foreign invaders and moved his own forces to the furthermost regions of the Continent, threatening to overtake all of Europe. His greatest accomplishment was the uniting of the Celtic kings and barons into a confederacy under his leadership.

Actual historical evidence to confirm these facts is slight. It is from the early Welsh chroniclers that we know the little we do about the historic Arthur. It is mainly his

heroic feats of arms about which they report, his twelve
great battles and his final bitter defeat.

What we actually find in the vast body of Arthurian
literature is a fusion of forces—that of British history and
the French courtly tradition, that of Christian dogma and
pagan mythology, that of Irish folklore and the folk tales
of the Welsh, Cornish and North Britons. The writers and
storytellers who found their inspiration in the Arthurian
legend blended the material in such a manner to satisfy the
tastes of their particular time and place.

Through the efforts of professional Breton storytellers,
conteurs, and the writing of Geoffrey of Monmouth, the
name and deeds of Arthur took root and spread throughout
Europe. Gradually he was transformed from an indigenous
English warrior into an international hero. The medieval
minstrels wandered from place to place, reciting their tales
of love and adventure and moving their audiences to tears
with their inventiveness and theatricality.

Geoffrey of Monmouth fused the oral tradition of the
storytellers with a pseudo history of Britain in writing a
chronicle of remarkable individuality and power. No other
single work succeeded in extending the fame of Arthur as
did Geoffrey's *Historiae regum Britanniae.* Written in
Latin (*c.* 1135), it was widely accepted as a definitive
history for nearly four centuries. Translations were made
into many languages, the best of which was done by the
French poet, Wace, in 1155, who toned down the barbaric
aspects of Geoffrey's chronicle and added much picturesque
detail. Wace also made one of the earliest references to
the famed Round Table, Arthur's circular conference
meeting board which prevented quarrels over rank and
ceremonial propriety.

Of the writers of Arthurian romance, two of the best
were Chrétien de Troyes and Wolfram von Eschenbach.
Chrétien began his literary career about 1170 and composed five long poems which created a sensation among the
aristocratic circles of Western Europe and added tre-
mendously to the vogue of the Arthurian cycle. Wolfram's
masterpiece, *Parzival* (*c.* 1210), a highly religious and
moral work, contains one of the most important renditions
of the story of the Holy Grail.

Perhaps the greatest Arthurian work of the Middle
Ages is Sir Thomas Malory's *Le Morte d'Arthur.* Printed
in 1485, it is the one work which is the principal source

for all later writings on the legend and the work which supplied the basis for most of Tennyson's *Idylls of the King*. While focusing on the story of the adulterous passion of Lancelot and Guinevere, Malory attempted to unify in a single work the various strains of Arthurian legend which had circulated through the Middle Ages. The book, filled with exaggerated feats of arms and brutal combats, remains one of the most popular pieces of chivalric literature.

The Arthurian legend continued through the centuries to serve as an inspiration to both writers and musicians. The poets Matthew Arnold, Algernon Swinburne, John Masefield and Edwin Arlington Robinson used the cycle to create some of their most enduring verse. Richard Wagner and Claude Debussy composed operas on the subject. Mark Twain's *A Connecticut Yankee in King Arthur's Court* drew a bleak, harsh picture of the Arthurian world strangled by the power of the Church and the authority of the ruling class. T. H. White's *The Once and Future King*, a book of great charm, gave us all the riches and pageantry of the legend, while depicting a very modern sort of Camelot, Arthur's capital city.

ii

No author probably had such high intentions in using the famous cycle of stories as did Alfred, Lord Tennyson, whose loosely connected idylls are bound together by the theme of the effect of evil and sin on virtue and hope. One of the most popular books of poetry ever printed in its time, the idylls were published over a number of years as separate pieces, the first complete ones appearing in 1859 and the final one in 1885. They were not written in sequence, and it was only later that they were collected into a single, unified work. There are twelve idylls in all, seven of which are printed here.

The Tennyson poems appealed widely to the Victorian mind, which was faced with the harsh realities of a growing materialism. Idealistic and remote, *The Idylls of the King* placed nineteenth-century earnestness in an atmosphere of twelfth-century pageantry and romance. The outer trappings of the poems are those of the Middle Ages, the heart and soul are that of Queen Victoria and Prince Albert.

Tennyson's Arthur represents the rational mind striving

to spread the cause of civilization in a world where chaos
and dissension breed in every corner. Arthur's real wars are
waged not so much against invaders and usurpers as
against lusts of the body and the weaknesses of the spirit.

The book begins on a note of hopefulness. Clear and
bright springlike sunshine covers a once ravaged land.
Arthur has rescued King Leodogran from his enemies
and has been rewarded with the King's daughter, the
beautiful Guinevere. In a series of battles he has driven
the heathens and warring factions from England and
united the remaining realms under his leadership. He has
set up the Order of the Round Table, a glorious, high-
thinking fellowship dedicated to the ideals of hardiness,
gentleness, faithfulness, generosity, love and obedience.
Its purpose is to right human wrongs, uphold purity and
truth, spread Christianity, and have each and every knight
seek and earn the love of one virtuous maiden only.

For a brief time the Round Table flourishes, remains
in close harmony, honors the dictums of the chivalric code,
promotes the cause of peace and brotherhood. There is
Lancelot, Arthur's greatest and most beloved warrior, the
darling of the court, the model of manhood; and Guinevere, the first lady of the land, the epitome of beauty and
queenliness; and Arthur, guileless and true, the prototype
of kingship. The knights are honest and courteous, the
tournaments cleanly and graciously fought, the atmosphere
full of color and ceremony, and the ideals cherished and
upheld.

But this bright state is not destined to endure. Confusion
and dissension slither in in various forms and disguises. The
glorious fellowship of the Round Table is slowly dispersed
and dissolved.

The seeds of the confusion and doubt are already evident
in the first idyll, "The Coming of Arthur." Here, it is
made evident that the King's reign is not without inner
strife. His throne sits like "ice on summer seas." There are
those within his kingdom who hate him, loathe his goodness and sweetness, call him baseborn and less than man.
We are introduced to the lighthearted Gawain and the
malicious Modred, Arthur's disloyal nephews. And we
meet the doom-forboding, eye-drooping Guinevere, with
whom the King feels he will have the power to make the
dead world live.

As we are carried from poem to poem, from situation

to situation, swept up by the beauty of Tennyson's verse, we witness, more and more, the corrosive effects of sin and guilt, of power misused, of love unfulfilled. We see sin breeding sin, corruption coupling with corruption.

In the early idylls "Gareth and Lynette," "The Marriage of Geraint," "Geraint and Enid," and "Balin and Balan," which are excluded from this edition, there are continual hints and suggestions of the terrible chaos that is to follow. Once we enter into the tale of "Merlin and Vivien," we no longer doubt what is in store for Arthur's kingdom. Merlin, the great pillar of Arthur's court, the presider over the King's youth and preparer of his royal destiny, the man who has been these many years Arthur's teacher and counselor, the builder of his ships and halls, allows himself to be seduced and destroyed by the Delilah-like Vivien, a woman who is the incarnation of evil.

The heartrending tale of "Lancelot and Elaine" carries the sense of sin and suffering much further. Elaine, the lily maid of Astolat, the embodiment of purity and virtue, dies of grief over her love for the remorseful, guilt-ridden Lancelot. The great knight, entering the twilight of his life, still possessed by his love for the Queen, is crippled with despair. He has been a brilliant warrior, a man who has continually tried to do the right thing, but has not had an easy time of it. He is more to be pitied than scorned. His happiness has been very brief. Fits of madness seize him. He wanders aimlessly, longing for release from a life in which love has proved to be more bondage and betrayal than joy and loyalty.

Tennyson's view of illicit love is in direct contrast to the courtly ideal of the Middle Ages. What is found in medieval romance is a frank glorification of adultery, a tribute to the lovers who can rise above the sanction of the Church and the claims of society. Tristram and Lancelot are examples of noble rebels, incarnations of the ideal of manhood, cursed and blessed with a forbidden passion that binds them to the wife of their liege.

In *The Idylls of the King* the emphasis is on the suffering, not the glorification. The violations of the bonds of marriage and friendship are not idealized but treated as the primary cause of the crumbling of the kingdom and the wrecking of the Order of the Round Table.

In the idyll of "The Holy Grail," the knights go recklessly off in search of the miraculous cup, forgetting their allegiance to the King and their importance to the realm. The quest, while full of high, holy intentions, should not have been undertaken by all. Not everyone is a Galahad, nor can claim his Christlike goodness and selflessness, attributes necessary for the attainment of the Grail. In swearing their vows the knights overreach themselves, and Arthur, knowing full well that few of his men will return from this impetuous quest, can only express his deepest regret.

The story of "Pelleas and Ettarre" describes the indoctrination of a strong but innocent knight into a world of deception and despair. Pelleas, having won the tournament prize for his beloved Ettarre, is cruelly rejected by her. It is from this heartless woman and from the frivolous Gawain that the devoted youth learns that all knights are not honorable and all ladies are not pure. His disillusionment is complete when Percivale tells him that not even Lancelot and Guinevere are what they seem. In "The Last Tournament" (excluded from this edition), Arthur's noble Round Table really no longer exists. The knights are lawless and fierce, and the sinful love of Tristram and Isolt is reduced to a petty exchange between two apprehensive lovers.

In "Guinevere" the pot of corruption has boiled over, the glorious ideals are smashed, the golden kingdom is no more. Camelot and all it has stood for is about to be destroyed. Guinevere and Lancelot, taking their final leave of each other, grasp at one last chance to right the wrong they have committed. Unfortunately, it is too late, and the lovers are exposed by the hateful Modred, who has stood in the shadows of the court waiting to enact his treachery. Arthur is forced to face the truth, a truth it would seem he has been desperately trying to avoid. He must now condemn the Queen and enter into a futile war with Lancelot. The King has no recourse but to do what he does. The sinful lovers have brought disgrace on themselves and on the court and all it has stood for.

Though it would be hard to defend Guinevere, it must be remembered that she of all women was loved by the two greatest men of her time. And if she did break the design and purpose of the Round Table, she suffered for her sin and closed out her days in nobleness and repentance. Guinevere was a passionate woman, forced to contain her emotions and spend most of her adult life hiding behind a disguise. Like most medieval maidens, she was obliged to marry by the will of her father. There was no period of courtship. She was simply sent to and joined with the King. But Guinevere was not bound by the marriage vows. She sought a love that was spontaneous and free. The King, far too remote and perfect for her, was not to her taste. It is in Lancelot that she finds the warmth and color of the earth, the fulfillment of her passion. Only later, after disaster has struck, does she perceive her error and see the greatness of Arthur, whose mercy sets her prostrate at his feet. She realizes that it was her own voluptuous pride, which sought all on this earth and nothing above, that brought ruin to everyone. When the King leaves her, he leaves her with the hope that, though they cannot come together again in this life, they can be united in the hereafter.

In the final idyll, "The Passing of Arthur," the cycle is completed. The earth has returned to the state it was in before Arthur was king. The land is ravaged and once again barren. What began in glorious, springlike sunshine, ends now in the dead of winter. Icy mists and frost cover all. We see Arthur afflicted with terrible despair. This war against the usurper, Modred, could not interest him less, for to win it means nothing. His golden kingdom has been laid to waste. Only at the very end does the King, dying of battle wounds, say that the suffering was not in vain, that it was God's way, and that a new order will arise and replace the old.

iii

When we leave *The Idylls of the King* and come to the court of Camelot as depicted in the Alan Jay Lerner–Frederick Loewe musical play, we enter a somewhat different Arthurian world. The cast of characters is primarily the same, but the atmosphere and tone are different. *Camelot* was designed as a musical entertainment, so the high moral earnestness which characterizes the Tennyson work gives way to fancifulness and fantasy. The world of *The Idylls of the King* is essentially tragic, lightened by a few brief moments of pleasure. *Camelot* is a happy world, filled with eccentrics, that becomes saddened through light-headedness and pranksterish tricks.

Arthur when we first met him in the *Idylls* was very

much a king, sternly bent on promoting his high purpose and in establishing his noble design. In *Camelot* when we first come upon him he is very much a boy, playacting and clever, an impatient youth, hiding in a tree, frightened over the prospects of being a husband and hardly ready to take on the burden of being a king. Waiting for the arrival of Guinevere, he clings to his childhood memories, more an avoider than a doer, more a gamester than a fearless warrior.

Guinevere, too, is quite different from the woman we encountered in the *Idylls*. Imaginative and naïve, she is still set in her medieval trappings, a young woman forced into a marriage that she has not picked for herself, a well-brought-up young lady reared on chivalric adventures and romantic fiction. But this Guinevere is also every inch a modern woman—headstrong and independent. She will not be bid and bargained for; to be wooed and won is what she wants. And if St. Genevieve cannot help her, she will seek elsewhere. In the *Idylls* Arthur had to engage in brave acts, rid the land of warring factions, prove his royal heritage, to win the Queen. But this Arthur has to do very little. Everything has been arranged for him. Guinevere, however, wants adventure. She wants to see a little blood spilled for her. She wants to be worshipped a while and competed for a bit. She is a modern girl, yes, but she desires some of those medieval formalities that set women apart as glorious creatures. What we find then is a young lady bridging two worlds—the old and the new—trying to get the best from both but having trouble getting satisfaction from either.

The royal marriage does take place as planned, the young couple finally being captivated by each other's charm. For the next few years the kingdom prospers, and Arthur and Guinevere grow into maturity. The King conducts his wars, leads his knights in battle, makes a few successful treaties, performs his duties as a husband. One day, however, he has a rude awakening. He realizes that being England's King and greatest warrior is not enough, for he has not achieved the real goals that Merlin sought for him and his country. He has not exerted strength and power in the cause of what is right and virtuous. His victorious battles have been no more than mass murders and plunderings. He has brought the world no closer to civilization. So like the Arthur of the *Idylls*, the Arthur of *Camelot* comes upon the idea of a *new* order of chivalry, an order in which might will be used for what is right, wrongs done in the past amended, lawlessness combated, the oppressed aided, the helpless protected. This new order, which is to be embodied in the idea of the Round Table, will have the best, youngest and most idealistic knights, "angels of armor, sword-swinging apostles battling to snuff out evil."

For a time this glorious ideal flourishes, but, as in the *Idylls,* soon the seeds of destruction take root. Lancelot, the great French knight, comes to Camelot. Joyless and iron-willed, he enters upon the scene bringing nothing but trouble. Professing uncanny purity and an ardent passion for Arthur's noble cause, he is disliked immediately by everyone. This is not the darling of the court that we knew in the *Idylls.* This Lancelot is an outcast, a fellow who might mean well but who is hard to admire. Guinevere herself finds him pompous and arrogant. She sees in him almost the very same features, the icy fervor and cold perfection that the Guinevere of the *Idylls* saw and disliked in Arthur. But the Queen is not long put off by the fanatical, unyielding knight. Upon seeing him perform a miracle, she falls hopelessly in love with him and so initiates the downfall of the King's noble civilization.

Arthur is much more aware of his fate in *Camelot* than he was in the *Idylls.* He immediately recognizes the love of his Queen for his favorite knight, but he fights his jealousy. And Guinevere, too, is much kinder. She remains faithful to the King, stifling her romance with Lancelot as best she can. One of the most touching scenes in the play is the duet between Arthur and Guinevere in which the pair, seeking to lighten their royal burden, indulge in the pleasures of simple folk.

Into the uncertain atmosphere at the court slips Modred, the King's serpentine nephew. Modred is still very much the incarnation of evil, a little livelier and precious perhaps, but nonetheless the begetter of discord and the debunker of virtue. It is not the earth the meek inherit, according to him, but the dirt. He exposes the lovers, tells the King that his whole existence has been a failure and that, to survive in this world, one needs ruthlessness not compassion.

Forced to publicly acknowledge the truth, Arthur is driven to the regrettable war. But where we witnessed in the *Idylls* a harsh and bitter ending, Arthur deserted by his men, fighting a losing, futile battle amid icy, death-like mists, drained of all faith, in *Camelot* we witness an ending that is more melancholic than fierce, more forlorn than devastating. The knights have again been dispersed and Arthur once more stands alone amid the ruins of his civilization, but he has not lost faith. He still believes in virtue. He is still capable of forgiving his Queen and her lover. The sadness and resentment in his heart have not defeated him. In the final scene he sends one of his new young recruits home from the battlefront to grow up in peace, instructing the boy to tell the story of the glory of Camelot.

In both works—Tennyson's moving allegory and Lerner and Loewe's lively musical play—we see a great idea brought to ruin. The King's high purpose is undermined by the very people in whom he puts his trust. Arthur's court, representing the most noble ideals in the world, flourishes only for a short time. In the end it is the frailties of human nature which win out. It is not hard to understand why this cycle of stories has excited the imagination of writers and audiences for nearly a thousand years.

—ALLAN KNEE

IDYLLS of the KING

by ALFRED, LORD TENNYSON

The Coming of Arthur

LEODOGRAN, the King of Cameliard,
Had one fair daughter, and none other child;
And she was fairest of all flesh on earth,
Guinevere, and in her his one delight.

For many a petty king ere Arthur came
Ruled in this isle, and ever waging war
Each upon other, wasted all the land;
And still from time to time the heathen host
Swarm'd overseas, and harried what was left.
And so there grew great tracts of wilderness,   10
Wherein the beast was ever more and more,
But man was less and less, till Arthur came.
For first Aurelius lived and fought and died,
And after him King Uther fought and died,
But either fail'd to make the kingdom one.
And after these King Arthur for a space,
And thro' the puissance of his Table Round,
Drew all their petty princedoms under him,
Their king and head, and made a realm, and reign'd.

And thus the land of Cameliard was waste,   20
Thick with wet woods, and many a beast therein,
And none or few to scare or chase the beast;
So that wild dog, and wolf and boar and bear
Came night and day, and rooted in the fields,
And wallow'd in the gardens of the King.
And ever and anon the wolf would steal
The children and devour, but now and then,
Her own brood lost or dead, lent her fierce teat
To human sucklings; and the children, housed
In her foul den, there at their meat would growl,   30
And mock their foster-mother on four feet,
Till, straighten'd, they grew up to wolf-like men,

Notes on the Idylls begin on p. 248.

Worse than the wolves. And King Leodogran
Groan'd for the Roman legions here again,
And Caesar's eagle: then his brother king,
Urien, assail'd him: last a heathen horde,
Reddening the sun with smoke and earth with blood,
And on the spike that split the mother's heart
Spitting the child, brake on him, till, amazed,
He knew not whither he should turn for aid.   40

But—for he heard of Arthur newly crown'd,
Tho' not without an uproar made by those
Who cried, "He is not Uther's son"—the King
Sent to him, saying, "Arise, and help us thou!
For here between the man and beast we die."

And Arthur yet had done no deed of arms,
But heard the call, and came: and Guinevere
Stood by the castle walls to watch him pass;
But since he neither wore on helm or shield
The golden symbol of his kinglihood,   50
But rode a simple knight among his knights,
And many of these in richer arms than he,
She saw him not, or mark'd not, if she saw,
One among many, tho' his face was bare.
But Arthur, looking downward as he past,
Felt the light of her eyes into his life
Smite on the sudden, yet rode on, and pitch'd
His tents beside the forest. Then he drave
The heathen; after, slew the beast, and fell'd
The forest, letting in the sun, and made   60
Broad pathways for the hunter and the knight
And so return'd.

                    For while he linger'd there,
A doubt that ever smoulder'd in the hearts
Of those great Lords and Barons of his realm
Flash'd forth and into war: for most of these,
Colleaguing with a score of petty kings,
Made head against him, crying, "Who is he
That he should rule us? who hath proven him
King Uther's son? for lo! we look at him,
And find nor face nor bearing, limbs nor voice,   70
Are like to those of Uther whom we knew.
This is the son of Gorloïs, not the King;

This is the son of Anton, not the King."

And Arthur, passing thence to battle, felt
Travail, and throes and agonies of the life,
Desiring to be join'd with Guinevere;
And thinking as he rode, "Her father said
That there between the man and beast they die.
Shall I not lift her from this land of beasts
Up to my throne, and side by side with me?   80
What happiness to reign a lonely king,
Vext—O ye stars that shudder over me,
O earth that soundest hollow under me,
Vext with waste dreams? for saving I be join'd
To her that is the fairest under heaven,
I seem as nothing in the mighty world,
And cannot will my will, nor work my work
Wholly, nor make myself in mine own realm
Victor and lord. But were I join'd with her,
Then might we live together as one life,   90
And reigning with one will in everything
Have power on this dark land to lighten it,
And power on this dead world to make it live."
Thereafter—as he speaks who tells the tale—
When Arthur reach'd a field-of-battle bright
With pitch'd pavilions of his foe, the world
Was all so clear about him, that he saw
The smallest rock far on the faintest hill,
And even in high day the morning star.
So when the King had set his banner broad,   100
At once from either side, with trumpet-blast,
And shouts, and clarions shrilling unto blood,
The long-lanced *battle* let their horses run.
And now the Barons and the kings prevail'd,
And now the King, as here and there that war
Went swaying; but the *Powers* who walk the world
Made lightnings and great thunders over him,
And dazed all eyes, till Arthur by main might,
And mightier of his hands with every blow,
And leading all his knighthood *threw* the kings   110
Carádos, Urien, Cradlemont of Wales,
Claudias, and Clariance of Northumberland,
The King Brandagoras of Latangor,
With Anguisant of Erin, Morganore,
And Lot of Orkney. Then, before a voice

As dreadful as the shout of one who sees
To one who sins, and deems himself alone
And all the world asleep, they swerved and brake
Flying, and Arthur call'd to stay the brands
That hack'd among the flyers, "Ho! they yield!"   120
So like a painted battle the war stood
Silenced, the living quiet as the dead,
And in the heart of Arthur joy was lord.
He laugh'd upon his warrior whom he loved
And honour'd most. "Thou dost not doubt me King,
So well thine arm hath wrought for me to-day."
"Sir and my liege," he cried, "the fire of God
Descends upon thee in the battle-field:
I know thee for my King!" Whereat the two,
For each had warded either in the fight,   130
Sware on the field of death a deathless love.
And Arthur said, "Man's word is God in man:
Let chance what will, I trust thee to the death."

Then quickly from the foughten field he sent
Ulfius, and Brastias, and Bedivere,
His new-made knights, to King Leodogran,
Saying, "If I in aught have served thee well,
Give me thy daughter Guinevere to wife."

Whom when he heard, Leodogran in heart
Debating—"How should I that am a king,   140
However much he holp me at my need,
Give my one daughter saving to a king,
And a king's son?"—lifted his voice, and call'd
A hoary man, his chamberlain, to whom
He trusted all things, and of him required
His counsel: "Knowest thou aught of Arthur's birth?"

Then spake the hoary chamberlain and said,
"Sir King, there be but two old men that know:
And each is twice as old as I; and one
Is Merlin, the wise man that ever served   150
King Uther thro' his magic art; and one
Is Merlin's master (so they call him) Bleys,
Who taught him magic; but the scholar ran
Before the master, and so far, that Bleys
Laid magic by, and sat him down, and wrote
All things and whatsoever Merlin did

In one great annal-book, where after-years
Will learn the secret of our Arthur's birth."

To whom the King Leodogran replied,
"O friend, had I been holpen half as well   160
By this King Arthur as by thee to-day,
Then beast and man had had their share of me:
But summon here before us yet once more
Ulfius, and Brastias, and Bedivere."

Then, when they came before him, the King said,
"I have seen the cuckoo chased by lesser fowl,
And reason in the chase: but wherefore now
Do these your lords stir up the heat of war,
Some calling Arthur born of Gorloïs,
Others of Anton? Tell me, ye yourselves,   170
Hold ye this Arthur for King Uther's son?"

And Ulfius and Brastias answer'd, "Ay."
Then Bedivere, the first of all his knights
Knighted by Arthur at his crowning, spake—
For bold in heart and act and word was he,
Whenever slander breathed against the King—

"Sir, there be many rumours on this head:
For there be those who hate him in their hearts,
Call him baseborn, and since his ways are sweet,
And theirs are bestial, hold him less than man: 180
And there be those who deem him more than man,
And dream he dropt from heaven: but my belief
In all this matter—so ye care to learn—
Sir, for ye know that in King Uther's time
The prince and warrior Gorloïs, he that held
Tintagil castle by the Cornish sea,
Was wedded with a winsome wife, Ygerne:
And daughters had she borne him,—one whereof,
Lot's wife, the Queen of Orkney, Bellicent,
Hath ever like a loyal sister cleaved   190
To Arthur,—but a son she had not borne.
And Uther cast upon her eyes of love:
But she, a stainless wife to Gorloïs,
So loathed the bright dishonour of his love,
That Gorloïs and King Uther went to war:
And overthrown was Gorloïs and slain.

Then Uther in his wrath and heat besieged
Ygerne within Tintagil, where her men,
Seeing the mighty swarm about their walls,
Left her and fled, and Uther enter'd in,   200
And there was none to call to but himself.
So, compass'd by the power of the King,
Enforced she was to wed him in her tears,
And with a shameful swiftness: afterward,
Not many moons, King Uther died himself,
Moaning and wailing for an heir to rule
After him, lest the realm should go to wrack.
And that same night, the night of the new year,
By reason of the bitterness and grief
That vext his mother, all before his time   210
Was Arthur born, and all as soon as born
Deliver'd at a secret postern-gate
To Merlin, to be holden far apart
Until his hour should come; because the lords
Of that fierce day were as the lords of this,
Wild beasts, and surely would have torn the child
Piecemeal among them, had they known; for each
But sought to rule for his own self and hand,
And many hated Uther for the sake
Of Gorloïs. Wherefore Merlin took the child,   220
And gave him to Sir Anton, an old knight
And ancient friend of Uther; and his wife
Nursed the young prince, and rear'd him with her own;
And no man knew. And ever since the lords
Have foughten like wild beasts among themselves,
So that the realm has gone to wrack: but now,
This year, when Merlin (for his hour had come)
Brought Arthur forth, and set him in the hall,
Proclaiming, 'Here is Uther's heir your king,'
A hundred voices cried, 'Away with him!   230
No king of ours! a son of Gorloïs he,
Or else the child of Anton, and no king,
Or else baseborn.' Yet Merlin thro' his craft,
And while the people clamour'd for a king,
Had Arthur crown'd; but after, the great lords
Banded, and so brake out in open war.''

    Then while the King debated with himself
If Arthur were the child of shamefulness,
Or born the son of Gorloïs, after death,

Or Uther's son, and born before his time,   240
Or whether there were truth in anything
Said by these three, there came to Cameliard,
With Gawain and young Modred, her two sons,
Lot's wife, the Queen of Orkney, Bellicent;
Whom as he could, not as he would, the King
Made feast for, saying, as they sat at meat,

"A doubtful throne is ice on summer seas.
Ye come from Arthur's court. Victor his men
Report him! Yea, but ye—think ye this king—
So many those that hate him, and so strong,   250
So few his knights, however brave they be—
Hath body enow to hold his foemen down?"

"O King," she cried, "and I will tell thee: few,
Few, but all brave, all of one mind with him;
For I was near him when the savage yells
Of Uther's peerage died, and Arthur sat
Crown'd on the daïs, and his warriors cried,
'Be thou the king, and we will work thy will
Who love thee.' Then the King in low deep tones,
And simple words of great authority,   260
Bound them by so strait vows to his own self,
That when they rose, knighted from kneeling, some
Were pale as at the passing of a ghost,
Some flush'd, and others dazed, as one who wakes
Half-blinded at the coming of a light.

"But when he spake and cheer'd his Table Round
With large, divine, and comfortable words,
Beyond my tongue to tell thee—I beheld
From eye to eye thro' all their Order flash
A momentary likeness of the King: 270
And ere it left their faces, thro' the cross
And those around it and the Crucified,
Down from the casement over Arthur, smote
Flame-colour, vert and azure, in three rays,
One falling upon each of three fair queens,
Who stood in silence near his throne, the friends
Of Arthur, gazing on him, tall, with bright
Sweet faces, who will help him at his need.

"And there I saw Mage Merlin, whose vast wit

And hundred winters are but as the hands   280
Of loyal vassals toiling for their liege.

"And near him stood the Lady of the Lake,
Who knows a subtler magic than his own—
Clothed in white samite, mystic, wonderful.
She gave the King his huge cross-hilted sword,
Whereby to drive the heathen out: a mist
Of incense curl'd about her, and her face
Wellnigh was hidden in the minster gloom;
But there was heard among the holy hymns
A voice as of the waters, for she dwells   290
Down in a deep; calm, whatsoever storms
May shake the world, and when the surface rolls,
Hath power to walk the waters like our Lord.

"There likewise I beheld Excalibur
Before him at his crowning borne, the sword
That rose from out the bosom of the lake,
And Arthur row'd across and took it—rich
With jewels, elfin Urim, on the hilt,
Bewildering heart and eye—the blade so bright
That men are blinded by it—on one side,   300
Graven in the oldest tongue of all this world,
'Take me,' but turn the blade and ye shall see,
And written in the speech ye speak yourself,
'Cast me away!' And sad was Arthur's face
Taking it, but old Merlin counsell'd him,
'Take thou and strike! the time to cast away
Is yet far-off.' So this great brand the King
Took, and by this will beat his foemen down."

Thereat Leodogran rejoiced, but thought
To sift his doubtings to the last, and ask'd,   310
Fixing full eyes of question on her face,
"The swallow and the swift are near akin,
But thou art closer to this noble prince,
Being his own dear sister;" and she said,
"Daughter of Gorloïs and Ygerne am I;"
"And therefore Arthur's sister?" ask'd the King.
She answer'd, "These be secret things," and sign'd
To those two sons to pass, and let them be.
And Gawain went, and breaking into song
Sprang out, and follow'd by his flying hair   320

Ran like a colt, and leapt at all he saw:
But Modred laid his ear beside the doors,
And there half-heard; the same that afterward
Struck for the throne, and striking found his doom.

And then the Queen made answer, "What know I?
For dark my mother was in eyes and hair,
And dark in hair and eyes am I; and dark
Was Gorloïs, yea and dark was Uther too,
Wellnigh to blackness; but this King is fair
Beyond the race of Britons and of men.   330
Moreover, always in my mind I hear
A cry from out the dawning of my life,
A mother weeping, and I hear her say,
'O that ye had some brother, pretty one,
To guard thee on the rough ways of the world.' "

"Ay," said the King, "and hear ye such a cry?
But when did Arthur chance upon thee first?"

"O King!" she cried, "and I will tell thee true:
He found me first when yet a little maid:
Beaten I had been for a little fault   340
Whereof I was not guilty; and out I ran
And flung myself down on a bank of heath,
And hated this fair world and all therein,
And wept, and wish'd that I were dead; and he—
I know not whether of himself he came,
Or brought by Merlin, who, they say, can walk
Unseen at pleasure—he was at my side,
And spake sweet words, and comforted my heart,
And dried my tears, being a child with me.
And many a time he came, and evermore   350
As I grew greater grew with me; and sad
At times he seem'd, and sad with him was I,
Stern too at times, and then I loved him not,
But sweet again, and then I loved him well.
And now of late I see him less and less,
But those first days had golden hours for me,
For then I surely thought he would be king.

"But let me tell thee now another tale:
For Bleys, our Merlin's master, as they say,
Died but of late, and sent his cry to me,   360

To hear him speak before he left his life.
Shrunk like a fairy changeling lay the mage;
And when I enter'd told me that himself
And Merlin ever served about the King,
Uther, before he died; and on the night
When Uther in Tintagil past away
Moaning and wailing for an heir, the two
Left the still King, and passing forth to breathe,
Then from the castle gateway by the chasm
Descending thro' the dismal night—a night   370
In which the bounds of heaven and earth were lost—
Beheld, so high upon the dreary deeps
It seem'd in heaven, a ship, the shape thereof
A dragon wing'd, and all from stem to stern
Bright with a shining people on the decks,
And gone as soon as seen. And then the two
Dropt to the cove, and watch'd the great sea fall,
Wave after wave, each mightier than the last,
Till last, a ninth one, gathering half the deep
And full of voices, slowly rose and plunged   380
Roaring, and all the wave was in a flame:
And down the wave and in the flame was borne
A naked babe, and rode to Merlin's feet,
Who stoopt and caught the babe, and cried, 'The King!
Here is an heir for Uther!' And the fringe
Of that great breaker, sweeping up the strand,
Lash'd at the wizard as he spake the word,
And all at once all round him rose in fire,
So that the child and he were clothed in fire.
And presently thereafter follow'd calm,   390
Free sky and stars: 'And this same child,' he said,
'Is he who reigns; nor could I part in peace
Till this were told,' And saying this the seer
Went thro' the strait and dreadful pass of death,
Not ever to be question'd any more
Save on the further side; but when I met
Merlin, and ask'd him if these things were truth—
The shining dragon and the naked child
Descending in the glory of the seas—
He laugh'd as is his wont, and answer'd me   400
In riddling triplets of old time, and said:

" 'Rain, rain, and sun! a rainbow in the sky!
A young man will be wiser by and by;

An old man's wit may wander ere he die.

   " 'Rain, rain, and sun! a rainbow on the lea!
And truth is this to me, and that to thee;
And truth or clothed or naked let it be.

   " 'Rain, sun, and rain! and the free blossom blows.
Sun, rain, and sun! and where is he who knows?
From the great deep to the great deep he goes.'   410

   "So Merlin riddling anger'd me; but thou
Fear not to give this King thine only child,
Guinevere: so great bards of him will sing
Hereafter; and dark sayings from of old
Ranging and ringing thro' the minds of men,
And echo'd by old folk beside their fires
For comfort after their wage-work is done,
Speak of the King; and Merlin in our time
Hath spoken also, not in jest, and sworn
Tho' men may wound him that he will not die,   420
But pass, again to come; and then or now
Utterly smite the heathen underfoot,
Till these and all men hail him for their king."

   She spake and King Leodogran rejoiced,
But musing, "Shall I answer yea or nay?"
Doubted, and drowsed, nodded and slept, and saw,
Dreaming, a slope of land that ever grew,
Field after field, up to a height, the peak
Haze-hidden, and thereon a phantom king,
Now looming, and now lost; and on the slope   430
The sword rose, the hind fell, the herd was driven,
Fire glimpsed; and all the land from roof and rick,
In drifts of smoke before a rolling wind,
Stream'd to the peak, and mingled with the haze
And made it thicker; while the phantom king
Sent out at times a voice; and here or there
Stood one who pointed toward the voice, the rest
Slew on and burnt, crying, "No king of ours,
No son of Uther, and no king of ours;"
Till with a wink his dream was changed, the haze   440
Descended, and the solid earth became
As nothing, but the King stood out in heaven,

Crown'd. And Leodogran awoke, and sent
Ulfius, and Brastias and Bedivere,
Back to the court of Arthur answering yea.

Then Arthur charged his warrior whom he loved
And honour'd most, Sir Lancelot, to ride forth
And bring the Queen;—and watch'd him from the gates:
And Lancelot past away among the flowers,
(For then was latter April) and return'd   450
Among the flowers, in May, with Guinevere.
To whom arrived, by Dubric the high saint,
Chief of the church in Britain, and before
The stateliest of her altar-shrines, the King
That morn was married, while in stainless white,
The fair beginners of a nobler time,
And glorying in their vows and him, his knights
Stood round him, and rejoicing in his joy.
Far shone the fields of May thro' open door,
The sacred altar blossom'd white with May,   460
The Sun of May descended on their King,
They gazed on all earth's beauty in their Queen,
Roll'd incense, and there past along the hymns
A voice as of the waters, while the two
Sware at the shrine of Christ a deathless love:
And Arthur said, "Behold, thy doom is mine.
Let chance what will, I love thee to the death!"
To whom the Queen replied with drooping eyes,
"King and my lord, I love thee to the death!"
And holy Dubric spread his hands and spake,   470
"Reign ye, and live and love, and make the world
Other, and may thy Queen be one with thee,
And all this Order of thy Table Round
Fulfil the boundless purpose of their King!"

So Dubric said; but when they left the shrine
Great Lords from Rome before the portal stood,
In scornful stillness gazing as they past;
Then while they paced a city all on fire
With sun and cloth of gold, the trumpets blew,
And Arthur's knighthood sang before the King:—   480

"Blow trumpet, for the world is white with May;
Blow trumpet, the long night hath roll'd away!
Blow thro' the living world—'Let the King reign.'

"Shall Rome or Heathen rule in Arthur's realm?
Flash brand and lance, fall battleaxe upon helm,
Fall battleaxe, and flash brand! Let the King reign.

"Strike for the King and live! his knights have heard
That God hath told the King a secret word.
Fall battleaxe, and flash brand! Let the King reign.

"Blow trumpet! he will lift us from the dust.   490
Blow trumpet! live the strength and die the lust!
Clang battleaxe, and clash brand! Let the King reign.

"Strike for the King and die! and if thou diest,
The King is King, and ever wills the highest.
Clang battleaxe, and clash brand! Let the King reign.

"Blow, for our Sun is mighty in his May!
Blow, for our Sun is mightier day by day!
Clang battleaxe, and clash brand! Let the King reign.

"The King will follow Christ, and we the King
In whom high God hath breathed a secret thing.   500
Fall battleaxe, and flash brand! Let the King reign."

So sang the knighthood, moving to their hall.
There at the banquet those great Lords from Rome,
The slowly-fading mistress of the world,
Strode in, and claim'd their tribute as of yore.
But Arthur spake, "Behold, for these have sworn
To wage my wars, and worship me their King;
The old order changeth, yielding place to new;
And we that fight for our fair father Christ,
Seeing that ye be grown too weak and old   510
To drive the heathen from your Roman wall,
No tribute will we pay:" so those great lords
Drew back in wrath, and Arthur strove with Rome.

And Arthur and his knighthood for a space
Were all one will, and thro' that strength the King
Drew in the petty princedoms under him,
Fought, and in twelve great battles overcame
The heathen hordes, and made a realm and reign'd.

Merlin and Vivien

A STORM was coming, but the winds were still,
And in the wild woods of Broceliande,
Before an oak, so hollow, huge and old
It look'd a tower of ivied masonwork,
At Merlin's feet the wily Vivien lay.

For he that always bare in bitter grudge
The slights of Arthur and his Table, Mark
The Cornish King, had heard a wandering voice,
A minstrel of Caerleon by strong storm
Blown into shelter at Tintagil, say   10
That out of naked knightlike purity
Sir Lancelot worshipt no unmarried girl
But the great Queen herself, fought in her name,
Sware by her—vows like theirs, that high in heaven
Love most, but neither marry, nor are given
In marriage, angels of our Lord's report.

He ceased, and then—for Vivien sweetly said
(She sat beside the banquet nearest Mark),
"And is the fair example follow'd, Sir,
In Arthur's household?"—answer'd innocently: 20

"Ay, by some few—ay, truly—youths that hold
It more beseems the perfect virgin knight
To worship woman as true wife beyond
All hopes of gaining, than as maiden girl.
They placed their pride in Lancelot and the Queen.
So passionate for an utter purity
Beyond the limit of their bond, are these,
For Arthur bound them not to singleness.
Brave hearts and clean! and yet—God guide them—
        young."

Then Mark was half in heart to hurl his cup   30
Straight at the speaker, but forbore: he rose
To leave the hall, and, Vivien following him,
Turn'd to her: "Here are snakes within the grass;
And you methinks, O Vivien, save ye fear
The monkish manhood, and the mask of pure
Worn by this court, can stir them till they sting."

And Vivien answer'd, smiling scornfully,
"Why fear? because that foster'd at *thy* court
I savour of thy—virtues? fear them? no.
As Love, if Love be perfect, casts out fear,   40
So Hate, if Hate be perfect, casts out fear.
My father died in battle against the King,
My mother on his corpse in open field;
She bore me there, for born from death was I
Among the dead and sown upon the wind—
And then on thee! and shown the truth betimes,
That old true filth, and bottom of the well,
Where Truth is hidden. Gracious lessons thine
And maxims of the mud! 'This Arthur pure!
Great Nature thro' the flesh herself hath made   50
Gives him the lie! There is no being pure,
My cherub; saith not Holy Writ the same?'—
If I were Arthur, I would have thy blood.
Thy blessing, stainless King! I bring thee back,
When I have ferreted out their burrowings,
The hearts of all this Order in mine hand—
Ay—so that fate and craft and folly close,
Perchance, one curl of Arthur's golden beard.
To me this narrow grizzled fork of thine
Is cleaner-fashion'd—Well, I loved thee first,   60
That warps the wit."

              Loud laugh'd the graceless Mark.
But Vivien, into Camelot stealing, lodged
Low in the city, and on a festal day
When Guinevere was crossing the great hall
Cast herself down, knelt to the Queen, and wail'd.

"Why kneel ye there? What evil have ye wrought?
Rise!" and the damsel bidden rise arose
And stood with folded hands and downward eyes
Of glancing corner, and all meekly said,

"None wrought, but suffer'd much, an orphan maid!   70
My father died in battle for thy King,
My mother on his corpse—in open field,
The sad sea-sounding wastes of Lyonnesse—
Poor wretch—no friend!—and now by Mark the King
For that small charm of feature mine, pursued—
If any such be mine—I fly to thee.
Save, save me thou—Woman of women—thine
The wreath of beauty, thine the crown of power,
Be thine the balm of pity, O Heaven's own white
Earth-angel, stainless bride of stainless King—   80
Help, for he follows! take me to thyself!
O yield me shelter for mine innocency
Among thy maidens!"

                    Here her slow sweet eyes
Fear-tremulous, but humbly hopeful, rose
Fixt on her hearer's, while the Queen who stood
All glittering like May sunshine on May leaves
In green and gold, and plumed with green replied,
"Peace, child! of overpraise and overblame
We choose the last. Our noble Arthur, him
Ye scarce can overpraise, will hear and know.   90
Nay—we believe all evil of thy Mark—
Well, we shall test thee farther; but this hour
We ride a-hawking with Sir Lancelot.
He hath given us a fair falcon which he train'd;
We go to prove it. Bide ye here the while."

    She past; and Vivien murmur'd after, "Go!
I bide the while." Then thro' the portal-arch
Peering askance, and muttering broken-wise,
As one that labours with an evil dream,
Beheld the Queen and Lancelot get to horse.   100

    "Is that the Lancelot? goodly—ay, but gaunt:
Courteous—amends for gauntness—takes her hand—
That glance of theirs, but for the street, had been
A clinging kiss—how hand lingers in hand!
Let go at last!—they ride away—to hawk
For waterfowl. Royaller game is mine.
For such a supersensual sensual bond
As that gray cricket chirpt of at our hearth—
Touch flax with flame—a glance will serve—the liars!

Ah little rat that borest in the dyke   110
Thy hole by night to let the boundless deep
Down upon far-off cities while they dance—
Or dream—of thee they dream'd not—nor of me
These—ay, but each of either: ride, and dream
The mortal dream that never yet was mine—
Ride, ride and dream until ye wake—to me!
Then, narrow court and lubber King, farewell!
For Lancelot will be gracious to the rat,
And our wise Queen, if knowing that I know,
Will hate, loathe, fear—but honour me the more."   120

Yet while they rode together down the plain,
Their talk was all of training, terms of art,
Diet and seeling, jesses, leash and lure.
"She is too noble" he said "to check at pies,
Nor will she rake: there is no baseness in her."
Here when the Queen demanded as by chance
"Know ye the stranger woman?" "Let her be,"
Said Lancelot and unhooded casting off
The goodly falcon free; she tower'd; her bells,
Tone under tone, shrill'd; and they lifted up   130
Their eager faces, wondering at the strength,
Boldness and royal knighthood of the bird
Who pounced her quarry and slew it. Many a time
As once—of old—among the flowers—they rode.

But Vivien half-forgotten of the Queen
Among her damsels broidering sat, heard, watch'd
And whisper'd: thro' the peaceful court she crept
And whisper'd: then as Arthur in the highest
Leaven'd the world, so Vivien in the lowest,
Arriving at a time of golden rest,   140
And sowing one ill hint from ear to ear,
While all the heathen lay at Arthur's feet,
And no quest came, but all was joust and play,
Leaven'd his hall. They heard and let her be.

Thereafter as an enemy that has left
Death in the living waters, and withdrawn,
The wily Vivien stole from Arthur's court.

She hated all the knights, and heard in thought
Their lavish comment when her name was named.

For once, when Arthur walking all alone,   150
Vext at a rumour issued from herself
Of some corruption crept among his knights,
Had met her, Vivien, being greeted fair,
Would fain have wrought upon his cloudy mood
With reverent eyes mock-loyal, shaken voice,
And flutter'd adoration, and at last
With dark sweet hints of some who prized him more
Than who should prize him most; at which the King
Had gazed upon her blankly and gone by:
But one had watch'd, and had not held his peace: 160
It made the laughter of an afternoon
That Vivien should attempt the blameless King.
And after that, she set herself to gain
Him, the most famous man of all those times,
Merlin, who knew the range of all their arts,
Had built the King his havens, ships, and halls,
Was also Bard, and knew the starry heavens;
The people call'd him Wizard; whom at first
She play'd about with slight and sprightly talk,
And vivid smiles, and faintly-venom'd points   170
Of slander, glancing here and grazing there;
And yielding to his kindlier moods, the Seer
Would watch her at her petulance, and play,
Ev'n when they seem'd unloveable, and laugh
As those that watch a kitten; thus he grew
Tolerant of what he half disdain'd, and she,
Perceiving that she was but half disdain'd,
Began to break her sports with graver fits,
Turn red or pale, would often when they met
Sigh fully, or all-silent gaze upon him   180
With such a fixt devotion, that the old man,
Tho' doubtful, felt the flattery, and at times
Would flatter his own wish in age for love,
And half believe her true: for thus at times
He waver'd; but that other clung to him,
Fixt in her will, and so the seasons went.

    Then fell on Merlin a great melancholy:
He walk'd with dreams and darkness, and he found
A doom that ever poised itself to fall,
An ever-moaning battle in the mist,   190
World-war of dying flesh against the life,
Death in all life and lying in all love,

The meanest having power upon the highest,
And the high purpose broken by the worm.

So leaving Arthur's court he gain'd the beach;
There found a little boat, and stept into it;
And Vivien follow'd, but he mark'd her not.
She took the helm and he the sail; the boat
Drave with a sudden wind across the deeps,
And touching Breton sands, they disembark'd.　　200
And then she follow'd Merlin all the way,
Ev'n to the wild woods of Broceliande.
For Merlin once had told her of a charm,
The which if any wrought on anyone
With woven paces and with waving arms,
The man so wrought on ever seem'd to lie
Closed in the four walls of a hollow tower,
From which was no escape for evermore;
And none could find that man for evermore,
Nor could he see but him who wrought the charm　　210
Coming and going, and he lay as dead
And lost to life and use and name and fame.
And Vivien ever sought to work the charm
Upon the great Enchanter of the Time,
As fancying that her glory would be great
According to his greatness whom she quench'd.

There lay she all her length and kiss'd his feet,
As if in deepest reverence and in love.
A twist of gold was round her hair; a robe
Of samite without price, that more exprest　　220
Than hid her, clung about her lissome limbs,
In colour like the satin-shining palm
On sallows in the windy gleams of March:
And while she kiss'd them, crying "Trample me,
Dear feet, that I have follow'd thro' the world,
And I will pay you worship; tread me down
And I will kiss you for it;" he was mute:
So dark a forethought roll'd about his brain,
As on a dull day in an Ocean cave
The blind wave feeling round his long sea-hall　　230
In silence: wherefore, when she lifted up
A face of sad appeal, and spake and said,
"O Merlin, do ye love me?" and again,
"O Merlin, do ye love me?" and once more,

"Great Master, do ye love me?" he was mute.
And lissome Vivien, holding by his heel,
Writhed toward him, slided up his knee and sat,
Behind his ankle twined her hollow feet
Together, curved an arm about his neck,
Clung like a snake; and letting her left hand   240
Droop from his mighty shoulder, as a leaf,
Made with her right a comb of pearl to part
The lists of such a beard as youth gone out
Had left in ashes: then he spoke and said,
Not looking at her, "Who are wise in love
Love most, say least," and Vivien answer'd quick,
"I saw the little elf-god eyeless once
In Arthur's arras hall at Camelot:
But neither eyes nor tongue—O stupid child!
Yet you are wise who say it; let me think   250
Silence is wisdom: I am silent then,
And ask no kiss;" then adding all at once,
"And lo, I clothe myself with wisdom," drew
The vast and shaggy mantle of his beard
Across her neck and bosom to her knee,
And call'd herself a gilded summer fly
Caught in a great old tyrant spider's web,
Who meant to eat her up in that wild wood
Without one word. So Vivien call'd herself,
But rather seem'd a lovely baleful star   260
Veil'd in gray vapour; till he sadly smiled:
"To what request for what strange boon," he said,
"Are these your pretty tricks and fooleries,
O Vivien, the preamble? yet my thanks,
For these have broken up my melancholy."

And Vivien answer'd smiling saucily,
"What, O my Master, have ye found your voice?
I bid the stranger welcome. Thanks at last!
But yesterday you never open'd lip,
Except indeed to drink: no cup had we: 270
In mine own lady palms I cull'd the spring
That gather'd trickling dropwise from the cleft,
And made a pretty cup of both my hands
And offer'd you it kneeling: then you drank
And knew no more, nor gave me one poor word;
O no more thanks than might a goat have given
With no more sign of reverence than a beard.

And when we halted at that other well,
And I was faint to swooning, and you lay
Foot-gilt with all the blossom-dust of those   280
Deep meadows we had traversed, did you know
That Vivien bathed your feet before her own?
And yet no thanks: and all thro' this wild wood
And all this morning when I fondled you:
Boon, ay, there was a boon, one not so strange—
How had I wrong'd you? surely ye are wise,
But such a silence is more wise than kind."

And Merlin lock'd his hand in hers and said:
"O did ye never lie upon the shore,
And watch the curl'd white of the coming wave   290
Glass'd in the slippery sand before it breaks?
Ev'n such a wave, but not so pleasurable,
Dark in the glass of some presageful mood,
Had I for three days seen, ready to fall.
And then I rose and fled from Arthur's court
To break the mood. You follow'd me unask'd;
And when I look'd, and saw you following still,
My mind involved yourself the nearest thing
In that mind-mist: for shall I tell you truth?
You seem'd that wave about to break upon me   300
And sweep me from my hold upon the world,
My use and name and fame. Your pardon, child.
Your pretty sports have brighten'd all again.
And ask your boon, for boon I owe you thrice,
Once for wrong done you by confusion, next
For thanks it seems till now neglected, last
For these your dainty gambols: wherefore ask;
And take this boon so strange and not so strange."

And Vivien answer'd smiling mournfully:
"O not so strange as my long asking it,   310
Not yet so strange as you yourself are strange,
Nor half so strange as that dark mood of yours.
I ever fear'd ye were not wholly mine;
And see, yourself have own'd ye did me wrong.
The people call you prophet: let it be:
But not of those that can expound themselves.
Take Vivien for expounder; she will call
That three-days-long presageful gloom of yours
No presage, but the same mistrustful mood

That makes you seem less noble than yourself,   320
Whenever I have ask'd this very boon,
Now ask'd again: for see you not, dear love,
That such a mood as that, which lately gloom'd
Your fancy when ye saw me following you,
Must make me fear still more you are not mine,
Must make me yearn still more to prove you mine,
And make me wish still more to learn this charm
Of woven paces and of waving hands,
As proof of trust. O Merlin, teach it me.
The charm so taught will charm us both to rest.   330
For, grant me some slight power upon your fate,
I, feeling that you felt me worthy trust,
Should rest and let you rest, knowing you mine.
And therefore be as great as ye are named,
Not muffled round with selfish reticence.
How hard you look and how denyingly!
O, if you think this wickedness in me,
That I should prove it on you unawares,
That makes me passing wrathful; then our bond
Had best be loosed for ever: but think or not,   340
By Heaven that hears I tell you the clean truth,
As clean as blood of babes, as white as milk:
O Merlin, may this earth, if ever I,
If these unwitty wandering wits of mine,
Ev'n in the jumbled rubbish of a dream,
Have tript on such conjectural treachery—
May this hard earth cleave to the Nadir hell
Down, down, and close again, and nip me flat,
If I be such a traitress. Yield my boon,
Till which I scarce can yield you all I am;   350
And grant my re-reiterated wish,
The great proof of your love: because I think,
However wise, ye hardly know me yet."

     And Merlin loosed his hand from hers and said,
"I never was less wise, however wise,
Too curious Vivien, tho' you talk of trust,
Than when I told you first of such a charm.
Yea, if ye talk of trust I tell you this,
Too much I trusted when I told you that,
And stirr'd this vice in you which ruin'd man   360
Thro' woman the first hour; for howsoe'er
In children a great curiousness be well,

Who have to learn themselves and all the world,
In you, that are no child, for still I find
Your face is practised when I spell the lines,
I call it,—well, I will not call it vice:
But since you name yourself the summer fly,
I well could wish a cobweb for the gnat,
That settles, beaten back, and beaten back
Settles, till one could yield for weariness: 370
But since I will not yield to give you power
Upon my life and use and name and fame,
Why will ye never ask some other boon?
Yea, by God's rood, I trusted you too much."

And Vivien, like the tenderest-hearted maid
That ever bided tryst at village stile,
Made answer, either eyelid wet with tears:
"Nay, Master, be not wrathful with your maid;
Caress her: let her feel herself forgiven
Who feels no heart to ask another boon.   380
I think ye hardly know the tender rhyme
Of 'trust me not at all or all in all.'
I heard the great Sir Lancelot sing it once,
And it shall answer for me. Listen to it.

      " 'In Love, if Love be Love, if Love be ours,
Faith and unfaith can ne'er be equal powers:
Unfaith in aught is want of faith in all.

      " 'It is the little rift within the lute,
That by and by will make the music mute,
And ever widening slowly silence all.   390

      " 'The little rift within the lover's lute
Or little pitted speck in garner'd fruit,
That rotting inward slowly moulders all.

      " 'It is not worth the keeping: let it go:
But shall it? answer, darling, answer, no.
And trust me not at all or all in all.'

      "O Master, do ye love my tender rhyme?"

And Merlin look'd and half believed her true,
So tender was her voice, so fair her face,

So sweetly gleam'd her eyes behind her tears   400
Like sunlight on the plain behind a shower:
And yet he answer'd half indignantly:

   "Far other was the song that once I heard
By this huge oak, sung nearly where we sit:
For here we met, some ten or twelve of us,
To chase a creature that was current then
In these wild woods, the hart with golden horns.
It was the time when first the question rose
About the founding of a Table Round,
That was to be, for love of God and men   410
And noble deeds, the flower of all the world.
And each incited each to noble deeds.
And while we waited, one, the youngest of us,
We could not keep him silent, out he flash'd,
And into such a song, such fire for fame,
Such trumpet-blowings in it, coming down
To such a stern and iron-clashing close,
That when he stopt we long'd to hurl together,
And should have done it; but the beauteous beast
Scared by the noise upstarted at our feet,   420
And like a silver shadow slipt away
Thro' the dim land; and all day long we rode
Thro' the dim land against a rushing wind,
That glorious roundel echoing in our ears,
And chased the flashes of his golden horns
Until they vanish'd by the fairy well
That laughs at iron—as our warriors did—
Where children cast their pins and nails, and cry,
'Laugh, little well!' but touch it with a sword,
It buzzes fiercely round the point; and there   430
We lost him: such a noble song was that.
But, Vivien, when you sang me that sweet rhyme,
I felt as tho' you knew this cursed charm,
Were proving it on me, and that I lay
And felt them slowly ebbing, name and fame."

   And Vivien answer'd smiling mournfully:
"O mine have ebb'd away for evermore,
And all thro' following you to this wild wood,
Because I saw you sad, to comfort you.
Lo now, what hearts have men! they never mount   440

As high as woman in her selfless mood.
And touching fame, howe'er ye scorn my song,
Take one verse more—the lady speaks it—this:

" 'My name, once mine, now thine, is closelier mine,
For fame, could fame be mine, that fame were thine,
And shame, could shame be thine, that shame were
      mine.
So trust me not at all or all in all.'

"Says she not well? and there is more—this rhyme
Is like the fair pearl-necklace of the Queen,
That burst in dancing, and the pearls were spilt;   450
Some lost, some stolen, some as relics kept.
But nevermore the same two sister pearls
Ran down the silken thread to kiss each other
On her white neck—so is it with this rhyme:
It lives dispersedly in many hands,
And every minstrel sings it differently;
Yet is there one true line, the pearl of pearls:
'Man dreams of Fame while woman wakes to love.'
Yea! Love, tho' Love were of the grossest, carves
A portion from the solid present, eats   460
And uses, careless of the rest; but Fame,
The Fame that follows death is nothing to us;
And what is Fame in life but half-disfame,
And counterchanged with darkness? ye yourself
Know well that Envy calls you Devil's son,
And since ye seem the Master of all Art,
They fain would make you Master of all vice."

And Merlin lock'd his hand in hers and said,
"I once was looking for a magic weed,
And found a fair young squire who sat alone,   470
Had carved himself a knightly shield of wood,
And then was painting on it fancied arms,
Azure, an Eagle rising or, the Sun
In dexter chief; the scroll, 'I follow fame.'
And speaking not, but leaning over him,
I took his brush and blotted out the bird,
And made a Gardener putting in a graff,
With this for motto, 'Rather use than fame.'
You should have seen him blush; but afterwards
He made a stalwart knight. O Vivien,   480

For you, methinks you think you love me well;
For me, I love you somewhat; rest: and Love
Should have some rest and pleasure in himself
Not ever be too curious for a boon,
Too prurient for a proof against the grain
Of him ye say ye love: but Fame with men,
Being but ampler means to serve mankind,
Should have small rest or pleasure in herself,
But work as vassal to the larger love,
That dwarfs the petty love of one to one.   490
Use gave me Fame at first, and Fame again
Increasing gave me use. Lo, there my boon!
What other? for men sought to prove me vile,
Because I fain had given them greater wits:
And then did Envy call me Devil's son:
The sick weak beast seeking to help herself
By striking at her better, miss'd, and brought
Her own claw back, and wounded her own heart.
Sweet were the days when I was all unknown,
But when my name was lifted up, the storm   500
Brake on the mountain and I cared not for it.
Right well know I that Fame is half-disfame,
Yet needs must work my work. That other fame,
To one at least, who hath not children, vague,
The cackle of the unborn about the grave,
I cared not for it: a single misty star,
Which is the second in a line of stars
That seem a sword beneath a belt of three,
I never gazed upon it but I dreamt
Of some vast charm concluded in that star   510
To make fame nothing. Wherefore, if I fear,
Giving you power upon me thro' this charm,
That you might play me falsely, having power,
However well ye think ye love me now
(As sons of kings loving in pupilage
Have turn'd to tyrants when they came to power)
I rather dread the loss of use than fame;
If you—and not so much from wickedness,
As some wild turn of anger, or a mood
Of overstrain'd affection, it may be,   520
To keep me all to your own self,—or else
A sudden spurt of woman's jealousy,—
Should try this charm on whom ye say ye love."

And Vivien answer'd smiling as in wrath:
"Have I not sworn? I am not trusted. Good!
Well, hide it, hide it; I shall find it out;
And being found take heed of Vivien.
A woman and not trusted, doubtless I
Might feel some sudden turn of anger born
Of your misfaith; and your fine epithet   530
Is accurate too, for this full love of mine
Without the full heart back may merit well
Your term of overstrain'd. So used as I,
My daily wonder is, I love at all.
And as to woman's jealousy, O why not?
O to what end, except a jealous one,
And one to make me jealous if I love,
Was this fair charm invented by yourself?
I well believe that all about this world
Ye cage a buxom captive here and there,   540
Closed in the four walls of a hollow tower
From which is no escape for evermore."

Then the great Master merrily answer'd her:
"Full many a love in loving youth was mine;
I needed then no charm to keep them mine
But youth and love; and that full heart of yours
Whereof ye prattle, may now assure you mine;
So live uncharm'd. For those who wrought it first,
The wrist is parted from the hand that waved,
The feet unmortised from their ankle-bones   550
Who paced it, ages back: but will ye hear
The legend as in guerdon for your rhyme?

"There lived a king in the most Eastern East,
Less old than I, yet older, for my blood
Hath earnest in it of far springs to be.
A tawny pirate anchor'd in his port,
Whose bark had plunder'd twenty nameless isles;
And passing one, at the high peep of dawn,
He saw two cities in a thousand boats
All fighting for a woman on the sea.   560
And pushing his black craft among them all,
He lightly scatter'd theirs and brought her off,
With loss of half his people arrow-slain;
A maid so smooth, so white, so wonderful,
They said a light came from her when she moved:

And since the pirate would not yield her up,
The King impaled him for his piracy;
Then made her Queen: but those isle-nurtured eyes
Waged such unwilling tho' successful war
On all the youth, they sicken'd; councils thinn'd,   570
And armies waned, for magnet-like she drew
The rustiest iron of old fighters' hearts;
And beasts themselves would worship; camels knelt
Unbidden, and the brutes of mountain back
That carry kings in castles, bow'd black knees
Of homage, ringing with their serpent hands,
To make her smile, her golden ankle-bells.
What wonder, being jealous, that he sent
His horns of proclamation out thro' all
The hundred under-kingdoms that he sway'd   580
To find a wizard who might teach the King
Some charm, which being wrought upon the Queen
Might keep her all his own: to such a one
He promised more than ever king has given,
A league of mountain full of golden mines,
A province with a hundred miles of coast,
A palace and a princess, all for him:
But on all those who tried and fail'd, the King
Pronounced a dismal sentence, meaning by it
To keep the list low and pretenders back.   590
Or like a king, not to be trifled with—
Their heads should moulder on the city gates.
And many tried and fail'd, because the charm
Of nature in her overbore their own:
And many a wizard brow bleach'd on the walls:
And many weeks a troop of carrion crows
Hung like a cloud above the gateway towers."

And Vivien breaking in upon him, said:
"I sit and gather honey; yet, methinks,
Thy tongue has tript a little: ask thyself.   600
The lady never made *unwilling* war
With those fine eyes: she had her pleasure in it,
And made her good man jealous with good cause.
And lived there neither dame nor damsel then
Wroth at a lover's loss? were all as tame,
I mean, as noble, as their Queen was fair?
Not one to flirt a venom at her eyes,
Or pinch a murderous dust into her drink,

Or make her paler with a poison'd rose?
Well, those were not our days: but did they find 610
A wizard? Tell me, was he like to thee?"

She ceased, and made her lithe arm round his neck
Tighten, and then drew back, and let her eyes
Speak for her, glowing on him, like a bride's
On her new lord, her own, the first of men.

He answer'd laughing, "Nay, not like to me.
At last they found—his foragers for charms—
A little glassy-headed hairless man,
Who lived alone in a great wild on grass;
Read but one book, and ever reading grew 620
So grated down and filed away with thought,
So lean his eyes were monstrous; while the skin
Clung but to crate and basket, ribs and spine.
And since he kept his mind on one sole aim,
Nor ever touch'd fierce wine, nor tasted flesh,
Nor own'd a sensual wish, to him the wall
That sunders ghosts and shadow-casting men
Became a crystal, and he saw them thro' it,
And heard their voices talk behind the wall,
And learnt their elemental secrets, powers 630
And forces; often o'er the sun's bright eye
Drew the vast eyelid of an inky cloud,
And lash'd it at the base with slanting storm;
Or in the noon of mist and driving rain,
When the lake whiten'd and the pinewood roar'd,
And the cairn'd mountain was a shadow, sunn'd
The world to peace again: here was the man.
And so by force they dragg'd him to the King.
And then he taught the King to charm the Queen
In such-wise, that no man could see her more, 640
Nor saw she save the King, who wrought the charm,
Coming and going, and she lay as dead,
And lost all use of life: but when the King
Made proffer of the league of golden mines,
The province with a hundred miles of coast,
The palace and the princess, that old man
Went back to his old wild, and lived on grass,
And vanish'd, and his book came down to me."

And Vivien answer'd smiling saucily:

"Ye have the book: the charm is written in it: 650
Good: take my counsel: let me know it at once:
For keep it like a puzzle chest in chest,
With each chest lock'd and padlock'd thirty-fold,
And whelm all this beneath as vast a mound
As after furious battle turfs the slain
On some wild down above the windy deep,
I yet should strike upon a sudden means
To dig, pick, open, find and read the charm:
Then, if I tried it, who should blame me then?"

And smiling as a master smiles at one   660
That is not of his school, nor any school
But that where blind and naked Ignorance
Delivers brawling judgments, unashamed,
On all things all day long, he answer'd her:

"Thou read the book, my pretty Vivien!
O ay, it is but twenty pages long,
But every page having an ample marge,
And every marge enclosing in the midst
A square of text that looks a little blot,
The text no larger than the limbs of fleas;   670
And every square of text an awful charm,
Writ in a language that has long gone by.
So long, that mountains have arisen since
With cities on their flanks—thou read the book!
And every margin scribbled, crost, and cramm'd
With comment, densest condensation, hard
To mind and eye; but the long sleepless nights
Of my long life have made it easy to me.
And none can read the text, not even I;
And none can read the comment but myself;   680
And in the comment did I find the charm.
O, the results are simple; a mere child
Might use it to the harm of anyone,
And never could undo it: ask no more:
For tho' you should not prove it upon me,
But keep that oath ye sware, ye might, perchance,
Assay it on some one of the Table Round,
And all because ye dream they babble of you."

And Vivien, frowning in true anger, said:
"What dare the full-fed liars say of me?   690

They ride abroad redressing human wrongs!
They sit with knife in meat and wine in horn!
They bound to holy vows of chastity!
Were I not woman, I could tell a tale.
But you are man, you well can understand
The shame that cannot be explain'd for shame.
Not one of all the drove should touch me: swine!"

Then answer'd Merlin careless of her words:
"You breathe but accusation vast and vague,
Spleen-born, I think, and proofless. If ye know,   700
Set up the charge ye know, to stand or fall!"

And Vivien answer'd frowning wrathfully:
"O ay, what say ye to Sir Valence, him
Whose kinsman left him watcher o'er his wife
And two fair babes, and went to distant lands;
Was one year gone, and on returning found
Not two but three? there lay the reckling, one
But one hour old! What said the happy sire?
A seven-months' babe had been a truer gift.
Those twelve sweet moons confused his fatherhood."   710

Then answer'd Merlin, "Nay, I know the tale.
Sir Valence wedded with an outland dame:
Some cause had kept him sunder'd from his wife:
One child they had: it lived with her: she died:
His kinsman travelling on his own affair
Was charged by Valence to bring home the child.
He brought, not found it therefore: take the truth."

"O ay," said Vivien, "overtrue a tale.
What say ye then to sweet Sir Sagramore,
That ardent man? 'to pluck the flower in season,'   720
So says the song, 'I trow it is no treason.'
O Master, shall we call him overquick
To crop his own sweet rose before the hour?"

And Merlin answer'd, "Overquick art thou
To catch a loathly plume fall'n from the wing
Of that foul bird of rapine whose whole prey
Is man's good name: he never wrong'd his bride.
I know the tale. An angry gust of wind
Puff'd out his torch among the myriad-room'd

And many-corridor'd complexities   730
Of Arthur's palace: then he found a door,
And darkling felt the sculptured ornament
That wreathen round it made it seem his own;
And wearied out made for the couch and slept,
A stainless man beside a stainless maid;
And either slept, nor knew of other there;
Till the high dawn piercing the royal rose
In Arthur's casement glimmer'd chastely down,
Blushing upon them blushing, and at once
He rose without a word and parted from her: 740
But when the thing was blazed about the court,
The brute world howling forced them into bonds,
And as it chanced they are happy, being pure."

    "O ay," said Vivien, "that were likely too.
What say ye then to fair Sir Percivale
And of the horrid foulness that he wrought,
The saintly youth, the spotless lamb of Christ,
Or some black wether of St. Satan's fold.
What, in the precincts of the chapel-yard,
Among the knightly brasses of the graves,   750
And by the cold Hic Jacets of the dead!"

    And Merlin answer'd careless of her charge,
"A sober man is Percivale and pure;
But once in life was fluster'd with new wine,
Then paced for coolness in the chapel-yard;
Where one of Satan's shepherdesses caught
And meant to stamp him with her master's mark;
And that he sinn'd is not believable;
For, look upon his face!—but if he sinn'd,
The sin that practice burns into the blood,   760
And not the one dark hour which brings remorse,
Will brand us, after, of whose fold we be:
Or else were he, the holy king, whose hymns
Are chanted in the minster, worse than all.
But is your spleen froth'd out, or have ye more?"

    And Vivien answer'd frowning yet in wrath:
"O ay; what say ye to Sir Lancelot, friend
Traitor or true? that commerce with the Queen,
I ask you, is it clamour'd by the child,
Or whisper'd in the corner? do ye know it?"   770

To which he answer'd sadly, "Yea, I know it.
Sir Lancelot went ambassador, at first,
To fetch her, and she watch'd him from her walls.
A rumour runs, she took him for the King,
So fixt her fancy on him: let them be.
But have ye no one word of loyal praise
For Arthur, blameless King and stainless man?"

She answer'd with a low and chuckling laugh:
"Man! is he man at all, who knows and winks?
Sees what his fair bride is and does, and winks?   780
By which the good King means to blind himself,
And blinds himself and all the Table Round
To all the foulness that they work. Myself
Could call him (were it not for womanhood)
The pretty, popular name such manhood earns,
Could call him the main cause of all their crime;
Yea, were he not crown'd King, coward, and fool."

Then Merlin to his own heart, loathing, said:
"O true and tender! O my liege and King!
O selfless man and stainless gentleman,   790
Who wouldst against thine own eye-witness fain
Have all men true and leal, all women pure;
How, in the mouths of base interpreters,
From over-fineness not intelligible
To things with every sense as false and foul
As the poach'd filth that floods the middle street,
Is thy white blamelessness accounted blame!"

But Vivien, deeming Merlin overborne
By instance, recommenced, and let her tongue
Rage like a fire among the noblest names,   800
Polluting, and imputing her whole self,
Defaming and defacing, till she left
Not even Lancelot brave, nor Galahad clean.

Her words had issue other than she will'd.
He dragg'd his eyebrow bushes down, and made
A snowy penthouse for his hollow eyes,
And mutter'd in himself, "Tell *her* the charm!
So, if she had it, would she rail on me
To snare the next, and if she have it not

So will she rail. What did the wanton say?   810
'Not mount as high;' we scarce can sink as low:
For men at most differ as Heaven and earth,
But women, worst and best, as Heaven and Hell.
I know the Table Round, my friends of old;
All brave, and many generous, and some chaste.
She cloaks the scar of some repulse with lies;
I well believe she tempted them and fail'd,
Being so bitter: for fine plots may fail,
Tho' harlots paint their talk as well as face
With colours of the heart that are not theirs.   820
I will not let her know: nine tithes of times
Face-flatterer and backbiter are the same.
And they, sweet soul, that most impute a crime
Are pronest to it, and impute themselves,
Wanting the mental range; or low desire
Not to feel lowest makes them level all;
Yea, they would pare the mountain to the plain,
To leave an equal baseness; and in this
Are harlots like the crowd, that if they find
Some stain or blemish in a name of note,   830
Not grieving that their greatest are so small,
Inflate themselves with some insane delight,
And judge all nature from her feet of clay,
Without the will to lift their eyes, and see
Her godlike head crown'd with spiritual fire,
And touching other worlds. I am weary of her."

    He spoke in words part heard, in whispers part,
Half-suffocated in the hoary fell
And many-winter'd fleece of throat and chin.
But Vivien, gathering somewhat of his mood,   840
And hearing "harlot" mutter'd twice or thrice,
Leapt from her session on his lap, and stood
Stiff as a viper frozen; loathsome sight,
How from the rosy lips of life and love,
Flash'd the bare-grinning skeleton of death!
White was her cheek; sharp breaths of anger puff'd
Her fairy nostril out; her hand half-clench'd
Went faltering sideways downward to her belt,
And feeling; had she found a dagger there
(For in a wink the false love turns to hate)   850
She would have stabb'd him; but she found it not:
His eye was calm, and suddenly she took

To bitter weeping like a beaten child,
A long, long weeping, not consolable.
Then her false voice made way, broken with sobs:

"O crueller than was ever told in tale,
Or sung in song! O vainly lavish'd love!
O cruel, there was nothing wild or strange,
Or seeming shameful—for what shame in love,
So love be true, and not as yours is—nothing   860
Poor Vivien had not done to win his trust
Who call'd her what he call'd her—all her crime,
All—all—the wish to prove him wholly hers."

She mused a little, and then clapt her hands
Together with a wailing shriek, and said:
"Stabb'd through the heart's affections to the heart!
Seethed like the kid in its own mother's milk!
Kill'd with a word worse than a life of blows!
I thought that he was gentle, being great:
O God, that I had loved a smaller man!   870
I should have found in him a greater heart.
O, I, that flattering my true passion, saw
The knights, the court, the King, dark in your light,
Who loved to make men darker than they are,
Because of that high pleasure which I had
To seat you sole upon my pedestal
Of worship—I am answer'd, and henceforth
The course of life that seem'd so flowery to me
With you for guide and master, only you,
Becomes the sea-cliff pathway broken short,   880
And ending in a ruin—nothing left,
But into some low cave to crawl, and there,
If the wolf spare me, weep my life away,
Kill'd with inutterable unkindliness."

She paused, she turn'd away, she hung her head,
The snake of gold slid from her hair, the braid
Slipt and uncoil'd itself, she wept afresh,
And the dark wood grew darker toward the storm
In silence, while his anger slowly died
Within him, till he let his wisdom go   890
For ease of heart, and half believed her true:
Call'd her to shelter in the hollow oak,
"Come from the storm," and having no reply,

Gazed at the heaving shoulder, and the face
Hand-hidden, as for utmost grief or shame;
Then thrice essay'd, by tenderest-touching terms,
To sleek her ruffled peace of mind, in vain.
At last she let herself be conquer'd by him,
And as the cageling newly flown returns,
The seeming-injured simple-hearted thing   900
Came to her old perch back, and settled there.
There while she sat, half-falling from his knees,
Half-nestled at his heart, and since he saw
The slow tear creep from her closed eyelid yet,
About her, more in kindness than in love,
The gentle wizard cast a shielding arm.
But she dislink'd herself at once and rose,
Her arms upon her breast across, and stood,
A virtuous gentlewoman deeply wrong'd,
Upright and flush'd before him: then she said: 910

    "There must be now no passages of love
Betwixt us twain henceforward evermore;
Since, if I be what I am grossly call'd,
What should be granted which your own gross heart
Would reckon worth the taking? I will go.
In truth, but one thing now—better have died
Thrice than have ask'd it once—could make me stay—
That proof of trust—so often ask'd in vain!
How justly, after that vile term of yours,
I find with grief! I might believe you then,   920
Who knows? once more. Lo! what was once to me
Mere matter of the fancy, now hath grown
The vast necessity of heart and life.
Farewell; think gently of me, for I fear
My fate or folly, passing gayer youth
For one so old, must be to love thee still.
But ere I leave thee let me swear once more
That if I schemed against thy peace in this,
May yon just heaven, that darkens o'er me, send
One flash, that, missing all things else, may make   930
My scheming brain a cinder, if I lie."

    Scarce had she ceased, when out of heaven a bolt
(For now the storm was close above them) struck,
Furrowing a giant oak, and javelining
With darted spikes and splinters of the wood

The dark earth round. He raised his eyes and saw
The tree that shone white-listed thro' the gloom.
But Vivien, fearing heaven had heard her oath,
And dazzled by the livid-flickering fork,
And deafen'd with the stammering cracks and claps   940
That follow'd, flying back and crying out,
"O Merlin, tho' you do not love me, save,
Yet save me!" clung to him and hugg'd him close;
And call'd him dear protector in her fright,
Nor yet forgot her practice in her fright,
But wrought upon his mood and hugg'd him close.
The pale blood of the wizard at her touch
Took gayer colours, like an opal warm'd.
She blamed herself for telling hearsay tales:
She shook from fear, and for her fault she wept   950
Of petulancy; she call'd him lord and liege,
Her seer, her bard, her silver star of eve,
Her God, her Merlin, the one passionate love
Of her whole life; and ever overhead
Bellow'd the tempest, and the rotten branch
Snapt in the rushing of the river-rain
Above them; and in change of glare and gloom
Her eyes and neck glittering went and came;
Till now the storm, its burst of passion spent,
Moaning and calling out of other lands,   960
Had left the ravaged woodland yet once more
To peace; and what should not have been had been,
For Merlin, overtalk'd and overworn,
Had yielded, told her all the charm, and slept.

Then, in one moment, she put forth the charm
Of woven paces and of waving hands,
And in the hollow oak he lay as dead,
And lost to life and use and name and fame.

Then crying "I have made his glory mine,"
And shrieking out "O fool!" the harlot leapt   970
Adown the forest, and the thicket closed
Behind her, and the forest echo'd "fool."

Lancelot and Elaine

ELAINE the fair, Elaine the loveable,
Elaine, the lily maid of Astolat,
High in her chamber up a tower to the east
Guarded the sacred shield of Lancelot;
Which first she placed where morning's earliest ray
Might strike it, and awake her with the gleam;
Then fearing rust or soilure fashion'd for it
A case of silk, and braided thereupon
All the devices blazon'd on the shield
In their own tinct, and added, of her wit,   10
A border fantasy of branch and flower,
And yellow-throated nestling in the nest.
Nor rested thus content, but day by day,
Leaving her household and good father, climb'd
That eastern tower, and entering barr'd her door,
Stript off the case, and read the naked shield,
Now guess'd a hidden meaning in his arms,
Now made a pretty history to herself
Of every dint a sword had beaten in it,
And every scratch a lance had made upon it,   20
Conjecturing when and where: this cut is fresh;
That ten years back; this dealt him at Caerlyle;
That at Caerleon; this at Camelot:
And ah God's mercy, what a stroke was there!
And here a thrust that might have kill'd, but God
Broke the strong lance, and roll'd his enemy down,
And saved him: so she lived in fantasy.

How came the lily maid by that good shield
Of Lancelot, she that knew not ev'n his name?
He left it with her, when he rode to tilt   30
For the great diamond in the diamond jousts,
Which Arthur had ordain'd, and by that name
Had named them, since a diamond was the prize.

For Arthur, long before they crown'd him King,
Roving the trackless realms of Lyonnesse,
Had found a glen, gray boulder and black tarn.
A horror lived about the tarn, and clave
Like its own mists to all the mountain side:
For here two brothers, one a king, had met
And fought together; but their names were lost: 40
And each had slain his brother at a blow;
And down they fell and made the glen abhorr'd:
And there they lay till all their bones were bleach'd,
And lichen'd into colour with the crags:
And he, that once was king, had on a crown
Of diamonds, one in front, and four aside.
And Arthur came, and labouring up the pass,
All in a misty moonshine, unawares
Had trodden that crown'd skeleton, and the skull
Brake from the nape, and from the skull the crown   50
Roll'd into light, and turning on its rims
Fled like a glittering rivulet to the tarn:
And down the shingly scaur he plunged, and caught,
And set it on his head, and in his heart
Heard murmurs, "Lo, thou likewise shalt be King."

  Thereafter, when a King, he had the gems
Pluck'd from the crown, and show'd them to his
    knights,
Saying, "These jewels, whereupon I chanced
Divinely, are the kingdom's, not the King's—
For public use: henceforward let there be,   60
Once every year, a joust for one of these:
For so by nine years' proof we needs must learn
Which is our mightiest, and ourselves shall grow
In use of arms and manhood, till we drive
The heathen, who, some say, shall rule the land
Hereafter, which God hinder." Thus he spoke:
And eight years past, eight jousts had been, and still
Had Lancelot won the diamond of the year,
With purpose to present them to the Queen,
When all were won; but meaning all at once   70
To snare her royal fancy with a boon
Worth half her realm, had never spoken word.

  Now for the central diamond and the last
And largest, Arthur, holding then his court

Hard on the river nigh the place which now
Is this world's hugest, let proclaim a joust
At Camelot, and when the time drew nigh
Spake (for she had been sick) to Guinevere,
"Are you so sick, my Queen, you cannot move
To these fair jousts?" "Yea, lord," she said, "ye know
     it."   80
"Then will ye miss," he answer'd, "the great deeds
Of Lancelot, and his prowess in the lists,
A sight ye love to look on." And the Queen
Lifted her eyes, and they dwelt languidly
On Lancelot, where he stood beside the King.
He thinking that he read her meaning there,
"Stay with me, I am sick; my love is more
Than many diamonds," yielded; and a heart
Love-loyal to the least wish of the Queen
(However much he yearn'd to make complete   90
The tale of diamonds for his destined boon)
Urged him to speak against the truth, and say,
"Sir King, mine ancient wound is hardly whole,
And lets me from the saddle;" and the King
Glanced first at him, then her, and went his way.
No sooner gone than suddenly she began:

     "To blame, my lord Sir Lancelot, much to blame!
Why go ye not to these fair jousts? the knights
Are half of them our enemies, and the crowd
Will murmur, 'Lo the shameless ones, who take   100
Their pastime now the trustful King is gone!' "
Then Lancelot vext at having lied in vain:
"Are ye so wise? ye were not once so wise,
My Queen, that summer, when ye loved me first.
Then of the crowd ye took no more account
Than of the myriad cricket of the mead,
When its own voice clings to each blade of grass,
And every voice is nothing. As to knights,
Then surely can I silence with all ease.
But now my loyal worship is allow'd   110
Of all men: many a bard, without offence,
Has link'd our names together in his lay,
Lancelot, the flower of bravery, Guinevere,
The pearl of beauty: and our knights at feast
Have pledged us in this union, while the King
Would listen smiling. How then? is there more?

Has Arthur spoken aught? or would yourself,
Now weary of my service and devoir,
Henceforth be truer to your faultless lord?"

    She broke into a little scornful laugh: 120
"Arthur, my lord, Arthur, the faultless King,
That passionate perfection, my good lord—
But who can gaze upon the Sun in heaven?
He never spake word of reproach to me,
He never had a glimpse of mine untruth,
He cares not for me: only here to-day
There gleam'd a vague suspicion in his eyes:
Some meddling rogue has tamper'd with him—else
Rapt in this fancy of his Table Round,
And swearing men to vows impossible,   130
To make them like himself: but, friend, to me
He is all fault who hath no fault at all:
For who loves me must have a touch of earth;
The low sun makes the colour: I am yours,
Not Arthur's, as ye know, save by the bond.
And therefore hear my words: go to the jousts:
The tiny-trumpeting gnat can break our dream
When sweetest; and the vermin voices here
May buzz so loud—we scorn them, but they sting."

    Then answer'd Lancelot, the chief of knights: 140
"And with what face, after my pretext made,
Shall I apear, O Queen, at Camelot, I
Before a King who honours his own word,
As if it were his God's?"

                   "Yea," said the Queen,
"A moral child without the craft to rule,
Else had he not lost me: but listen to me,
If I must find you wit: we hear it said
That men go down before your spear at a touch,
But knowing you are Lancelot; your great name,
This conquers: hide it therefore; go unknown: 150
Win! by this kiss you will: and our true King
Will then allow your pretext, O my knight,
As all for glory; for to speak him true,
Ye know right well, how meek soe'er he seem,
No keener hunter after glory breathes.
He loves it in his knights more than himself:

They prove to him his work: win and return."

Then got Sir Lancelot suddenly to horse,
Wroth at himself. Not willing to be known,
He left the barren-beaten thoroughfare,   160
Chose the green path that show'd the rarer foot,
And there among the solitary downs,
Full often lost in fancy, lost his way;
Till as he traced a faintly-shadow'd track,
That all in loops and links among the dales
Ran to the Castle of Astolat, he saw
Fired from the west, far on a hill, the towers.
Thither he made, and blew the gateway horn.
Then came an old, dumb, myriad-wrinkled man,
Who let him into lodging and disarm'd.   170
And Lancelot marvell'd at the wordless man;
And issuing found the Lord of Astolat
With two strong sons, Sir Torre and Sir Lavaine,
Moving to meet him in the castle court;
And close behind them stept the lily maid
Elaine, his daughter: mother of the house
There was not: some light jest among them rose
With laughter dying down as the great knight
Approach'd them: then the Lord of Astolat:
"Whence comest thou, my guest, and by what name   180
Livest between the lips? for by thy state
And presence I might guess thee chief of those,
After the King, who eat in Arthur's halls.
Him have I seen: the rest, his Table Round,
Known as they are, to me they are unknown."

Then answer'd Lancelot, the chief of knights:
"Known am I, and of Arthur's hall, and known,
What I by mere mischance have brought, my shield.
But since I go to joust as one unknown
At Camelot for the diamond, ask me not,   190
Hereafter ye shall know me—and the shield—
I pray you lend me one, if such you have,
Blank, or at least with some device not mine."

Then said the Lord of Astolat, "Here is Torre's:
Hurt in his first tilt was my son, Sir Torre.
And so, God wot, his shield is blank enough.
His ye can have." Then added plain Sir Torre,

"Yea, since I cannot use it, ye may have it."
Here laugh'd the father saying, "Fie, Sir Churl,
Is that an answer for a noble knight?   200
Allow him! but Lavaine, my younger here,
He is so full of lustihood, he will ride,
Joust for it, and win, and bring it in an hour,
And set it in this damsel's golden hair,
To make her thrice as wilful as before."

    "Nay, father, nay good father, shame me not
Before this noble knight," said young Lavaine,
"For nothing. Surely I but play'd on Torre:
He seem'd so sullen, vext he could not go:
A jest, no more! for, knight, the maiden dreamt   210
That some one put this diamond in her hand,
And that it was too slippery to be held,
And slipt and fell into some pool or stream,
The castle-well, belike; and then I said
That *if* I went and *if* I fought and won it
(But all was jest and joke among ourselves)
Then must she keep it safelier. All was jest.
But, father, give me leave, an if he will,
To ride to Camelot with this noble knight:
Win shall I not, but do my best to win: 220
Young as I am, yet would I do my best."

    "So ye will grace me," answer'd Lancelot,
Smiling a moment, "with your fellowship
O'er these waste downs whereon I lost myself,
Then were I glad of you as guide and friend:
And you shall win this diamond,—as I hear
It is a fair large diamond,—if ye may,
And yield it to this maiden, if ye will."
"A fair large diamond," added plain Sir Torre,
"Such be for queens, and not for simple maids."   230
Then she, who held her eyes upon the ground,
Elaine, and heard her name so tost about,
Flush'd slightly at the slight disparagement
Before the stranger knight, who, looking at her,
Full courtly, yet not falsely, thus return'd:
"If what is fair be but for what is fair,
And only queens are to be counted so,
Rash were my judgment then, who deem this maid
Might wear as fair a jewel as is on earth,

Not violating the bond of like to like."

He spoke and ceased: the lily maid Elaine,
Won by the mellow voice before she look'd,
Lifted her eyes, and read his lineaments.
The great and guilty love he bare the Queen,
In battle with the love he bare his lord,
Had marr'd his face, and mark'd it ere his time.
Another sinning on such heights with one,
The flower of all the west and all the world,
Had been the sleeker for it: but in him
His mood was often like a fiend, and rose   250
And drove him into wastes and solitudes
For agony, who was yet a living soul.
Marr'd as he was, he seem'd the goodliest man
That ever among ladies ate in hall,
And noblest, when she lifted up her eyes.
However marr'd, of more than twice her years,
Seam'd with an ancient swordcut on the cheek,
And bruised and bronzed, she lifted up her eyes
And loved him, with that love which was her doom.

Then the great knight, the darling of the court,   260
Loved of the loveliest, into that rude hall
Stept with all grace, and not with half disdain
Hid under grace, as in a smaller time,
But kindly man moving among his kind:
Whom they with meats and vintage of their best
And talk and minstrel melody entertain'd.
And much they ask'd of court and Table Round,
And ever well and readily answer'd he:
But Lancelot, when they glanced at Guinevere,
Suddenly speaking of the wordless man,   270
Heard from the Baron that, ten years before,
The heathen caught and reft him of his tongue.
"He learnt and warn'd me of their fierce design
Against my house, and him they caught and maim'd;
But I, my sons, and little daughter fled
From bonds or death, and dwelt among the woods
By the great river in a boatman's hut.
Dull days were those, till our good Arthur broke
The Pagan yet once more on Badon hill."

"O there, great lord, doubtless," Lavaine said, rapt   280

By all the sweet and sudden passion of youth
Toward greatness in its elder, "you have fought.
O tell us—for we live apart—you know
Of Arthur's glorious wars." And Lancelot spoke
And answer'd him at full, as having been
With Arthur in the fight which all day long
Rang by the white mouth of the violent Glem;
And in the four loud battles by the shore
Of Duglas; that on Bassa; then the war
That thunder'd in and out the gloomy skirts   290
Of Celidon the forest; and again
By castle Gurnion, where the glorious King
Had on his cuirass worn our Lady's Head,
Carved of one emerald center'd in a sun
Of silver rays, that lighten'd as he breathed;
And at Caerleon had he help'd his lord,
When the strong neighings of the wild white Horse
Set every gilded parapet shuddering;
And up in Agned-Cathregonion too,
And down the waste sand-shores of Trath Treroit,   300
Where many a heathen fell; "and on the mount
Of Badon I myself beheld the King
Charge at the head of all his Table Round,
And all his legions crying Christ and him,
And break them; and I saw him, after, stand
High on a heap of slain, from spur to plume
Red as the rising sun with heathen blood,
And seeing me, with a great voice he cried,
'They are broken, they are broken!' for the King
However mild he seems at home, nor cares   310
For triumph in our mimic wars, the jousts—
For if his own knight cast him down, he laughs
Saying, his knights are better men than he—
Yet in this heathen war the fire of God
Fills him: I never saw his like: there lives
No greater leader."

                 While he utter'd this,
Low to her own heart said the lily maid,
"Save your great self, fair lord;" and when he fell
From talk of war to traits of pleasantry—
Being mirthful he, but in a stately kind—   320
She still took note that when the living smile
Died from his lips, across him came a cloud

Of melancholy severe, from which again,
Whenever in her hovering to and fro
The lily maid had striven to make him cheer,
There brake a sudden-beaming tenderness
Of manners and of nature: and she thought
That all was nature, all, perchance, for her.
And all night long his face before her lived,
As when a painter, poring on a face, 330
Divinely thro' all hindrance finds the man
Behind it, and so paints him that his face,
The shape and colour of a mind and life,
Lives for his children, ever at his best
And fullest; so the face before her lived,
Dark-splendid, speaking in the silence, full
Of noble things, and held her from her sleep.
Till rathe she rose, half-cheated in the thought
She needs must bid farewell to sweet Lavaine.
First as in fear, step after step, she stole 340
Down the long tower-stairs, hesitating:
Anon, she heard Sir Lancelot cry in the court,
"This shield, my friend, where is it?" and Lavaine
Past inward, as she came from out the tower.
There to his proud horse Lancelot turn'd, and smooth'd
The glossy shoulder, humming to himself.
Half-envious of the flattering hand, she drew
Nearer and stood. He look'd, and more amazed
Than if seven men had set upon him, saw
The maiden standing in the dewy light. 350
He had not dream'd she was so beautiful.
Then came on him a sort of sacred fear,
For silent, tho' he greeted her, she stood
Rapt on his face as if it were a God's.
Suddenly flash'd on her a wild desire,
That he should wear her favour at the tilt.
She braved a riotous heart in asking for it.
"Fair lord, whose name I know not—noble it is,
I well believe, the noblest—will you wear
My favour at this tourney?" "Nay," said he, 360
"Fair lady, since I never yet have worn
Favour of any lady in the lists.
Such is my wont, as those, who know me, know."
"Yea, so," she answer'd; "then in wearing mine
Needs must be lesser likelihood, noble lord,

That those who know should know you." And he
    turn'd
Her counsel up and down within his mind,
And found it true, and answer'd, "True, my child.
Well, I will wear it: fetch it out to me:
What is it?" and she told him, "A red sleeve   370
Broider'd with pearls," and brought it: then he bound
Her token on his helmet, with a smile
Saying, "I never yet have done so much
For any maiden living," and the blood
Sprang to her face and fill'd her with delight;
But left her all the paler, when Lavaine
Returning brought the yet-unblazon'd shield,
His brother's; which he gave to Lancelot,
Who parted with his own to fair Elaine:
"Do me this grace, my child, to have my shield   380
In keeping till I come." "A grace to me,"
She answer'd, "twice to-day. I am your squire!"
Whereat Lavaine said, laughing, "Lily maid,
For fear our people call you lily maid
In earnest, let me bring your colour back;
Once, twice, and thrice: now get you hence to bed:"
So kiss'd her, and Sir Lancelot his own hand,
And thus they moved away: she stay'd a minute,
Then made a sudden step to the gate, and there—
Her bright hair blown about the serious face   390
Yet rosy-kindled with her brother's kiss—
Paused by the gateway, standing near the shield
In silence, while she watch'd their arms far-off
Sparkle, until they dipt below the downs.
Then to her tower she climb'd, and took the shield,
There kept it, and so lived in fantasy.

Meanwhile the new companions past away
Far o'er the long backs of the bushless downs,
To where Sir Lancelot knew there lived a knight
Not far from Camelot, now for forty years   400
A hermit, who had pray'd, labour'd and pray'd,
And ever labouring had scoop'd himself
In the white rock a chapel and a hall
On massive columns, like a shorecliff cave,
And cells and chambers: all were fair and dry;
The green light from the meadows underneath

Struck up and lived along the milky roofs;
And in the meadows tremulous aspen-trees
And poplars made a noise of falling showers.
And thither wending there that night they bode.   410

But when the next day broke from underground,
And shot red fire and shadows thro' the cave,
They rose, heard mass, broke fast, and rode away:
Then Lancelot saying, "Hear, but hold my name
Hidden, you ride with Lancelot of the Lake,"
Abash'd Lavaine, whose instant reverence,
Dearer to true young hearts than their own praise,
But left him leave to stammer, "Is it indeed?"
And after muttering, "The great Lancelot,"
At last he got his breath and answer'd, "One,   420
One have I seen—that other, our liege lord,
The dread Pendragon, Britain's King of kings,
Of whom the people talk mysteriously,
He will be there—then were I stricken blind
That minute, I might say that I had seen."

So spake Lavaine, and when they reach'd the lists
By Camelot in the meadow, let his eyes
Run thro' the peopled gallery which half round
Lay like a rainbow fall'n upon the grass,
Until they found the clear-faced King, who sat   430
Robed in red samite, easily to be known,
Since to his crown the golden dragon clung,
And down his robe the dragon writhed in gold,
And from the carven-work behind him crept
Two dragons gilded, sloping down to make
Arms for his chair, while all the rest of them
Thro' knots and loops and folds innumerable
Fled ever thro' the woodwork, till they found
The new design wherein they lost themselves,
Yet with all ease, so tender was the work: 440
And, in the costly canopy o'er him set,
Blazed the last diamond of the nameless king.

Then Lancelot answer'd young Lavaine and said,
"Me you call great: mine is the firmer seat,
The truer lance: but there is many a youth
Now crescent, who will come to all I am
And overcome it; and in me there dwells

No greatness, save it be some far-off touch
Of greatness to know well I am not great:
There is the man." And Lavaine gaped upon him   450
As on a thing miraculous, and anon
The trumpets blew; and then did either side,
They that assail'd, and they that held the lists,
Set lance in rest, strike spur, suddenly move,
Meet in the midst, and there so furiously
Shock, that a man far-off might well perceive,
If any man that day were left afield,
The hard earth shake, and a low thunder of arms.
And Lancelot bode a little, till he saw
Which were the weaker; then he hurl'd into it   460
Against the stronger: little need to speak
Of Lancelot in his glory! King, duke, earl,
Count, baron—whom he smote, he overthrew.

But in the field were Lancelot's kith and kin,
Ranged with the Table Round that held the lists,
Strong men, and wrathful that a stranger knight
Should do and almost overdo the deeds
Of Lancelot; and one said to the other, "Lo!
What is he? I do not mean the force alone—
The grace and versatility of the man!   470
Is it not Lancelot?" "When has Lancelot worn
Favour of any lady in the lists?
Not such his wont, as we, that know him, know."
"How then? who then?" a fury seized them all,
A fiery family passion for the name
Of Lancelot, and a glory one with theirs.
They couch'd their spears and prick'd their steeds, and
        thus,
Their plumes driv'n backward by the wind they made
In moving, all together down upon him
Bare, as a wild wave in the wide North-sea,   480
Green-glimmering toward the summit, bears, with all
Its stormy crests that smoke against the skies,
Down on a bark, and overbears the bark,
And him that helms it, so they overbore
Sir Lancelot and his charger, and a spear
Down-glancing lamed the charger, and a spear
Prick'd sharply his own cuirass, and the head
Pierced thro' his side, and there snapt, and remain'd.

Then Sir Lavaine did well and worshipfully;
He bore a knight of old repute to the earth,   490
And brought his horse to Lancelot where he lay.
He up the side, sweating with agony, got,
But thought to do while he might yet endure,
And being lustily holpen by the rest,
His party,—tho' it seem'd half-miracle
To those he fought with,—drave his kith and kin,
And all the Table Round that held the lists,
Back to the barrier; then the trumpets blew
Proclaiming his the prize, who wore the sleeve
Of scarlet, and the pearls; and all the knights,   500
His party, cried, "Advance and take thy prize
The diamond;" but he answer'd, "Diamond me
No diamonds! for God's love, a little air!
Prize me no prizes, for my prize is death!
Hence will I, and I charge you, follow me not."

He spoke, and vanish'd suddenly from the field
With young Lavaine into the poplar grove.
There from his charger down he slid, and sat,
Gasping to Sir Lavaine, "Draw the lance-head:"
"Ah my sweet lord Sir Lancelot," said Lavaine,   510
"I dread me, if I draw it, you will die."
But he, "I die already with it: draw—
Draw,"—and Lavaine drew, and Sir Lancelot gave
A marvellous great shriek and ghastly groan,
And half his blood burst forth, and down he sank
For the pure pain, and wholly swoon'd away.
Then came the hermit out and bare him in,
There stanch'd his wound; and there, in daily doubt
Whether to live or die, for many a week
Hid from the wide world's rumour by the grove   520
Of poplars with their noise of falling showers,
And ever-tremulous aspen-trees, he lay.

But on that day when Lancelot fled the lists,
His party, knights of utmost North and West,
Lords of waste marches, kings of desolate isles,
Came round their great Pendragon, saying to him,
"Lo, Sire, our knight, thro' whom we won the day,
Hath gone sore wounded, and hath left his prize
Untaken, crying that his prize is death."
"Heaven hinder," said the King, "that such an one,   530

So great a knight as we have seen to-day—
He seem'd to me another Lancelot—
Yea, twenty times I thought him Lancelot—
He must not pass uncared for. Wherefore, rise,
O Gawain, and ride forth and find the knight.
Wounded and wearied needs must he be near.
I charge you that you get at once to horse.
And, knights and kings, there breathes not one of you
Will deem this prize of ours is rashly given:
His prowess was too wondrous. We will do him   540
No customary honour: since the knight
Came not to us, of us to claim the prize,
Ourselves will send it after. Rise and take
This diamond, and deliver it, and return,
And bring us where he is, and how he fares,
And cease not from your quest until ye find."

So saying, from the carven flower above,
To which it made a restless heart, he took,
And gave, the diamond: then from where he sat
At Arthur's right, with smiling face arose,   550
With smiling face and frowning heart, a Prince
In the mid might and flourish of his May,
Gawain, surnamed The Courteous, fair and strong,
And after Lancelot, Tristram, and Geraint
And Gareth, a good knight, but therewithal
Sir Modred's brother, and the child of Lot,
Nor often loyal to his word, and now
Wroth that the King's command to sally forth
In quest of whom he knew not, made him leave
The banquet, and concourse of knights and kings.   560

So all in wrath he got to horse and went;
While Arthur to the banquet, dark in mood,
Past, thinking, "Is it Lancelot who hath come
Despite the wound he spake of, all for gain
Of glory, and hath added wound to wound,
And ridd'n away to die?" So fear'd the King,
And, after two days' tarriance there, return'd.
Then when he saw the Queen, embracing ask'd,
"Love, are you yet so sick?" "Nay, lord," she said.
"And where is Lancelot?" Then the Queen amazed,   570
"Was he not with you? won he not your prize?"
"Nay, but one like him." "Why that like was he."

And when the King demanded how she knew,
Said, "Lord, no sooner had ye parted from us,
Than Lancelot told me of a common talk
That men went down before his spear at a touch,
But knowing he was Lancelot; his great name
Conquer'd; and therefore would he hide his name
From all men, ev'n the King, and to this end
Had made the pretext of a hindering wound,   580
That he might joust unknown of all, and learn
If his old prowess were in aught decay'd;
And added, 'Our true Arthur, when he learns,
Will well allow my pretext, as for gain
Of purer glory.' "

        Then replied the King:
"Far lovelier in our Lancelot had it been,
In lieu of idly dallying with the truth,
To have trusted me as he hath trusted thee.
Surely his King and most familiar friend
Might well have kept his secret. True, indeed,   590
Albeit I know my knights fantastical,
So fine a fear in our large Lancelot
Must needs have moved my laughter: now remains
But little cause for laughter: his own kin—
Ill news, my Queen, for all who love him, this!—
His kith and kin, not knowing, set upon him;
So that he went sore wounded from the field:
Yet good news too: for goodly hopes are mine
That Lancelot is no more a lonely heart.
He wore, against his wont, upon his helm   600
A sleeve of scarlet, broider'd with great pearls,
Some gentle maiden's gift."

        "Yea, lord," she said,
"Thy hopes are mine," and saying that, she choked,
And sharply turn'd about to hide her face,
Past to her chamber, and there flung herself
Down on the great King's couch, and writhed upon it,
And clench'd her fingers till they bit the palm,
And shriek'd out "Traitor" to the unhearing wall,
Then flash'd into wild tears, and rose again,
And moved about her palace, proud and pale.   610

  Gawain the while thro' all the region round

Rode with his diamond, wearied of the quest,
Touch'd at all points, except the poplar grove,
And came at last, tho' late, to Astolat:
Whom glittering in enamell'd arms the maid
Glanced at, and cried, "What news from Camelot,
    lord?
What of the knight with the red sleeve?" "He won."
"I knew it," she said. "But parted from the jousts
Hurt in the side," whereat she caught her breath;
Thro' her own side she felt the sharp lance go;   620
Thereon she smote her hand: wellnigh she swoon'd:
And, while he gazed wonderingly at her, came
The Lord of Astolat out, to whom the Prince
Reported who he was, and on what quest
Sent, that he bore the prize and could not find
The victor, but had ridd'n a random round
To seek him, and had wearied of the search.
To whom the Lord of Astolat, "Bide with us,
And ride no more at random, noble Prince!
Here was the knight, and here he left a shield;   630
This will he send or come for: furthermore
Our son is with him; we shall hear anon,
Needs must we hear." To this the courteous Prince
Accorded with his wonted courtesy,
Courtesy with a touch of traitor in it,
And stay'd; and cast his eyes on fair Elaine:
Where could be found face dainter? than her shape
From forehead down to foot, perfect—again
From foot to forehead exquisitely turn'd:
"Well—if I bide, lo! this wild flower for me!"   640
And oft they met among the garden yews,
And there he set himself to play upon her
With sallying wit, free flashes from a height
Above her, graces of the court, and songs,
Sighs, and slow smiles, and golden eloquence
And amorous adulation, till the maid
Rebell'd against it, saying to him, "Prince,
O loyal nephew of our noble King,
Why ask you not to see the shield he left,
Whence you might learn his name? Why slight your
    King,   650
And lose the quest he sent you on, and prove
No surer than our falcon yesterday,
Who lost the hern we slipt her at, and went

To all the winds?" "Nay, by mine head," said he,
"I lose it, as we lose the lark in heaven,
O damsel, in the light of your blue eyes;
But an ye will it let me see the shield."
And when the shield was brought, and Gawain saw
Sir Lancelot's azure lions, crown'd with gold,
Ramp in the field, he smote his thigh, and mock'd: 660
"Right was the King! our Lancelot! that true man!"
"And right was I," she answer'd merrily, "I,
Who dream'd my knight the greatest knight of all."
"And if *I* dream'd," said Gawain, "that you love
This greatest knight, your pardon! lo, ye know it!
Speak therefore: shall I waste myself in vain?"
Full simple was her answer, "What know I,
My brethren have been all my fellowship;
And I, when often they have talk'd of love,
Wish'd it had been my mother, for they talk'd,   670
Meseem'd, of what they knew not; so myself—
I know not if I know what true love is,
But if I know, then, if I love not him,
I know there is none other I can love."
"Yea, by God's death," said he, "ye love him well,
But would not, knew ye what all others know,
And whom he loves." "So be it," cried Elaine,
And lifted her fair face and moved away:
But he pursued her, calling, "Stay a little!
One golden minute's grace! he wore your sleeve: 680
Would he break faith with one I may not name?
Must our true man change like a leaf at last?
Nay—like enow: why then, far be it from me
To cross our mighty Lancelot in his loves!
And, damsel, for I deem you know full well
Where your great knight is hidden, let me leave
My quest with you; the diamond also: here!
For if you love, it will be sweet to give it;
And if he love, it will be sweet to have it
From your own hand; and whether he love or not,   690
A diamond is a diamond. Fare you well
A thousand times!—a thousand times farewell!
Yet, if he love, and his love hold, we two
May meet at court hereafter: there, I think,
So ye will learn the courtesies of the court,
We two shall know each other."

　　　　　　　　Then he gave,
And slightly kiss'd the hand to which he gave,
The diamond, and all wearied of the quest
Leapt on his horse, and carolling as he went
A true-love ballad, lightly rode away.　　　　　700

　　Thence to the court he past; there told the King
What the King knew, "Sir Lancelot is the knight."
And added, "Sire, my liege, so much I learnt;
But fail'd to find him, tho' I rode all round
The region: but I lighted on the maid
Whose sleeve he wore; she loves him; and to her,
Deeming our courtesy is the truest law,
I gave the diamond: she will render it;
For by mine head she knows his hiding-place."

　　The seldom-frowning King frown'd, and replied,　　710
"Too courteous truly! ye shall go no more
On quest of mine, seeing that ye forget
Obedience is the courtesy due to kings."

　　He spake and parted. Wroth, but all in awe,
For twenty strokes of the blood, without a word,
Linger'd that other, staring after him;
Then shook his hair, strode off, and buzz'd abroad
About the maid of Astolat, and her love.
All ears were prick'd at once, all tongues were loosed:
"The maid of Astolat loves Sir Lancelot,　　　　720
Sir Lancelot loves the maid of Astolat."
Some read the King's face, some the Queen's, and all
Had marvel what the maid might be, but most
Predoom'd her as unworthy. One old dame
Came suddenly on the Queen with the sharp news.
She, that had heard the noise of it before,
But sorrowing Lancelot should have stoop'd so low,
Marr'd her friend's aim with pale tranquillity.
So ran the tale like fire about the court,
Fire in dry stubble a nine-days' wonder flared:　　730
Till ev'n the knights at banquet twice or thrice
Forgot to drink to Lancelot and the Queen,
And pledging Lancelot and the lily maid
Smiled at each other, while the Queen, who sat
With lips severely placid, felt the knot

Climb in her throat, and with her feet unseen
Crush'd the wild passion out against the floor
Beneath the banquet, where the meats became
As wormwood, and she hated all who pledged.

But far away the maid in Astolat,   740
Her guiltless rival, she that ever kept
The one-day-seen Sir Lancelot in her heart,
Crept to her father, while he mused alone,
Sat on his knee, stroked his gray face and said,
"Father, you call me wilful, and the fault
Is yours who let me have my will, and now,
Sweet father, will you let me lose my wits?"
"Nay," said he, "surely." "Wherefore, let me hence,"
She answer'd, "and find out our dear Lavaine."
"Ye will not lose your wits for dear Lavaine: 750
Bide," answer'd he: "we needs must hear anon
Of him, and of that other." "Ay," she said,
"And of that other, for I needs must hence
And find that other, wheresoe'er he be,
And with mine own hand give his diamond to him,
Lest I be found as faithless in the quest
As yon proud Prince who left the quest to me.
Sweet father, I behold him in my dreams
Gaunt as it were the skeleton of himself,
Death-pale, for lack of gentle maiden's aid.   760
The gentler-born the maiden, the more bound,
My father, to be sweet and serviceable
To noble knights in sickness, as ye know
When these have worn their tokens: let me hence
I pray you." Then her father nodding said,
"Ay, ay, the diamond: wit ye well, my child,
Right fain were I to learn this knight were whole,
Being our greatest: yea, and you must give it—
And sure I think this fruit is hung too high
For any mouth to gape for save a queen's—   770
Nay, I mean nothing: so then; get you gone,
Being so very wilful you must go."

Lightly, her suit allow'd, she slipt away,
And while she made her ready for her ride,
Her father's latest word humm'd in her ear,
"Being so very wilful you must go,"
And changed itself and echo'd in her heart,

"Being so very wilful you must die."
But she was happy enough and shook it off,
As we shake off the bee that buzzes at us;   780
And in her heart she answer'd it and said,
"What matter, so I help him back to life?"
Then far away with good Sir Torre for guide
Rode o'er the long backs of the bushless downs
To Camelot, and before the city-gates
Came on her brother with a happy face
Making a roan horse caper and curvet
For pleasure all about a field of flowers:
Whom when she saw, "Lavaine," she cried, "Lavaine,
How fares my lord Sir Lancelot?" He amazed,   790
"Torre and Elaine! why here? Sir Lancelot!
How know ye my lord's name is Lancelot?"
But when the maid had told him all her tale,
Then turn'd Sir Torre, and being in his moods
Left them, and under the strange-statued gate,
Where Arthur's wars were render'd mystically,
Past up the still rich city to his kin,
His own far blood, which dwelt at Camelot;
And her, Lavaine across the poplar grove
Led to the caves: there first she saw the casque   800
Of Lancelot on the wall: her scarlet sleeve,
Tho' carved and cut, and half the pearls away,
Stream'd from it still; and in her heart she laugh'd,
Because he had not loosed it from his helm,
But meant once more perchance to tourney in it.
And when they gain'd the cell wherein he slept,
His battle-writhen arms and mighty hands
Lay naked on the wolfskin, and a dream
Of dragging down his enemy made them move.
Then she that saw him lying unsleek, unshorn,   810
Gaunt as it were the skeleton of himself,
Utter'd a little tender dolorous cry.
The sound not wonted in a place so still
Woke the sick knight, and while he roll'd his eyes
Yet blank from sleep, she started to him, saying,
"Your prize the diamond sent you by the King:"
His eyes glisten'd: she fancied, "Is it for me?"
And when the maid had told him all the tale
Of King and Prince, the diamond sent, the quest
Assign'd to her not worthy of it, she knelt   820
Full lowly by the corners of his bed,

And laid the diamond in his open hand.
Her face was near, and as we kiss the child
That does the task assign'd, he kiss'd her face.
At once she slipt like water to the floor.
"Alas," he said, "your ride hath wearied you.
Rest must you have." "No rest for me," she said;
"Nay, for near you, fair lord, I am at rest."
What might she mean by that? his large black eyes,
Yet larger thro' his leanness, dwelt upon her,   830
Till all her heart's sad secret blazed itself
In the heart's colours on her simple face;
And Lancelot look'd and was perplext in mind,
And being weak in body said no more;
But did not love the colour; woman's love,
Save one, he not regarded, and so turn'd
Sighing, and feign'd a sleep until he slept.

Then rose Elaine and glided thro' the fields,
And past beneath the weirdly-sculptured gates
Far up the dim rich city to her kin;   840
There bode the night: but woke with dawn, and past
Down thro' the dim rich city to the fields,
Thence to the cave: so day by day she past
In either twilight ghost-like to and fro
Gliding, and every day she tended him,
And likewise many a night: and Lancelot
Would, tho' he call'd his wound a little hurt
Whereof he should be quickly whole, at times
Brain-feverous in his heat and agony, seem
Uncourteous, even he: but the meek maid   850
Sweetly forebore him ever, being to him
Meeker than any child to a rough nurse,
Milder than any mother to a sick child,
And never woman yet, since man's first fall,
Did kindlier unto man, but her deep love
Upbore her; till the hermit, skill'd in all
The simples and the science of that time,
Told him that her fine care had saved his life.
And the sick man forgot her simple blush,
Would call her friend and sister, sweet Elaine,   860
Would listen for her coming and regret
Her parting step, and held her tenderly,
And loved her with all love except the love
Of man and woman when they love their best,

Closest and sweetest, and had died the death
In any knightly fashion for her sake.
And peradventure had he seen her first
She might have made this and that other world
Another world for the sick man; but now
The shackles of an old love straiten'd him,   870
His honour rooted in dishonour stood,
And faith unfaithful kept him falsely true.

Yet the great knight in his mid-sickness made
Full many a holy vow and pure resolve.
These, as but born of sickness, could not live:
For when the blood ran lustier in him again,
Full often the bright image of one face,
Making a treacherous quiet in his heart,
Dispersed his resolution like a cloud.
Then if the maiden, while that ghostly grace   880
Beam'd on his fancy, spoke, he answer'd not,
Or short and coldly, and she knew right well
What the rough sickness meant, but what this meant
She knew not, and the sorrow dimm'd her sight,
And drave her ere her time across the fields
Far into the rich city, where alone
She murmur'd, "Vain, in vain: it cannot be.
He will not love me: how then? must I die?"
Then as a little helpless innocent bird,
That has but one plain passage of few notes,   890
Will sing the simple passage o'er and o'er
For all an April morning, till the ear
Wearies to hear it, so the simple maid
Went half the night repeating, "Must I die?"
And now to right she turn'd, and now to left,
And found no ease in turning or in rest;
And, "Him or death," she mutter'd, "death or him,"
Again and like a burthen, "Him or death."

But when Sir Lancelot's deadly hurt was whole,
To Astolat returning rode the three.   900
There morn by morn, arraying her sweet self
In that wherein she deem'd she look'd her best,
She came before Sir Lancelot, for she thought
"If I be loved, these are my festal robes,
If not, the victim's flowers before he fall."
And Lancelot ever prest upon the maid

That she should ask some goodly gift of him
For her own self or hers; "and do not shun
To speak the wish most near to your true heart;
Such service have ye done me, that I make 910
My will of yours, and Prince and Lord am I
In mine own land, and what I will I can."
Then like a ghost she lifted up her face,
But like a ghost without the power to speak.
And Lancelot saw that she withheld her wish,
And bode among them yet a little space
Till he should learn it; and one morn it chanced
He found her in among the garden yews,
And said, "Delay no longer, speak your wish,
Seeing I go to-day:" then out she brake: 920
"Going? and we shall never see you more.
And I must die for want of one bold word."
"Speak: that I live to hear," he said, "is yours."
Then suddenly and passionately she spoke:
"I have gone mad. I love you: let me die."
"Ah, sister," answer'd Lancelot, "what is this?"
And innocently extending her white arms,
"Your love," she said, "your love—to be your wife."
And Lancelot answer'd, "Had I chosen to wed,
I had been wedded earlier, sweet Elaine: 930
But now there never will be wife of mine."
"No, no," she cried, "I care not to be wife,
But to be with you still, to see your face,
To serve you, and to follow you thro' the world."
And Lancelot answer'd, "Nay, the world, the world,
All ear and eye, with such a stupid heart
To interpret ear and eye, and such a tongue
To blare its own interpretation—nay,
Full ill then should I quit your brother's love,
And your good father's kindness." And she said, 940
"Not to be with you, not to see your face—
Alas for me then, my good days are done."
"Nay, noble maid," he answer'd, "ten times nay!
This is not love: but love's first flash in youth,
Most common: yea, I know it of mine own self:
And you yourself will smile at your own self
Hereafter, when you yield your flower of life
To one more fitly yours, not thrice your age:
And then will I, for true you are and sweet
Beyond mine old belief in womanhood, 950

More specially should your good knight be poor,
Endow you with broad land and territory
Even to the half my realm beyond the seas,
So that would make you happy: furthermore,
Ev'n to the death, as tho' ye were my blood,
In all your quarrels will I be your knight.
This will I do, dear damsel, for your sake,
And more than this I cannot."

                         While he spoke
She neither blush'd nor shook, but deathly-pale
Stood grasping what was nearest, then replied: 960
"Of all this will I nothing;" and so fell,
And thus they bore her swooning to her tower.

      Then spake, to whom thro' those black walls of yew
Their talk had pierced, her father: "Ay, a flash,
I fear me, that will strike my blossom dead.
Too courteous are ye, fair Lord Lancelot.
I pray you, use some rough discourtesy
To blunt or break her passion."

                         Lancelot said,
"That were against me: what I can I will;"
And there that day remain'd, and toward even   970
Sent for his shield: full meekly rose the maid,
Stript off the case, and gave the naked shield;
Then, when she heard his horse upon the stones,
Unclasping flung the casement back, and look'd
Down on his helm, from which her sleeve had gone.
And Lancelot knew the little clinking sound;
And she by tact of love was well aware
That Lancelot knew that she was looking at him.
And yet he glanced not up, nor waved his hand,
Nor bad farewell, but sadly rode away.   980
This was the one discourtesy that he used.

      So in her tower alone the maiden sat:
His very shield was gone; only the case,
Her own poor work, her empty labour, left.
But still she heard him, still his picture form'd
And grew between her and the pictured wall.
Then came her father, saying in low tones,
"Have comfort," whom she greeted quietly.

Then came her brethren saying, "Peace to thee,
Sweet sister," whom she answer'd with all calm.   990
But when they left her to herself again,
Death, like a friend's voice from a distant field
Approaching thro' the darkness, call'd; the owls
Wailing had power upon her, and she mixt
Her fancies with the sallow-rifted glooms
Of evening, and the moanings of the wind.

And in those days she made a little song,
And call'd her song "The Song of Love and Death,"
And sang it: sweetly could she make and sing.

"Sweet is true love tho' given in vain, in vain;   1000
And sweet is death who puts an end to pain:
I know not which is sweeter, no, not I.

"Love, art thou sweet? then bitter death must be:
Love, thou art bitter; sweet is death to me.
O Love, if death be sweeter, let me die.

"Sweet love, that seems not made to fade away,
Sweet death, that seems to make us loveless clay,
I know not which is sweeter, no, not I.

"I fain would follow love, if that could be;
I needs must follow death, who calls for me;   1010
Call and I follow, I follow! let me die."

High with the last line scaled her voice, and this,
All in a fiery dawning wild with wind
That shook her tower, the brothers heard, and thought
With shuddering, "Hark the Phantom of the house
That ever shrieks before a death," and call'd
The father, and all three in hurry and fear
Ran to her, and lo! the blood-red light of dawn
Flared on her face, she shrilling, "Let me die!"

As when we dwell upon a word we know,   1020
Repeating, till the word we know so well
Becomes a wonder, and we know not why,
So dwelt the father on her face, and thought
"Is this Elaine?" till back the maiden fell,
Then gave a languid hand to each, and lay,

Speaking a still good-morrow with her eyes.
At last she said, "Sweet brothers, yesternight
I seem'd a curious little maid again,
As happy as when we dwelt among the woods,
And when ye used to take me with the flood   1030
Up the great river in the boatman's boat.
Only ye would not pass beyond the cape
That has the poplar on it: there ye fixt
Your limit, oft returning with the tide.
And yet I cried because ye would not pass
Beyond it, and far up the shining flood
Until we found the palace of the King.
And yet ye would not; but this night I dream'd
That I was all alone upon the flood,
And then I said, 'Now shall I have my will:'   1040
And there I woke, but still the wish remain'd.
So let me hence that I may pass at last
Beyond the poplar and far up the flood,
Until I find the palace of the King.
There will I enter in among them all,
And no man there will dare to mock at me;
But there the fine Gawain will wonder at me,
And there the great Sir Lancelot muse at me;
Gawain, who bad a thousand farewells to me,
Lancelot, who coldly went, nor bad me one: 1050
And there the King will know me and my love,
And there the Queen herself will pity me,
And all the gentle court will welcome me,
And after my long voyage I shall rest!"

"Peace," said her father, "O my child, ye seem
Light-headed, for what force is yours to go
So far, being sick? and wherefore would ye look
On this proud fellow again, who scorns us all?"

Then the rough Torre began to heave and move,
And bluster into stormy sobs and say,   1060
"I never loved him: an I meet with him,
I care not howsoever great he be,
Then will I strike at him and strike him down,
Give me good fortune, I will strike him dead,
For this discomfort he hath done the house."

To whom the gentle sister made reply,

"Fret not yourself, dear brother, nor be wroth,
Seeing it is no more Sir Lancelot's fault
Not to love me, than it is mine to love
Him of all men who seems to me the highest."   1070

"Highest?" the father answer'd, echoing "highest?"
(He meant to break the passion in her) "nay,
Daughter, I know not what you call the highest;
But this I know, for all the people know it,
He loves the Queen, and in an open shame;
And she returns his love in open shame:
If this be high, what is it to be low?"

Then spake the lily maid of Astolat:
"Sweet father, all too faint and sick am I
For anger: these are slanders: never yet   1080
Was noble man but made ignoble talk.
He makes no friend who never made a foe.
But now it is my glory to have loved
One peerless, without stain: so let me pass,
My father, howsoe'er I seem to you,
Not all unhappy, having loved God's best
And greatest, tho' my love had no return:
Yet, seeing you desire your child to live,
Thanks, but you work against your own desire;
For if I could believe the things you say   1090
I should but die the sooner; wherefore cease,
Sweet father, and bid call the ghostly man
Hither, and let me shrive me clean, and die."

So when the ghostly man had come and gone,
She with a face, bright as for sin forgiven,
Besought Lavaine to write as she devised
A letter, word for word; and when he ask'd
"Is it for Lancelot, is it for my dear lord?
Then will I bear it gladly;" she replied,
"For Lancelot and the Queen and all the world,   1100
But I myself must bear it." Then he wrote
The letter she devised; which being writ
And folded, "O sweet father, tender and true,
Deny me not," she said—"ye never yet
Denied my fancies—this, however strange,
My latest: lay the letter in my hand
A little ere I die, and close the hand

Upon it; I shall guard it even in death.
And when the heat is gone from out my heart,
Then take the little bed on which I died   1110
For Lancelot's love, and deck it like the Queen's
For richness, and me also like the Queen
In all I have of rich, and lay me on it.
And let there be prepared a chariot-bier
To take me to the river, and a barge
Be ready on the river, clothed in black.
I go in state to court, to meet the Queen.
There surely I shall speak for mine own self,
And none of you can speak for me so well.
And therefore let our dumb old man alone   1120
Go with me, he can steer and row, and he
Will guide me to that palace, to the doors."

   She ceased: her father promised; whereupon
She grew so cheerful that they deem'd her death
Was rather in the fantasy than the blood.
But ten slow mornings past, and on the eleventh
Her father laid the letter in her hand,
And closed the hand upon it, and she died.
So that day there was dole in Astolat.

   But when the next sun brake from underground,   1130
Then, those two brethren slowly with bent brows
Accompanying, the sad chariot-bier
Past like a shadow thro' the field, that shone
Full-summer, to that stream whereon the barge,
Pall'd all its length in blackest samite, lay.
There sat the lifelong creature of the house,
Loyal, the dumb old servitor, on deck,
Winking his eyes, and twisted all his face.
So those two brethren from the chariot took
And on the black decks laid her in her bed,   1140
Set in her hand a lily, o'er her hung
The silken case with braided blazonings,
And kiss'd her quiet brows, and saying to her
"Sister, farewell for ever," and again
"Farewell, sweet sister," parted all in tears.
Then rose the dumb old servitor, and the dead,
Oar'd by the dumb, went upward with the flood—
In her right hand the lily, in her left
The letter—all her bright hair streaming down—

And all the coverlid was cloth of gold   1150
Drawn to her waist, and she herself in white
All but her face, and that clear-featured face
Was lovely, for she did not seem as dead,
But fast asleep, and lay as tho' she smiled.

That day Sir Lancelot at the palace craved
Audience of Guinevere, to give at last
The price of half a realm, his costly gift,
Hard-won and hardly won with bruise and blow,
With deaths of others, and almost his own,
The nine-years-fought-for diamonds: for he saw   1160
One of her house, and sent him to the Queen
Bearing his wish, whereto the Queen agreed
With such and so unmoved a majesty
She might have seem'd her statue, but that he,
Low-drooping till he wellnigh kiss'd her feet
For loyal awe, saw with a sidelong eye
The shadow of some piece of pointed lace,
In the Queen's shadow, vibrate on the walls,
And parted, laughing in his courtly heart.

All in an oriel on the summer side,   1170
Vine-clad, of Arthur's palace toward the stream,
They met, and Lancelot kneeling utter'd, "Queen,
Lady, my liege, in whom I have my joy,
Take, what I had not won except for you,
These jewels, and make me happy, making them
An armlet for the roundest arm on earth,
Or necklace for a neck to which the swan's
Is tawnier than her cygnet's: these are words:
Your beauty is your beauty, and I sin
In speaking, yet O grant my worship of it   1180
Words, as we grant grief tears. Such sin in words
Perchance, we both can pardon: but, my Queen,
I hear of rumours flying thro' your court.
Our bond, as not the bond of man and wife,
Should have in it an absoluter trust
To make up that defect: let rumours be:
When did not rumours fly? these, as I trust
That you trust me in your own nobleness,
I may not well believe that you believe."

While thus he spoke, half turn'd away, the Queen   1190

Brake from the vast oriel-embowering vine
Leaf after leaf, and tore, and cast them off,
Till all the place whereon she stood was green;
Then, when he ceased, in one cold passive hand
Received at once and laid aside the gems
There on a table near her, and replied:

"It may be, I am quicker of belief
Than you believe me, Lancelot of the Lake.
Our bond is not the bond of man and wife.
This good is in it, whatsoe'er of ill,   1200
It can be broken easier. I for you
This many a year have done despite and wrong
To one whom ever in my heart of hearts
I did acknowledge nobler. What are these?
Diamonds for me! they had been thrice their worth
Being your gift, had you not lost your own.
To loyal hearts the value of all gifts
Must vary as the giver's. Not for me!
For her! for your new fancy. Only this
Grant me, I pray you: have your joys apart.   1210
I doubt not that however changed, you keep
So much of what is graceful: and myself
Wound shun to break those bounds of courtesy
In which as Arthur's Queen I move and rule:
So cannot speak my mind. An end to this!
A strange one! yet I take it with Amen.
So pray you, add my diamonds to her pearls;
Deck her with these; tell her, she shines me down:
An armlet for an arm to which the Queen's
Is haggard, or a necklace for a neck   1220
O as much fairer—as a faith once fair
Was richer than these diamonds—hers not mine—
Nay, by the mother of our Lord himself,
Or hers or mine, mine now to work my will—
She shall not have them."

     Saying which she seized,
And, thro' the casement standing wide for heat,
Flung them, and down they flash'd, and smote the
  stream.
Then from the smitten surface flash'd, as it were,
Diamonds to meet them, and they past away.
Then while Sir Lancelot leant, in half disdain   1230

At love, life, all things, on the window ledge,
Close underneath his eyes, and right across
Where these had fallen, slowly past the barge
Whereon the lily maid of Astolat
Lay smiling, like a star in blackest night.

But the wild Queen, who saw not, burst away
To weep and wail in secret; and the barge,
On to the palace-doorway sliding, paused.
There two stood arm'd, and kept the door; to whom,
All up the marble stair, tier over tier,   1240
Were added mouths that gaped, and eyes that ask'd
"What is it?" but that oarsman's haggard face,
As hard and still as is the face that men
Shape to their fancy's eye from broken rocks
On some cliff-side, appall'd them, and they said,
"He is enchanted, cannot speak—and she,
Look how she sleeps—the Fairy Queen, so fair!
Yea, but how pale! what are they? flesh and blood?
Or come to take the King to Fairyland?
For some do hold our Arthur cannot die,   1250
But that he passes into Fairyland."

While thus they babbled of the King, the King
Came girt with knights: then turn'd the tongueless man
From the half-face to the full eye, and rose
And pointed to the damsel, and the doors.
So Arthur bad the meek Sir Percivale
And pure Sir Galahad to uplift the maid;
And reverently they bore her into hall.
Then came the fine Gawain and wonder'd at her,
And Lancelot later came and mused at her,   1260
And last the Queen herself, and pitied her:
But Arthur spied the letter in her hand,
Stoopt, took, brake seal, and read it; this was all:

"Most noble lord, Sir Lancelot of the Lake,
I, sometime call'd the maid of Astolat,
Come, for you left me taking no farewell,
Hither, to take my last farewell of you.
I loved you, and my love had no return,
And therefore my true love has been my death.
And therefore to our Lady Guinevere,   1270
And to all other ladies, I make moan:

Pray for my soul, and yield me burial.
Pray for my soul thou too, Sir Lancelot,
As thou art a knight peerless."

> Thus he read;
And ever in the reading, lords and dames
Wept, looking often from his face who read
To hers which lay so silent, and at times,
So touch'd were they, half-thinking that her lips,
Who had devised the letter, moved again.

Then freely spoke Sir Lancelot to them all: 1280
"My lord liege Arthur, and all ye that hear,
Know that for this most gentle maiden's death
Right heavy am I; for good she was and true,
But loved me with a love beyond all love
In women, whomsoever I have known.
Yet to be loved makes not to love again;
Not at my years, however it hold in youth.
I swear by truth and knighthood that I gave
No cause, not willingly, for such a love:
To this I call my friends in testimony, 1290
Her brethren, and her father, who himself
Besought me to be plain and blunt, and use,
To break her passion, some discourtesy
Against my nature: what I could, I did.
I left her and I bad her no farewell;
Tho', had I dreamt the damsel would have died,
I might have put my wits to some rough use,
And help'd her from herself."

> Then said the Queen
(Sea was her wrath, yet working after storm)
"Ye might at least have done her so much grace, 1300
Fair lord, as would have help'd her from her death."
He raised his head, their eyes met and hers fell,
He adding,

> "Queen, she would not be content
Save that I wedded her, which could not be.
Then might she follow me thro' the world, she ask'd;
It could not be. I told her that her love
Was but the flash of youth, would darken down
To rise hereafter in a stiller flame

Toward one more worthy of her—then would I,
More specially were he, she wedded, poor,   1310
Estate them with large land and territory
In mine own realm beyond the narrow seas,
To keep them in all joyance: more than this
I could not; this she would not, and she died."

He´pausing, Arthur answer'd, "O my knight,
It will be to thy worship, as my knight,
And mine, as head of all our Table Round,
To see that she be buried worshipfully."

So toward that shrine which then in all the realm
Was richest, Arthur leading, slowly went   1320
The marshall'd Order of their Table Round,
And Lancelot sad beyond his wont, to see
The maiden buried, not as one unknown,
Nor meanly, but with gorgeous obsequies,
And mass, and rolling music, like a queen.
And when the knights had laid her comely head
Low in the dust of half-forgotten kings,
Then Arthur spake among them, "Let her tomb
Be costly, and her image thereupon,
And let the shield of Lancelot at her feet   1330
Be carven, and her lily in her hand.
And let the story of her dolorous voyage
For all true hearts be blazon'd on her tomb
In letters gold and azure!" which was wrought
Thereafter; but when now the lords and dames
And people, from the high door streaming, brake
Disorderly, as homeward each, the Queen,
Who mark'd Sir Lancelot where he moved apart,
Drew near, and sigh'd in passing, "Lancelot,
Forgive me; mine was jealousy in love."   1340
He answer'd with his eyes upon the ground,
"That is love's curse; pass on, my Queen, forgiven."
But Arthur, who beheld his cloudy brows,
Approach'd him, and with full affection said,

"Lancelot, my Lancelot, thou in whom I have
Most joy and most affiance, for I know
What thou hast been in battle by my side,
And many a time have watch'd thee at the tilt
Strike down the lusty and long practised knight,

And let the younger and unskill'd go by 1350
To win his honour and to make his name,
And loved thy courtesies and thee, a man
Made to be loved; but now I would to God,
Seeing the homeless trouble in thine eyes,
Thou couldst have loved this maiden, shaped, it seems,
By God for thee alone, and from her face,
If one may judge the living by the dead,
Delicately pure and marvellously fair,
Who might have brought thee, now a lonely man
Wifeless and heirless, noble issue, sons 1360
Born to the glory of thy name and fame,
My knight, the great Sir Lancelot of the Lake."

Then answer'd Lancelot, "Fair she was, my King,
Pure, as you ever wish your knights to be.
To doubt her fairness were to want an eye,
To doubt her pureness were to want a heart—
Yea, to be loved, if what is worthy love
Could bind him, but free love will not be bound."

"Free love, so bound, were freëst," said the King.
"Let love be free; free love is for the best: 1370
And, after heaven, on our dull side of death,
What should be best, if not so pure a love
Clothed in so pure a loveliness? yet thee
She fail'd to bind, tho' being, as I think,
Unbound as yet, and gentle, as I know."

And Lancelot answer'd nothing, but he went,
And at the inrunning of a little brook
Sat by the river in a cove, and watch'd
The high reed wave, and lifted up his eyes
And saw the barge that brought her moving down, 1380
Far-off, a blot upon the stream, and said
Low in himself, "Ah simple heart and sweet,
Ye loved me, damsel, surely with a love
Far tenderer than my Queen's. Pray for thy soul?
Ay, that will I. Farewell too—now at last—
Farewell, fair lily. 'Jealousy in love?'
Not rather dead love's harsh heir, jealous pride?
Queen, if I grant the jealousy as of love,
May not your crescent fear for name and fame
Speak, as it waxes, of a love that wanes? 1390

Why did the King dwell on my name to me?
Mine own name shames me, seeming a reproach,
Lancelot, whom the Lady of the Lake
Caught from his mother's arms—the wondrous one
Who passes thro' the vision of the night—
She chanted snatches of mysterious hymns
Heard on the winding waters, eve and morn
She kiss'd me saying, 'Thou art fair, my child,
As a king's son,' and often in her arms
She bare me, pacing on the dusky mere.   1400
Would she had drown'd me in it, where'er it be!
For what am I? what profits me my name
Of greatest knight? I fought for it, and have it:
Pleasure to have it, none; to lose it, pain;
Now grown a part of me: but what use in it?
To make men worse by making my sin known?
Or sin seem less, the sinner seeming great?
Alas for Arthur's greatest knight, a man
Not after Arthur's heart! I needs must break
These bonds that so defame me: not without   1410
She wills it: would I, if she will'd it? nay,
Who knows? but if I would not, then may God,
I pray him, send a sudden Angel down
To seize me by the hair and bear me far,
And fling me deep in that forgotten mere,
Among the tumbled fragments of the hills."

     So groan'd Sir Lancelot in remorseful pain,
Not knowing he should die a holy man.

The Holy Grail

FROM noiseful arms, and acts of prowess done
In tournament or tilt, Sir Percivale,
Whom Arthur and his knighthood call'd The Pure,
Had pass'd into the silent life of prayer,
Praise, fast, and alms; and leaving for the cowl

The helmet in an abbey far away
From Camelot, there, and not long after, died.

And one, a fellow-monk among the rest,
Ambrosius, loved him much beyond the rest,
And honour'd him, and wrought into his heart   10
A way by love that waken'd love within,
To answer that which came: and as they sat
Beneath a world-old yew-tree, darkening half
The cloisters, on a gustful April morn
That puff'd the swaying branches into smoke
Above them, ere the summer when he died,
The monk Ambrosius question'd Percivale:

"O brother, I have seen this yew-tree smoke,
Spring after spring, for half a hundred years:
For never have I known the world without,   20
Nor ever stray'd beyond the pale: but thee,
When first thou camest—such a courtesy
Spake thro' the limbs and in the voice—I knew
For one of those who eat in Arthur's hall;
For good ye are and bad, and like to coins,
Some true, some light, but every one of you
Stamp'd with the image of the King; and now
Tell me, what drove thee from the Table Round,
My brother? was it earthly passion crost?"

"Nay," said the knight; "for no such passion mine.   30
But the sweet vision of the Holy Grail
Drove me from all vainglories, rivalries,
And earthly heats that spring and sparkle out
Among us in the jousts, while women watch
Who wins, who falls; and waste the spiritual strength
Within us, better offer'd up to Heaven."

To whom the monk: "The Holy Grail!—I trust
We are green in Heaven's eyes; but here too much
We moulder—as to things without I mean—
Yet one of your own knights, a guest of ours,   40
Told us of this in our refectory,
But spake with such a sadness and so low
We heard not half of what he said. What is it?
The phantom of a cup that comes and goes?"

"Nay, monk! what phantom?" answer'd Percivale.
"The cup, the cup itself, from which our Lord
Drank at the last sad supper with his own.
This, from the blessed land of Aromat—
After the day of darkness, when the dead
Went wandering o'er Moriah—the good saint   50
Arimathaean Joseph, journeying brought
To Glastonbury, where the winter thorn
Blossoms at Christmas, mindful of our Lord.
And there awhile it bode; and if a man
Could touch or see it, he was heal'd at once,
By faith, of all his ills. But then the times
Grew to such evil that the holy cup
Was caught away to Heaven, and disappear'd."

To whom the monk: "From our old books I know
That Joseph came of old to Glastonbury,   60
And there the heathen Prince, Arviragus,
Gave him an isle of marsh whereon to build;
And there he built with wattles from the marsh
A little lonely church in days of yore,
For so they say, these books of ours, but seem
Mute of this miracle, far as I have read.
But who first saw the holy thing to-day?"

"A woman," answer'd Percivale, "a nun,
And one no further off in blood from me
Than sister; and if ever holy maid   70
With knees of adoration wore the stone,
A holy maid; tho' never maiden glow'd,
But that was in her earlier maidenhood,
With such a fervent flame of human love,
Which being rudely blunted, glanced and shot
Only to holy things; to prayer and praise
She gave herself, to fast and alms. And yet,
Nun as she was, the scandal of the Court,
Sin against Arthur and the Table Round,
And the strange sound of an adulterous race,   80
Across the iron grating of her cell
Beat, and she pray'd and fasted all the more.

"And he to whom she told her sins, or what
Her all but utter whiteness held for sin,
A man wellnigh a hundred winters old

Spake often with her of the Holy Grail,
A legend handed down thro' five or six,
And each of these a hundred winters old,
From our Lord's time. And when King Arthur made
His Table Round, and all men's hearts became   90
Clean for a season, surely he had thought
That now the Holy Grail would come again;
But sin broke out. Ah, Christ, that it would come,
And heal the world of all their wickedness!
'Oh Father!' ask'd the maiden, 'might it come
To me by prayer and fasting?' 'Nay,' said he,
'I know not, for thy heart is pure as snow.'
And so she pray'd and fasted, till the sun
Shone, and the wind blew, thro' her, and I thought
She might have risen and floated when I saw her.   100

    "For on a day she sent to speak with me.
And when she came to speak, behold her eyes
Beyond my knowing of them, beautiful,
Beyond all knowing of them, wonderful,
Beautiful in the light of holiness.
And 'O my brother Percivale,' she said,
'Sweet brother, I have seen the Holy Grail:
For, waked at dead of night, I heard a sound
As of a silver horn from o'er the hills
Blown, and I thought, "It is not Arthur's use   110
To hunt by moonlight;" and the slender sound
As from a distance beyond distance grew
Coming upon me—O never harp nor horn,
Nor aught we blow with breath, or touch with hand,
Was like that music as it came; and then
Stream'd thro' my cell a cold and silver beam,
And down the long beam stole the Holy Grail,
Rose-red with beatings in it, as if alive,
Till all the white walls of my cell were dyed
With rosy colours leaping on the wall;   120
And then the music faded, and the Grail,
Past, and the beam decay'd, and from the walls
The rosy quiverings died into the night.
So now the Holy Thing is here again
Among us, brother, fast thou too and pray,
And tell thy brother knights to fast and pray,
That so perchance the vision may be seen
By thee and those, and all the world be heal'd.'

"Then leaving the pale nun, I spake of this
To all men; and myself fasted and pray'd   130
Always, and many among us many a week
Fasted and pray'd even to the uttermost,
Expectant of the wonder that would be.

"And one there was among us, ever moved
Among us in white armour, Galahad.
'God make thee good as thou art beautiful,'
Said Arthur, when he dubb'd him knight; and none,
In so young youth, was ever made a knight
Till Galahad; and this Galahad, when he heard
My sister's vision, fill'd me with amaze;   140
His eyes became so like her own, they seem'd
Hers, and himself her brother more than I.

"Sister or brother none had he; but some
Call'd him a son of Lancelot, and some said
Begotten by enchantment—chatterers they,
Like birds of passage piping up and down,
That gape for flies—we know not whence they come;
For when was Lancelot wanderingly lewd?

"But she, the wan sweet maiden, shore away
Clean from her forehead all that wealth of hair   150
Which made a silken mat-work for her feet;
And out of this she plaited broad and long
A strong sword-belt, and wove with silver thread
And crimson in the belt a strange device,
A crimson grail within a silver beam;
And saw the bright boy-knight, and bound it on him,
Saying, 'My knight, my love, my knight of heaven,
O thou, my love, whose love is one with mine,
I, maiden, round thee, maiden, bind my belt.
Go forth, for thou shalt see what I have seen,   160
And break thro' all, till one will crown thee king
Far in the spiritual city:' and as she spake
She sent the deathless passion in her eyes
Thro' him, and made him hers, and laid her mind
On him, and he believed in her belief.

"Then came a year of miracle: O brother,
In our great hall there stood a vacant chair,
Fashion'd by Merlin ere he past away,

And carven with strange figures; and in and out
The figures, like a serpent, ran a scroll   170
Of letters in a tongue no man could read.
And Merlin call'd it 'The Siege perilous,'
Perilous for good and ill; 'for there,' he said,
'No man could sit but he should lose himself:'
And once by misadventure Merlin sat
In his own chair, and so was lost; but he,
Galahad, when he heard of Merlin's doom,
Cried, 'If I lose myself, I save myself!'

"Then on a summer night it came to pass,
While the great banquet lay along the hall,   180
That Galahad would sit down in Merlin's chair.

"And all at once, as there we sat, we heard
A cracking and a riving of the roofs,
And rending, and a blast, and overhead
Thunder, and in the thunder was a cry.
And in the blast there smote along the hall
A beam of light seven times more clear than day:
And down the long beam stole the Holy Grail
All over cover'd with a luminous cloud,
And none might see who bare it, and it past.   190
But every knight beheld his fellow's face
As in a glory, and all the knights arose,
And staring each at other like dumb men
Stood, till I found a voice and sware a vow.

"I sware a vow before them all, that I,
Because I had not seen the Grail, would ride
A twelvemonth and a day in quest of it,
Until I found and saw it, as the nun
My sister saw it; and Galahad sware the vow,
And good Sir Bors, our Lancelot's cousin, sware.   200
And Lancelot sware, and many among the knights,
And Gawain sware, and louder than the rest."

Then spake the monk Ambrosius, asking him,
"What said the King? Did Arthur take the vow?"

"Nay, for my lord," said Percivale, "the King,
Was not in hall: for early that same day,
Scaped thro' a cavern from a bandit hold,

An outraged maiden sprang into the hall
Crying on help: for all her shining hair
Was smear'd with earth, and either milky arm   210
Red-rent with hooks of bramble, and all she wore
Torn as a sail that leaves the rope is torn
In tempest: so the King arose and went
To smoke the scandalous hive of those wild bees
That made such honey in his realm. Howbeit
Some little of this marvel he too saw,
Returning o'er the plain that then began
To darken under Camelot; whence the King
Look'd up, calling aloud, 'Lo, there! the roofs
Of our great hall are roll'd in thunder-smoke!   220
Pray Heaven, they be not smitten by the bolt.'
For dear to Arthur was that hall of ours,
As having there so oft with all his knights
Feasted, and as the stateliest under heaven.

"O brother, had you known our mighty hall,
Which Merlin built for Arthur long ago!
For all the sacred mount of Camelot,
And all the dim rich city, roof by roof,
Tower after tower, spire beyond spire,
By grove, and garden-lawn, and rushing brook,   230
Climbs to the mighty hall that Merlin built.
And four great zones of sculpture, set betwixt
With many a mystic symbol, gird the hall:
And in the lowest beasts are slaying men,
And in the second men are slaying beasts,
And on the third are warriors, perfect men,
And on the fourth are men with growing wings,
And over all one statue in the mould
Of Arthur, made by Merlin, with a crown,
And peak'd wings pointed to the Northern Star.   240
And eastward fronts the statue, and the crown
And both the wings are made of gold, and flame
At sunrise till the people in far fields,
Wasted so often by the heathen hordes,
Behold it, crying, 'We have still a King.'

"And, brother, had you known our hall within,
Broader and higher than any in all the lands!
Where twelve great windows blazon Arthur's wars,
And all the light that falls upon the board

Streams thro' the twelve great battles of our King.   250
Nay, one there is, and at the eastern end,
Wealthy with wandering lines of mount and mere,
Where Arthur finds the brand Excalibur.
And also one to the west, and counter to it,
And blank: and who shall blazon it? when and how?—
O there, perchance, when all our wars are done,
The brand Excalibur will be cast away.

"So to this hall full quickly rode the King,
In horror lest the work by Merlin wrought,
Dreamlike, should on the sudden vanish, wrapt   260
In unremorseful folds of rolling fire.
And in he rode, and up I glanced, and saw
The golden dragon sparkling over all:
And many of those who burnt the hold, their arms
Hack'd, and their foreheads grimed with smoke, and
     sear'd,
Follow'd, and in among bright faces, ours,
Full of the vision, prest: and then the King
Spake to me, being nearest, 'Percivale,'
(Because the hall was all in tumult—some
Vowing, and some protesting), 'what is this?'   270

"O brother, when I told him what had chanced,
My sister's vision, and the rest, his face
Darken'd, as I have seen it more than once,
When some brave deed seem'd to be done in vain,
Darken; and 'Woe is me, my knights,' he cried,
'Had I been here, ye had not sworn the vow.'
Bold was mine answer, 'Had thyself been here,
My King, thou wouldst have sworn.' 'Yea, yea,' said he,
'Art thou so bold and hast not seen the Grail?'

" 'Nay, lord, I heard the sound, I saw the light,   280
But since I did not see the Holy Thing,
I sware a vow to follow it till I saw.'

"Then when he ask'd us, knight by knight, if any
Had seen it, all their answers were as one:
'Nay, lord, and therefore have we sworn our vows.'

" 'Lo now,' said Arthur, 'have ye seen a cloud?
What go ye into the wilderness to see?'

"Then Galahad on the sudden, and in a voice
Shrilling along the hall to Arthur, call'd,
'But I, Sir Arthur, saw the Holy Grail,   290
I saw the Holy Grail and heard a cry—
"O Galahad, and O Galahad, follow me." '

" 'Ah, Galahad, Galahad,' said the King, 'for such
As thou art is the vision, not for these.
Thy holy nun and thou have seen a sign—
Holier is none, my Percivale, than she—
A sign to maim this Order which I made.
But ye, that follow but the leader's bell'
(Brother, the King was hard upon his knights)
'Taliessin is our fullest throat of song,   300
And one hath sung and all the dumb will sing.
Lancelot is Lancelot, and hath overborne
Five knights at once, and every younger knight,
Unproven, holds himself as Lancelot,
Till overborne by one, he learns—and ye,
What are ye? Galahads?—no, nor Percivales'
(For thus it pleased the King to range me close
After Sir Galahad); 'nay,' said he, 'but men
With strength and will to right the wrong'd, of power
To lay the sudden heads of violence flat,   310
Knights that in twelve great battles splash'd and dyed
The strong White Horse in his own heathen blood—
But one hath seen, and all the blind will see.
Go, since your vows are sacred, being made:
Yet—for ye know the cries of all my realm
Pass thro' this hall—how often, O my knights,
Your places being vacant at my side,
This chance of noble deeds will come and go
Unchallenged, while ye follow wandering fires
Lost in the quagmire! Many of you, yea most,   320
Return no more: ye think I show myself
Too dark a prophet: come now, let us meet
The morrow morn once more in one full field
Of gracious pastime, that once more the King,
Before ye leave him for this Quest, may count
The yet-unbroken strength of all his knights,
Rejoicing in that Order which he made.'

"So when the sun broke next from underground,
All the great table of our Arthur closed

And clash'd in such a tourney and so full,   330
So many lances broken—never yet
Had Camelot seen the like, since Arthur came;
And I myself and Galahad, for a strength
Was in us from the vision, overthrew
So many knights that all the people cried,
And almost burst the barriers in their heat,
Shouting, 'Sir Galahad and Sir Percivale!'

  "But when the next day brake from underground—
O brother, had you known our Camelot,
Built by old kings, age after age, so old   340
The King himself had fears that it would fall,
So strange, and rich, and dim; for where the roofs
Totter'd toward each other in the sky,
Met foreheads all along the street of those
Who watch'd us pass; and lower, and where the long
Rich galleries, lady-laden, weigh'd the necks
Of dragons clinging to the crazy walls,
Thicker than drops from thunder, showers of flowers
Fell as we past; and men and boys astride
On wyvern, lion, dragon, griffin, swan,   350
At all the corners, named us each by name,
Calling, 'God speed!' but in the ways below
The knights and ladies wept, and rich and poor
Wept, and the King himself could hardly speak
For grief, and all in middle street the Queen,
Who rode by Lancelot, wail'd and shriek'd aloud,
'This madness has come on us for our sins.'
So to the Gate of the three Queens we came,
Where Arthur's wars are render'd mystically,
And thence departed every one his way.   360

  "And I was lifted up in heart, and thought
Of all my late-shown prowess in the lists,
How my strong lance had beaten down the knights,
So many and famous names; and never yet
Had heaven appear'd so blue, nor earth so green,
For all my blood danced in me, and I knew
That I should light upon the Holy Grail.

  "Thereafter, the dark warning of our King,
That most of us would follow wandering fires
Came like a driving gloom across my mind.   370

Then every evil word I had spoken once,
And every evil thought I had thought of old,
And every evil deed I ever did,
Awoke and cried, 'This Quest is not for thee.'
And lifting up mine eyes, I found myself
Alone, and in a land of sand and thorns,
And I was thirsty even unto death;
And I, too, cried, 'This Quest is not for thee.'

"And on I rode, and when I thought my thirst
Would slay me, saw deep lawns, and then a brook,   380
With one sharp rapid, where the crisping white
Play'd ever back upon the sloping wave,
And took both ear and eye; and o'er the brook
Were apple-trees, and apples by the brook
Fallen, and on the lawns. 'I will rest here,'
I said, 'I am not worthy of the Quest;'
But even while I drank the brook, and ate
The goodly apples, all these things at once
Fell into dust, and I was left alone,
And thirsting, in a land of sand and thorns.   390

"And then behold a woman at a door
Spinning; and fair the house whereby she sat,
And kind the woman's eyes and innocent,
And all her bearing gracious; and she rose
Opening her arms to meet me, as who should say,
'Rest here;' but when I touch'd her, lo! she, too,
Fell into dust and nothing, and the house
Became no better than a broken shed,
And in it a dead babe; and also this
Fell into dust, and I was left alone.   400

"And on I rode, and greater was my thirst.
Then flash'd a yellow gleam across the world,
And where it smote the plowshare in the field,
The plowman left his plowing, and fell down
Before it; where it glitter'd on her pail
The milkmaid left her milking, and fell down
Before it, and I knew not why, but thought
'The sun is rising,' tho' the sun had risen.
Then was I ware of one that on me moved
In golden armour with a crown of gold   410
About a casque all jewels; and his horse

In golden armour jewell'd everywhere:
And on the splendour came, flashing me blind;
And seem'd to me the Lord of all the world,
Being so huge. But when I thought he meant
To crush me, moving on me, lo! he, too,
Open'd his arms to embrace me as he came,
And up I went and touch'd him, and he, too,
Fell into dust, and I was left alone
And wearying in a land of sand and thorns.   420

"And I rode on and found a mighty hill,
And on the top, a city wall'd: the spires
Prick'd with incredible pinnacles into heaven.
And by the gateway stirr'd a crowd; and these
Cried to me climbing, 'Welcome, Percivale!
Thou mightiest and thou purest among men!'
And glad was I and clomb, but found at top
No man, nor any voice. And thence I past
Far thro' a ruinous city, and I saw
That man had once dwelt there; but there I found   430
Only one man of an exceeding age.
'Where is that goodly company,' said I,
'That so cried out upon me?' and he had
Scarce any voice to answer, and yet gasp'd,
'Whence and what art thou?' and even as he spoke
Fell into dust, and disappear'd, and I
Was left alone once more, and cried in grief,
'Lo, if I find the Holy Grail itself
And touch it, it will crumble into dust.'

"And thence I dropt into a lowly vale,   440
Low as the hill was high, and where the vale
Was lowest, found a chapel, and thereby
A holy hermit in a hermitage,
To whom I told my phantoms, and he said:

" 'O son, thou hast not true humility,
The highest virtue, mother of them all;
For when the Lord of all things made Himself
Naked of glory for His mortal change,
"Take thou my robe," she said, "for all is thine,"
And all her form shone forth with sudden light   450
So that the angels were amazed, and she
Follow'd Him down, and like a flying star

Led on the gray-hair'd wisdom of the east;
But her thou hast not known: for what is this
Thou thoughtest of thy prowess and thy sins?
Thou hast not lost thyself to save thyself
As Galahad.' When the hermit made an end,
In silver armour suddenly Galahad shone
Before us, and against the chapel door
Laid lance, and enter'd, and we knelt in prayer.   460
And there the hermit slaked my burning thirst,
And at the sacring of the mass I saw
The holy elements alone; but he,
'Saw ye no more? I, Galahad, saw the Grail,
The Holy Grail, descend upon the shrine:
I saw the fiery face as of a child
That smote itself into the bread, and went;
And hither am I come; and never yet
Hath what thy sister taught me first to see,
This Holy Thing, fail'd from my side, nor come   470
Cover'd, but moving with me night and day,
Fainter by day, but always in the night
Blood-red, and sliding down the blacken'd marsh
Blood-red, and on the naked mountain top
Blood-red, and in the sleeping mere below
Blood-red. And in the strength of this I rode,
Shattering all evil customs everywhere,
And past thro' Pagan realms, and made them mine,
And clash'd with Pagan hordes, and bore them down
And broke thro' all, and in the strength of this   480
Come victor. But my time is hard at hand,
And hence I go; and one will crown me king
Far in the spiritual city; and come thou, too,
For thou shalt see the vision when I go.'

    "While thus he spake, his eye, dwelling on mine,
Drew me, with power upon me, till I grew
One with him, to believe as he believed.
Then, when the day began to wane, we went.

    "There rose a hill that none but man could climb,
Scarr'd with a hundred wintry water-courses—   490
Storm at the top, and when we gain'd it, storm
Round us and death; for every moment glanced
His silver arms and gloom'd: so quick and thick
The lightnings here and there to left and right

Struck, till the dry old trunks about us, dead,
Yea, rotten with a hundred years of death,
Sprang into fire: and at the base we found
On either hand, as far as eye could see,
A great black swamp and of an evil smell,
Part black, part whiten'd with the bones of men,   500
Not to be crost, save that some ancient king
Had built a way, where, link'd with many a bridge,
A thousand piers ran into the great Sea.
And Galahad fled along them bridge by bridge,
And every bridge as quickly as he crost
Sprang into fire and vanish'd, tho' I yearn'd
To follow; and thrice above him all the heavens
Open'd and blazed with thunder such as seem'd
Shoutings of all the sons of God: and first
At once I saw him far on the great Sea,   510
In silver-shining armour starry-clear;
And o'er his head the Holy Vessel hung
Clothed in white samite or a luminous cloud.
And with exceeding swiftness ran the boat,
If boat it were—I saw not whence it came.
And when the heavens open'd and blazed again
Roaring, I saw him like a silver star—
And had he set the sail, or had the boat
Become a living creature clad with wings?
And o'er his head the Holy Vessel hung   520
Redder than any rose, a joy to me,
For now I knew the veil had been withdrawn.
Then in a moment when they blazed again
Opening, I saw the least of little stars
Down on the waste, and straight beyond the star
I saw the spiritual city and all her spires
And gateways in a glory like one pearl—
No larger, tho' the goal of all the saints—
Strike from the sea; and from the star there shot
A rose-red sparkle to the city, and there   530
Dwelt, and I knew it was the Holy Grail,
Which never eyes on earth again shall see.
Then fell the floods of heaven drowning the deep.
And how my feet recrost the deathful ridge
No memory in me lives; but that I touch'd
The chapel-doors at dawn I know; and thence
Taking my war-horse from the holy man,
Glad that no phantom vext me more, return'd

To whence I came, the gate of Arthur's wars."

"O brother," ask'd Ambrosius,—"for in sooth   540
These ancient books—and they would win thee—teem.
Only I find not there this Holy Grail,
With miracles and marvels like to these,
Not all unlike; which oftentime I read,
Who read but on my breviary with ease,
Till my head swims; and then go forth and pass
Down to the little thorpe that lies so close,
And almost plaster'd like a martin's nest
To these old walls—and mingle with our folk;
And knowing every honest face of theirs   550
As well as ever shepherd knew his sheep,
And every homely secret in their hearts,
Delight myself with gossip and old wives,
And ills and aches, and teethings, lyings-in,
And mirthful sayings, children of the place,
That have no meaning half a league away:
Or lulling random squabbles when they rise,
Chafferings and chatterings at the market-cross,
Rejoice, small man, in this small world of mine,
Yea, even in their hens and in their eggs—   560
O brother, saving this Sir Galahad,
Came ye on none but phantoms in your quest,
No man, no woman?"

                    Then Sir Percivale:
"All men, to one so bound by such a vow,
And women were as phantoms. O, my brother,
Why wilt thou shame me to confess to thee
How far I falter'd from my quest and vow?
For after I had lain so many nights,
A bedmate of the snail and eft and snake,
In grass and burdock, I was changed to wan   570
And meagre, and the vision had not come;
And then I chanced upon a goodly town
With one great dwelling in the middle of it;
Thither I made, and there was I disarm'd
By maidens each as fair as any flower:
But when they led me into hall, behold,
The Princess of that castle was the one,
Brother, and that one only, who had ever
Made my heart leap; for when I moved of old

A slender page about her father's hall,   580
And she a slender maiden, all my heart
Went after her with longing: yet we twain
Had never kiss'd a kiss, or vow'd a vow.
And now I came upon her once again,
And one had wedded her, and he was dead,
And all his land and wealth and state were hers.
And while I tarried, every day she set
A banquet richer than the day before
By me; for all her longing and her will
Was toward me as of old; till one fair morn,   590
I walking to and fro beside a stream
That flash'd across her orchard underneath
Her castle-walls, she stole upon my walk,
And calling me the greatest of all knights,
Embraced me, and so kiss'd me the first time,
And gave herself and all her wealth to me.
Then I remember'd Arthur's warning word,
That most of us would follow wandering fires,
And the Quest faded in my heart. Anon,
The heads of all her people drew to me,   600
With supplication both of knees and tongue:
'We have heard of thee: thou art our greatest knight,
Our Lady says it, and we well believe:
Wed thou our Lady, and rule over us,
And thou shalt be as Arthur in our land.'
O me, my brother! but one night my vow
Burnt me within, so that I rose and fled,
But wail'd and wept, and hated mine own self,
And ev'n the Holy Quest, and all but her;
Then after I was join'd with Galahad   610
Cared not for her, nor anything upon earth."

Then said the monk, "Poor men, when yule is cold,
Must be content to sit by little fires.
And this am I, so that ye care for me
Ever so little; yea, and blest be Heaven
That brought thee here to this poor house of ours
Where all the brethren are so hard, to warm
My cold heart with a friend: but O the pity
To find thine own first love once more—to hold,
Hold her a wealthy bride within thine arms,   620
Or all but hold, and then—cast her aside,
Forgoing all her sweetness, like a weed.

For we that want the warmth of double life,
We that are plagued with dreams of something sweet
Beyond all sweetness in a life so rich,—
Ah, blessed Lord, I speak too earthlywise,
Seeing I never stray'd beyond the cell,
But live like an old badger in his earth,
With earth about him everywhere, despite
All fast and penance. Saw ye none beside,   630
None of your knights?"

                         "Yea so," said Percivale:
"One night my pathway swerving east, I saw
The pelican on the casque of our Sir Bors
All in the middle of the rising moon:
And toward him spurr'd, and hail'd him, and he me,
And each made joy of either; then he ask'd,
'Where is he? hast thou seen him—Lancelot?—Once,'
Said good Sir Bors, 'he dash'd across me—mad,
And maddening what he rode: and when I cried,
"Ridest thou then so hotly on a quest   640
So holy," Lancelot shouted, "Stay me not!
I have been the sluggard, and I ride apace,
For now there is a lion in the way."
So vanish'd.'

                         "Then Sir Bors had ridden on
Softly, and sorrowing for our Lancelot,
Because his former madness, once the talk
And scandal of our table, had return'd;
For Lancelot's kith and kin so worship him
That ill to him is ill to them; to Bors
Beyond the rest: he well had been content   650
Not to have seen, so Lancelot might have seen,
The Holy Cup of healing; and, indeed,
Being so clouded with his grief and love,
Small heart was his after the Holy Quest:
If God would send the vision, well: if not,
The Quest and he were in the hands of Heaven.

    "And then, with small adventure met, Sir Bors
Rode to the lonest tract of all the realm,
And found a people there among their crags,
Our race and blood, a remnant that were left   660
Paynim amid their circles, and the stones

They pitch up straight to heaven: and their wise men
Were strong in that old magic which can trace
The wandering of the stars, and scoff'd at him
And this high Quest as at a simple thing:
Told him he follow'd—almost Arthur's words—
A mocking fire: 'what other fire than he,
Whereby the blood beats, and the blossom blows,
And the sea rolls, and all the world is warm'd?'
And when his answer chafed them, the rough crowd,   670
Hearing he had a difference with their priests,
Seized him, and bound and plunged him into a cell
Of great piled stones; and lying bounden there
In darkness thro' innumerable hours
He heard the hollow-ringing heavens sweep
Over him till by miracle—what else?—
Heavy as it was, a great stone slipt and fell,
Such as no wind could move: and thro' the gap
Glimmer'd the streaming scud: then came a night
Still as the day was loud; and thro' the gap   680
The seven clear stars of Arthur's Table Round—
For, brother, so one night, because they roll
Thro' such a round in heaven, we named the stars,
Rejoicing in ourselves and in our King—
And these, like bright eyes of familiar friends,
In on him shone: 'And then to me, to me,'
Said good Sir Bors, 'beyond all hopes of mine,
Who scarce had pray'd or ask'd it for myself—
Across the seven clear stars—O grace to me—
In colour like the fingers of a hand   690
Before a burning taper, the sweet Grail
Glided and past, and close upon it peal'd
A sharp quick thunder.' Afterwards, a maid,
Who kept our holy faith among her kin
In secret, entering, loosed and let him go."

To whom the monk: "And I remember now
That pelican on the casque: Sir Bors it was
Who spake so low and sadly at our board;
And mighty reverent at our grace was he:
A square-set man and honest; and his eyes,   700
An out-door sign of all the warmth within,
Smiled with his lips—a smile beneath a cloud,
But heaven had meant it for a sunny one:
Ay, ay, Sir Bors, who else? But when ye reach'd

The city, found ye all your knights return'd,
Or was there sooth in Arthur's prophecy,
Tell me, and what said each, and what the King?"

Then answer'd Percivale: "And that can I,
Brother, and truly; since the living words
Of so great men as Lancelot and our King   710
Pass not from door to door and out again,
But sit within the house. O, when we reach'd
The city, our horses stumbling as they trode
On heaps of ruin, hornless unicorns,
Crack'd basilisks, and splinter'd cockatrices,
And shatter'd talbots, which had left the stones
Raw, that they fell from, brought us to the hall.

"And there sat Arthur on the daïs-throne,
And those that had gone out upon the Quest,
Wasted and worn, and but a tithe of them,   720
And those that had not, stood before the King,
Who, when he saw me, rose, and bad me hail,
Saying, 'A welfare in thine eyes reproves
Our fear of some disastrous chance for thee
On hill, or plain, at sea, or flooding ford.
So fierce a gale made havoc here of late
Among the strange devices of our kings;
Yea, shook this newer, stronger hall of ours,
And from the statue Merlin moulded for us
Half-wrench'd a golden wing; but now—the Quest,   730
This vision—hast thou seen the Holy Cup,
That Joseph brought of old to Glastonbury?'

"So when I told him all thyself hast heard,
Ambrosius, and my fresh but fixt resolve
To pass away into the quiet life,
He answer'd not, but, sharply turning, ask'd
Of Gawain, 'Gawain, was this Quest for thee?'

" 'Nay, lord,' said Gawain, 'not for such as I.
Therefore I communed with a saintly man,
Who made me sure the Quest was not for me;   740
For I was much awearied of the Quest:
But found a silk pavilion in a field,
And merry maidens in it; and then this gale
Tore my pavilion from the tenting-pin,

And blew my merry maidens all about
With all discomfort; yea, and but for this,
My twelvemonth and a day were pleasant to me.'

  "He ceased; and Arthur turn'd to whom at first
He saw not, for Sir Bors, on entering, push'd
Athwart the throng to Lancelot, caught his hand,   750
Held it, and there, half-hidden by him, stood,
Until the King espied him, saying to him,
'Hail, Bors! if ever loyal man and true
Could see it, thou hast seen the Grail;' and Bors,
'Ask me not, for I may not speak of it:
I saw it;' and the tears were in his eyes.

  "Then there remain'd but Lancelot, for the rest
Spake but of sundry perils in the storm;
Perhaps, like him of Cana in Holy Writ,
Our Arthur kept his best until the last;   760
'Thou, too, my Lancelot,' ask'd the King, 'my friend,
Our mightiest, hath this Quest avail'd for thee?'

  " 'Our mightiest!' answer'd Lancelot, with a groan;
'O King!'—and when he paused, methought I spied
A dying fire of madness in his eyes—
'O King, my friend, if friend of thine I be,
Happier are those that welter in their sin,
Swine in the mud, that cannot see for slime,
Slime of the ditch: but in me lived a sin
So strange, of such a kind, that all of pure,   770
Noble, and knightly in me twined and clung
Round that one sin, until the wholesome flower
And poisonous grew together, each as each,
Not to be pluck'd asunder; and when thy knights
Sware, I sware with them only in the hope
That could I touch or see the Holy Grail
They might be pluck'd asunder. Then I spake
To one most holy saint, who wept and said,
That save they could be pluck'd asunder, all
My quest were but in vain; to whom I vow'd   780
That I would work according as he will'd.
And forth I went, and while I yearn'd and strove
To tear the twain asunder in my heart,
My madness came upon me as of old,
And whipt me into waste fields far away;

There was I beaten down by little men,
Mean knights, to whom the moving of my sword
And shadow of my spear had been enow
To scare them from me once; and then I came
All in my folly to the naked shore,   790
Wide flats, where nothing but coarse grasses grew;
But such a blast, my King, began to blow,
So loud a blast along the shore and sea,
Ye could not hear the waters for the blast,
Tho' heapt in mounds and ridges all the sea
Drove like a cataract, and all the sand
Swept like a river, and the clouded heavens
Were shaken with the motion and the sound.
And blackening in the sea-foam sway'd a boat,
Half-swallow'd in it, anchor'd with a chain;   800
And in my madness to myself I said,
"I will embark and I will lose myself,
And in the great sea wash away my sin."
I burst the chain, I sprang into the boat.
Seven days I drove along the dreary deep,
And with me drove the moon and all the stars;
And the wind fell, and on the seventh night
I heard the shingle grinding in the surge,
And felt the boat shock earth, and looking up,
Behold, the enchanted towers of Carbonek,   810
A castle like a rock upon a rock,
With chasm-like portals open to the sea,
And steps that met the breaker! there was none
Stood near it but a lion on each side
That kept the entry, and the moon was full.
Then from the boat I leapt, and up the stairs.
There drew my sword. With sudden-flaring manes
Those two great beasts rose upright like a man,
Each gript a shoulder, and I stood between;
And, when I would have smitten them, heard a voice,   820
"Doubt not, go forward; if thou doubt, the beasts
Will tear thee piecemeal." Then with violence
The sword was dash'd from out my hand, and fell.
And up into the sounding hall I past;
But nothing in the sounding hall I saw,
No bench nor table, painting on the wall
Or shield of knight; only the rounded moon
Thro' the tall oriel on the rolling sea.
But always in the quiet house I heard,

Clear as a lark, high o'er me as a lark,   830
A sweet voice singing in the topmost tower
To the eastward: up I climb'd a thousand steps
With pain: as in a dream I seem'd to climb
For ever: at the last I reach'd a door,
A light was in the crannies, and I heard,
"Glory and joy and honour to our Lord
And to the Holy Vessel of the Grail."
Then in my madness I essay'd the door;
It gave; and thro' a stormy glare, a heat
As from a seventimes-heated furnace, I,   840
Blasted and burnt, and blinded as I was,
With such a fierceness that I swoon'd away—
O, yet methought I saw the Holy Grail,
All pall'd in crimson samite, and around
Great angels, awful shapes, and wings and eyes.
And but for all my madness and my sin,
And then my swooning, I had sworn I saw
That which I saw; but what I saw was veil'd
And cover'd; and this Quest was not for me.'

"So speaking, and here ceasing, Lancelot left   850
The hall long silent, till Sir Gawain—nay,
Brother, I need not tell thee foolish words,—
A reckless and irreverent knight was he,
Now bolden'd by the silence of his King,—
Well, I will tell thee: 'O King, my liege,' he said,
'Hath Gawain fail'd in any quest of thine?
When have I stinted stroke in foughten field?
But as for thine, my good friend Percivale,
Thy holy nun and thou have driven men mad,
Yea, made our mightiest madder than our least.   860
But by mine eyes and by mine ears I swear,
I will be deafer than the blue-eyed cat,
And thrice as blind as any noonday owl,
To holy virgins in their ecstasies,
Henceforward.'

            " 'Deafer,' said the blameless King,
'Gawain, and blinder unto holy things
Hope not to make thyself by idle vows,
Being too blind to have desire to see.
But if indeed there came a sign from heaven,
Blessed are Bors, Lancelot and Percivale,   870

For these have seen according to their sight.
For every fiery prophet in old times,
And all the sacred madness of the bard,
When God made music thro' them, could but speak
His music by the framework and the chord;
And as ye saw it ye have spoken truth.

" 'Nay—but thou errest, Lancelot: never yet
Could all of true and noble in knight and man
Twine round one sin, whatever it might be,
With such a closeness, but apart there grew,   880
Save that he were the swine thou spakest of,
Some root of knighthood and pure nobleness;
Whereto see thou, that it may bear its flower.

" 'And spake I not too truly, O my knights?
Was I too dark a prophet when I said
To those who went upon the Holy Quest,
That most of them would follow wandering fires,
Lost in the quagmire?—lost to me and gone,
And left me gazing at a barren board,
And a lean Order—scarce return'd a tithe—   890
And out of those to whom the vision came
My greatest hardly will believe he saw;
Another hath beheld it afar off,
And leaving human wrongs to right themselves,
Cares but to pass into the silent life.
And one hath had the vision face to face,
And now his chair desires him here in vain,
However they may crown him otherwhere.

" 'And some among you held, that if the King
Had seen the sight he would have sworn the vow: 900
Not easily, seeing that the King must guard
That which he rules, and is but as the hind
To whom a space of land is given to plow.
Who may not wander from the allotted field
Before his work be done; but, being done,
Let visions of the night or of the day
Come, as they will; and many a time they come,
Until this earth he walks on seems not earth,
This light that strikes his eyeball is not light,
This air that smites his forehead is not air   910

But vision—yea, his very hand and foot—
In moments when he feels he cannot die,
And knows himself no vision to himself,
Nor the high God a vision, nor that One
Who rose again: ye have seen what ye have seen.'

"So spake the King: I knew not all he meant."

Pelleas and Ettarre

KING ARTHUR made new knights to fill the gap
Left by the Holy Quest; and as he sat
In hall at old Caerleon, the high doors
Were softly sunder'd, and thro' these a youth,
Pelleas, and the sweet smell of the fields
Past, and the sunshine came along with him.

"Make me thy knight, because I know, Sir King,
All that belongs to knighthood, and I love."
Such was his cry: for having heard the King
Had let proclaim a tournament—the prize   10
A golden circlet and a knightly sword,
Full fain had Pelleas for his lady won
The golden circlet, for himself the sword:
And there were those who knew him near the King,
And promised for him: and Arthur made him knight.

And this new knight, Sir Pelleas of the isles—
But lately come to his inheritance,
And lord of many a barren isle was he—
Riding at noon, a day or twain before,
Across the forest call'd of Dean, to find   20
Caerleon and the King, had felt the sun
Beat like a strong knight on his helm, and reel'd
Almost to falling from his horse; but saw
Near him a mound of even-sloping side,

Whereon a hundred stately beeches grew,
And here and there great hollies under them;
But for a mile all round was open space,
And fern and heath: and slowly Pelleas drew
To that dim day, then binding his good horse
To a tree, cast himself down; and as he lay   30
At random looking over the brown earth
Thro' that green-glooming twilight of the grove,
It seem'd to Pelleas that the fern without
Burnt as a living fire of emeralds,
So that his eyes were dazzled looking at it.
Then o'er it crost the dimness of a cloud
Floating, and once the shadow of a bird
Flying, and then a fawn; and his eyes closed.
And since he loved all maidens, but no maid
In special, half-awake he whisper'd, "Where?   40
O where? I love thee, tho' I know thee not.
For fair thou art and pure as Guinevere,
And I will make thee with my spear and sword
As famous—O my Queen, my Guinevere,
For I will be thine Arthur when we meet."

    Suddenly waken'd with a sound of talk
And laughter at the limit of the wood,
And glancing thro' the hoary boles, he saw,
Strange as to some old prophet might have seem'd
A vision hovering on a sea of fire,   50
Damsels in divers colours like the cloud
Of sunset and sunrise, and all of them
On horses, and the horses richly trapt
Breast-high in that bright line of bracken stood:
And all the damsels talk'd confusedly,
And one was pointing this way, and one that,
Because the way was lost.

                        And Pelleas rose,
And loosed his horse, and led him to the light.
There she that seem'd the chief among them said,
"In happy time behold our pilot-star!   60
Youth, we are damsels-errant, and we ride,
Arm'd as ye see, to tilt against the knights
There at Caerleon, but have lost our way:
To right? to left? straight forward? back again?
Which? tell us quickly."

Pelleas gazing thought,
"Is Guinevere herself so beautiful?"
For large her violet eyes look'd, and her bloom
A rosy dawn kindled in stainless heavens,
And round her limbs, mature in womanhood;
And slender was her hand and small her shape;   70
And but for those large eyes, the haunts of scorn,
She might have seem'd a toy to trifle with,
And pass and care no more. But while he gazed
The beauty of her flesh abash'd the boy,
As tho' it were the beauty of her soul:
For as the base man, judging of the good,
Puts his own baseness in him by default
Of will and nature, so did Pelleas lend
All the young beauty of his own soul to hers,
Believing her; and when she spake to him,   80
Stammer'd, and could not make her a reply.
For out of the waste islands had he come,
Where saving his own sisters he had known
Scarce any but the women of his isles,
Rough wives, that laugh'd and scream'd against the
     gulls,
Makers of nets, and living from the sea.

Then with a slow smile turn'd the lady round
And look'd upon her people; and as when
A stone is flung into some sleeping tarn,
The circle widens till it lip the marge,   90
Spread the slow smile thro' all her company.
Three knights were thereamong; and they too smiled,
Scorning him; for the lady was Ettarre,
And she was a great lady in her land.

Again she said, "O wild and of the woods,
Knowest thou not the fashion of our speech?
Or have the Heavens but given thee a fair face,
Lacking a tongue?"

"O damsel," answer'd he,
"I woke from dreams; and coming out of gloom
Was dazzled by the sudden light, and crave   100
Pardon: but will ye to Caerleon? I
Go likewise: shall I lead you to the King?"

"Lead then," she said; and thro' the woods they went
And while they rode, the meaning in his eyes,
His tenderness of manner, and chaste awe,
His broken utterances and bashfulness,
Were all a burthen to her, and in her heart
She mutter'd, "I have lighted on a fool,
Raw, yet so stale!" But since her mind was bent
On hearing, after trumpet blown, her name   110
And title, "Queen of Beauty," in the lists
Cried—and beholding him so strong, she thought
That peradventure he will fight for me,
And win the circlet: therefore flatter'd him,
Being so gracious, that he wellnigh deem'd
His wish by hers was echo'd; and her knights
And all her damsels too were gracious to him,
For she was a great lady.

              And when they reach'd
Caerleon, ere they past to lodging, she,
Taking his hand, "O the strong hand," she said,   120
"See! look at mine! but wilt thou fight for me,
And win me this fine circlet, Pelleas,
That I may love thee?"

              Then his helpless heart
Leapt, and he cried, "Ay! wilt thou if I win?"
"Ay, that will I," she answer'd, and she laugh'd,
And straitly nipt the hand, and flung it from her;
Then glanced askew at those three knights of hers,
Till all her ladies laugh'd along with her.

"O happy world," thought Pelleas, "all, meseems,
Are happy; I the happiest of them all."   130
Nor slept that night for pleasure in his blood,
And green wood-ways, and eyes among the leaves;
Then being on the morrow knighted, sware
To love one only. And as he came away,
The men who met him rounded on their heels
And wonder'd after him, because his face
Shone like the countenance of a priest of old
Against the flame about a sacrifice
Kindled by fire from heaven: so glad was he.

Then Arthur made vast banquets, and strange
   knights   140

From the four winds came in: and each one sat,
Tho' served with choice from air, land, stream, and sea,
Oft in mid-banquet measuring with his eyes
His neighbour's make and might: and Pelleas look'd
Noble among the noble, for he dream'd
His lady loved him, and he knew himself
Loved of the King; and him his new-made knight
Worshipt, whose lightest whisper moved him more
Than all the ranged reasons of the world.

Then blush'd and brake the morning of the jousts,   150
And this was call'd "The Tournament of Youth:"
For Arthur, loving his young knight, withheld
His older and his mightier from the lists,
That Pelleas might obtain his lady's love,
According to her promise, and remain
Lord of the tourney. And Arthur had the jousts
Down in the flat field by the shore of Usk
Holden: the gilded parapets were crown'd
With faces, and the great tower fill'd with eyes
Up to the summit, and the trumpets blew.   160
There all day long Sir Pelleas kept the field
With honour: so by that strong hand of his
The sword and golden circlet were achieved.

Then rang the shout his lady loved: the heat
Of pride and glory fired her face; her eye
Sparkled; she caught the circlet from his lance,
And there before the people crown'd herself:
So for the last time she was gracious to him.

Then at Caerleon for a space—her look
Bright for all others, cloudier on her knight—   170
Linger'd Ettarre: and seeing Pelleas droop,
Said Guinevere, "We marvel at thee much,
O damsel, wearing this unsunny face
To him who won thee glory!" And she said,
"Had ye not held your Lancelot in your bower,
My Queen, he had not won." Whereat the Queen,
As one whose foot is bitten by an ant,
Glanced down upon her, turn'd and went her way.

But after, when her damsels, and herself,
And those three knights all set their faces home,   180

Sir Pelleas follow'd. She that saw him cried,
"Damsels—and yet I should be shamed to say it—
I cannot bide Sir Baby. Keep him back
Among yourselves. Would rather that we had
Some rough old knight who knew the worldly way,
Albeit grizzlier than a bear, to ride
And jest with: take him to you, keep him off,
And pamper him with papmeat, if ye will,
Old milky fables of the wolf and sheep,
Such as the wholesome mothers tell their boys   190
Nay, should ye try him with a merry one
To find his mettle, good: and if he fly us,
Small matter! let him." This her damsels heard,
And mindful of her small and cruel hand,
They, closing round him thro' the journey home,
Acted her hest, and always from her side
Restrain'd him with all manner of device,
So that he could not come to speech with her.
And when she gain'd her castle, upsprang the bridge,
Down rang the grate of iron thro' the groove,   200
And he was left alone in open field.

    "These be the ways of ladies," Pelleas thought,
"To those who love them, trials of our faith.
Yea, let her prove me to the uttermost,
For loyal to the uttermost am I."
So made his moan; and, darkness falling, sought
A priory not far off, there lodged, but rose
With morning every day, and, moist or dry,
Full-arm'd upon his charger all day long
Sat by the walls, and no one open'd to him.   210

    And this persistence turn'd her scorn to wrath.
Then calling her three knights, she charged them,
          "Out!
And drive him from the walls." And out they came,
But Pelleas overthrew them as they dash'd
Against him one by one; and these return'd,
But still he kept his watch beneath the wall.

    Thereon her wrath became a hate; and once,
A week beyond, while walking on the walls
With her three knights, she pointed downward, "Look,
He haunts me—I cannot breathe—besieges me;   220

Down! strike him! put my hate into your strokes,
And drive him from my walls." And down they went,
And Pelleas overthrew them one by one;
And from the tower above him cried Ettarre,
"Bind him, and bring him in."

                     He heard her voice;
Then let the strong hand, which had overthrown
Her minion-knights, by those he overthrew
Be bounden straight, and so they brought him in.

Then when he came before Ettarre, the sight
Of her rich beauty made him at one glance   230
More bondsman in his heart than in his bonds.
Yet with good cheer he spake, "Behold me, Lady,
A prisoner, and the vassal of thy will;
And if thou keep me in thy donjon here,
Content am I so that I see thy face
But once a day: for I have sworn my vows,
And thou hast given thy promise, and I know
That all these pains are trials of my faith,
And that thyself, when thou hast seen me strain'd
And sifted to the utmost, wilt at length   240
Yield me thy love and know me for thy knight."

Then she began to rail so bitterly,
With all her damsels, he was stricken mute;
But when she mock'd his vows and the great King,
Lighted on words: "For pity of thine own self,
Peace, Lady, peace: is he not thine and mine?"
"Thou fool," she said, "I never heard his voice
But long'd to break away. Unbind him now,
And thrust him out of doors; for save he be
Fool to the midmost marrow of his bones,   250
He will return no more." And those, her three,
Laugh'd, and unbound, and thrust him from the gate.

And after this, a week beyond, again
She call'd them, saying, "There he watches yet,
There like a dog before his master's door!
Kick'd, he returns: do ye not hate him, ye?
Ye know yourselves: how can ye bide at peace,
Affronted with his fulsome innocence?
Are ye but creatures of the board and bed,

No men to strike? Fall on him all at once,   260
And if ye slay him I reck not: if ye fail,
Give ye the slave mine order to be bound,
Bind him as heretofore, and bring him in:
It may be ye shall slay him in his bonds."

She spake; and at her will they couch'd their spears,
Three against one: and Gawain passing by,
Bound upon solitary adventure, saw
Low down beneath the shadow of those towers
A villainy, three to one: and thro' his heart
The fire of honour and all noble deeds   270
Flash'd, and he call'd, "I strike upon thy side—
The caitiffs!" "Nay," said Pelleas, "but forbear;
He needs no aid who doth his lady's will."

So Gawain, looking at the villainy done,
Forbore, but in his heat and eagerness
Trembled and quiver'd, as the dog, withheld
A moment from the vermin that he sees
Before him, shivers, ere he springs and kills.

And Pelleas overthrew them, one to three;
And they rose up, and bound, and brought him in.   280
Then first her anger, leaving Pelleas, burn'd
Full on her knights in many an evil name
Of craven, weakling, and thrice-beaten hound:
"Yet, take him, ye that scarce are fit to touch,
Far less to bind, your victor, and thrust him out,
And let who will release him from his bonds.
And if he comes again"—there she brake short;
And Pelleas answer'd, "Lady, for indeed
I loved you and I deem'd you beautiful,
I cannot brook to see your beauty marr'd   290
Thro' evil spite: and if ye love me not,
I cannot bear to dream you so forsworn:
I had liefer ye were worthy of my love,
Than to be loved again of you—farewell;
And tho' ye kill my hope, not yet my love,
Vex not yourself: ye will not see me more."

While thus he spake, she gazed upon the man
Of princely bearing, tho' in bonds, and thought,
"Why have I push'd him from me? this man loves,

If love there be: yet him I loved not. Why? 300
I deem'd him fool? yea, so? or that in him
A something—was it nobler than myself?—
Seem'd my reproach? He is not of my kind.
He could not love me, did he know me well.
Nay, let him go—and quickly." And her knights
Laugh'd not, but thrust him bounden out of door.

Forth sprang Gawain, and loosed him from his
bonds
And flung them o'er the walls; and afterward,
Shaking his hands, as from a lazar's rag,
"Faith of my body," he said, "and art thou not— 310
Yea thou art he, whom late our Arthur made
Knight of his table; yea and he that won
The circlet? wherefore hast thou so defamed
Thy brotherhood in me and all the rest,
As let these caitiffs on thee work their will?"

And Pelleas answer'd, "O, their wills are hers
For whom I won the circlet; and mine, hers,
Thus to be bounden, so to see her face,
Marr'd tho' it be with spite and mockery now,
Other than when I found her in the woods; 320
And tho' she hath me bounden but in spite,
And all to flout me, when they bring me in,
Let me be bounden, I shall see her face;
Else must I die thro' mine unhappiness."

And Gawain answer'd kindly tho' in scorn,
"Why, let my lady bind me if she will,
And let my lady beat me if she will:
But an she send her delegate to thrall
These fighting hands of mine—Christ kill me then
But I will slice him handless by the wrist, 330
And let my lady sear the stump for him,
Howl as he may. But hold me for your friend:
Come, ye know nothing: here I pledge my troth,
Yea, by the honour of the Table Round,
I will be leal to thee and work thy work,
And tame thy jailing princess to thine hand.
Lend me thine horse and arms, and I will say
That I have slain thee. She will let me in
To hear the manner of thy fight and fall;

Then, when I come within her counsels, then   340
From prime to vespers will I chant thy praise
As prowest knight and truest lover, more
Than any have sung thee living, till she long
To have thee back in lusty life again,
Not to be bound, save by white bonds and warm,
Dearer than freedom. Wherefore now thy horse
And armour: let me go: be comforted:
Give me three days to melt her fancy, and hope
The third night hence will bring thee news of gold."

Then Pelleas lent his horse and all his arms,   350
Saving the goodly sword, his prize, and took
Gawain's, and said, "Betray me not, but help—
Art thou not he whom men call light-of-love?"

"Ay," said Gawain, "for women be so light."
Then bounded forward to the castle walls,
And raised a bugle hanging from his neck,
And winded it, and that so musically
That all the old echoes hidden in the wall
Rang out like hollow woods at hunting-tide.

Up ran a score of damsels to the tower;   360
"Avaunt," they cried, "our lady loves thee not."
But Gawain lifting up his vizor said,
"Gawain am I, Gawain of Arthur's court,
And I have slain this Pelleas whom ye hate:
Behold his horse and armour. Open gates,
And I will make you merry."

                              And down they ran,
Her damsels, crying to their lady, "Lo!
Pelleas is dead—he told us—he that hath
His horse and armour: will ye let him in?
He slew him! Gawain of the court,
Sir Gawain—there he waits below the wall,   370
Blowing his bugle as who should say him nay."

And so, leave given, straight on thro' open door
Rode Gawain, whom she greeted courteously.
"Dead, is it so?" she ask'd. "Ay, ay," said he,
"And oft in dying cried upon your name."
"Pity on him," she answer'd, "a good knight,

But never let me bide one hour at peace."
"Ay," thought Gawain, "and you be fair enow:
But I to your dead man have given my troth,   380
That whom ye loathe, him will I make you love."

So those three days, aimless about the land,
Lost in a doubt, Pelleas wandering
Waited, until the third night brought a moon
With promise of large light on woods and ways.

Hot was the night and silent; but a sound
Of Gawain ever coming, and this lay—
Which Pelleas had heard sung before the Queen,
And seen her sadden listening—vext his heart,
And marr'd his rest—"A worm within the rose."   390

"A rose, but one, none other rose had I,
A rose, one rose, and this was wondrous fair,
One rose, a rose that gladden'd earth and sky,
One rose, my rose, that sweeten'd all mine air—
I cared not for the thorns; the thorns were there.

"One rose, a rose to gather by and by,
One rose, a rose, to gather and to wear,
No rose but one—what other rose had I?
One rose, my rose; a rose that will not die,—
He dies who loves it,—if the worm be there."   400

This tender rhyme, and evermore the doubt,
"Why lingers Gawain with his golden news?"
So shook him that he could not rest, but rode
Ere midnight to her walls, and bound his horse
Hard by the gates. Wide open were the gates,
And no watch kept; and in thro' these he past,
And heard but his own steps, and his own heart
Beating, for nothing moved but his own self,
And his own shadow. Then he crost the court,
And spied not any light in hall or bower,   410
But saw the postern portal also wide
Yawning; and up a slope of garden, all
Of roses white and red, and brambles mixt
And overgrowing them, went on, and found,
Here too, all hush'd below the mellow moon,
Save that one rivulet from a tiny cave

Came lightening downward, and so spilt itself
Among the roses, and was lost again.

Then was he ware of three pavilions rear'd
Above the bushes, gilden-peakt: in one,   420
Red after revel, droned her lurdane knights
Slumbering, and their three squires across their feet:
In one, their malice on the placid lip
Froz'n by sweet sleep, four of her damsels lay:
And in the third, the circlet of the jousts
Bound on her brow, were Gawain and Ettarre.

Back, as a hand that pushes thro' the leaf
To find a nest and feels a snake, he drew:
Back, as a coward slinks from what he fears
To cope with, or a traitor proven, or hound   430
Beaten, did Pelleas in an utter shame
Creep with his shadow thro' the court again,
Fingering at his sword-handle until he stood
There on the castle-bridge once more, and thought,
"I will go back, and slay them where they lie."

And so went back, and seeing them yet in sleep
Said, "Ye, that so dishallow the holy sleep,
Your sleep is death," and drew the sword, and thought,
"What! slay a sleeping knight? the King hath bound
And sworn me to this brotherhood;" again,   440
"Alas that ever a knight should be so false."
Then turn'd, and so return'd, and groaning laid
The naked sword athwart their naked throats,
There left it, and them sleeping; and she lay,
The circlet of the tourney round her brows,
And the sword of the tourney across her throat.

And forth he past, and mounting on his horse
Stared at her towers that, larger than themselves
In their own darkness, throng'd into the moon.
Then crush'd the saddle with his thighs, and clench'd   450
His hands, and madden'd with himself and moan'd:

"Would they have risen against me in their blood
At the last day? I might have answer'd them
Even before high God. O towers so strong,
Huge, solid, would that even while I gaze

The crack of earthquake shivering to your base
Split you, and Hell burst up your harlot roofs
Bellowing, and charr'd you thro' and thro' within,
Black as the harlot's heart—hollow as a skull!
Let the fierce east scream thro' your eyelet-holes,   460
And whirl the dust of harlots round and round
In dung and nettles! hiss, snake—I saw him there—
Let the fox bark, let the wolf yell. Who yells
Here in the still sweet summer night, but I—
I, the poor Pelleas whom she call'd her fool?
Fool, beast—he, she, or I? myself most fool;
Beast too, as lacking human wit—disgraced,
Dishonour'd all for trial of true love—
Love?—we be all alike: only the King
Hath made us fools and liars. O noble vows!   470
O great and sane and simple race of brutes
That own no lust because they have no law!
For why should I have loved her to my shame?
I loathe her, as I loved her to my shame.
I never loved her, I but lusted for her—
Away—"

He dash'd the rowel into his horse,
And bounded forth and vanish'd thro' the night.

Then she, that felt the cold touch on her throat,
Awaking knew the sword, and turn'd herself
To Gawain: "Liar, for thou hast not slain   480
This Pelleas! here he stood, and might have slain
Me and thyself." And he that tells the tale
Says that her ever-veering fancy turn'd
To Pelleas, as the one true knight on earth,
And only lover; and thro' her love her life
Wasted and pined, desiring him in vain.

But he by wild and way, for half the night,
And over hard and soft, striking the sod
From out the soft, the spark from off the hard,
Rode till the star above the wakening sun,   490
Beside that tower where Percivale was cowl'd,
Glanced from the rosy forehead of the dawn.
For so the words were flash'd into his heart
He knew not whence or wherefore: "O sweet star,
Pure on the virgin forehead of the dawn!"

And there he would have wept, but felt his eyes
Harder and drier than a fountain bed
In summer: thither came the village girls
And linger'd talking, and they come no more
Till the sweet heavens have fill'd it from the heights   500
Again with living waters in the change
Of seasons: hard his eyes; harder his heart
Seem'd; but so weary were his limbs, that he,
Gasping, "Of Arthur's hall am I, but here,
Here let me rest and die," cast himself down,
And gulf'd his griefs in inmost sleep; so lay,
Till shaken by a dream, that Gawain fired
The hall of Merlin, and the morning star
Reel'd in the smoke, brake into flame, and fell.

He woke, and being ware of some one nigh,   510
Sent hands upon him, as to tear him, crying,
"False! and I held thee pure as Guinevere."

But Percivale stood near him and replied,
"Am I but false as Guinevere is pure?
Or art thou mazed with dreams? or being one
Of our free-spoken Table hast not heard
That Lancelot"—there he check'd himself and paused.

Then fared it with Sir Pelleas as with one
Who gets a wound in battle, and the sword
That made it plunges thro' the wound again,   520
And pricks it deeper: and he shrank and wail'd,
"Is the Queen false?" and Percivale was mute.
"Have any of our Round Table held their vows?"
And Percivale made answer not a word.
"Is the King true?" "The King!" said Percivale.
"Why then let men couple at once with wolves.
What! art thou mad?"

                              But Pelleas, leaping up,
Ran thro' the doors and vaulted on his horse
And fled: small pity upon his horse had he,
Or on himself, or any, and when he met   530
A cripple, one that held a hand for alms—
Hunch'd as he was, and like an old dwarf-elm
That turns its back on the salt blast, the boy
Paused not, but overrode him, shouting, "False,

And false with Gawain!" and so left him bruised
And batter'd, and fled on, and hill and wood
Went ever streaming by him till the gloom,
That follows on the turning of the world,
Darken'd the common path: he twitch'd the reins,
And made his beast that better knew it, swerve   540
Now off it and now on; but when he saw
High up in heaven the hall that Merlin built,
Blackening against the dead-green stripes of even,
"Black nest of rats," he groan'd, "ye build too high."

Not long thereafter from the city gates
Issued Sir Lancelot riding airily,
Warm with a gracious parting from the Queen,
Peace at his heart, and gazing at a star
And marvelling what it was: on whom the boy,
Across the silent seeded meadow-grass   550
Borne, clash'd: and Lancelot, saying, "What name hast
    thou
That ridest here so blindly and so hard?"
"No name, no name," he shouted, "a scourge am I
To lash the treasons of the Table Round."
"Yea, but thy name?" "I have many names," he cried:
"I am wrath and shame and hate and evil fame,
And like a poisonous wind I pass to blast
And blaze the crime of Lancelot and the Queen."
"First over me," said Lancelot, "shalt thou pass."
"Fight therefore," yell'd the youth, and either knight   560
Drew back a space, and when they closed, at once
The weary steed of Pelleas floundering flung
His rider, who call'd out from the dark field,
"Thou art false as Hell: slay me: I have no sword."
Then Lancelot, "Yea, between thy lips—and sharp:
But here will I disedge it by thy death."
"Slay then," he shriek'd, "my will is to be slain,"
And Lancelot, with his heel upon the fall'n,
Rolling his eyes, a moment stood, then spake:
"Rise, weakling; I am Lancelot; say thy say."   570

And Lancelot slowly rode his warhorse back
To Camelot, and Sir Pelleas in brief while
Caught his unbroken limbs from the dark field,
And follow'd to the city. It chanced that both
Brake into hall together, worn and pale.

There with her knights and dames was Guinevere.
Full wonderingly she gazed on Lancelot
So soon return'd, and then on Pelleas, him
Who had not greeted her, but cast himself
Down on a bench, hard-breathing. "Have ye fought?"   580
She ask'd of Lancelot. "Ay, my Queen," he said.
"And thou hast overthrown him?" "Ay, my Queen."
Then she, turning to Pelleas, "O young knight,
Hath the great heart of knighthood in thee fail'd
So far thou canst not bide, unfrowardly,
A fall from *him?*" Then, for he answer'd not,
"Or hast thou other griefs? If I, the Queen,
May help them, loose thy tongue, and let me know."
But Pelleas lifted up an eye so fierce
She quail'd; and he, hissing, "I have no sword,"   590
Sprang from the door into the dark. The Queen
Look'd hard upon her lover, he on her;
And each foresaw the dolorous day to be:
And all talk died, as in a grove all song
Beneath the shadow of some bird of prey;
Then a long silence came upon the hall,
And Modred thought, "The time is hard at hand."

Guinevere

QUEEN GUINEVERE had fled the court, and sat
There in the holy house at Almesbury
Weeping, none with her save a little maid,
A novice: one low light betwixt them burn'd
Blurr'd by the creeping mist, for all abroad,
Beneath a moon unseen albeit at full,
The white mist, like a face-cloth to the face,
Clung to the dead earth, and the land was still.

For hither had she fled, her cause of flight
Sir Modred; he that like a subtle beast   10

Lay couchant with his eyes upon the throne,
Ready to spring, waiting a chance: for this
He chill'd the popular praises of the King
With silent smiles of slow disparagement;
And tamper'd with the Lords of the White Horse,
Heathen, the brood by Hengist left; and sought
To make disruption in the Table Round
Of Arthur, and to splinter it into feuds
Serving his traitorous end; and all his aims
Were sharpen'd by strong hate for Lancelot.   20

For thus it chanced one morn when all the court,
Green-suited, but with plumes that mock'd the may,
Had been, their wont, a-maying and return'd,
That Modred still in green, all ear and eye,
Climb'd to the high top of the garden-wall
To spy some secret scandal if he might,
And saw the Queen who sat betwixt her best
Enid, and lissome Vivien, of her court
The wiliest and the worst; and more than this
He saw not, for Sir Lancelot passing by   30
Spied where he couch'd, and as the gardener's hand
Picks from the colewort a green caterpillar,
So from the high wall and the flowering grove
Of grasses Lancelot pluck'd him by the heel,
And cast him as a worm upon the way;
But when he knew the Prince tho' marr'd with dust,
He, reverencing king's blood in a bad man,
Made such excuses as he might, and these
Full knightly without scorn; for in those days
No knight of Arthur's noblest dealt in scorn;   40
But, if a man were halt or hunch'd, in him
By those whom God had made full-limb'd and tall,
Scorn was allow'd as part of his defect,
And he was answer'd softly by the King
And all his Table. So Sir Lancelot holp
To raise the Prince, who rising twice or thrice
Full sharply smote his knees, and smiled, and went:
But, ever after, the small violence done
Rankled in him and ruffled all his heart,
As the sharp wind that ruffles all day long   50
A little bitter pool about a stone
On the bare coast.

                    But when Sir Lancelot told
This matter to the Queen, at first she laugh'd
Lightly, to think of Modred's dusty fall,
Then shudder'd, as the village wife who cries,
"I shudder, some one steps across my grave;"
Then laugh'd again, but faintlier, for indeed
She half-foresaw that he, the subtle beast,
Would track her guilt until he found, and hers
Would be for evermore a name of scorn.   60
Henceforward rarely could she front in hall,
Or elsewhere, Modred's narrow foxy face,
Heart-hiding smile, and gray persistent eye:
Henceforward too, the Powers that tend the soul,
To help it from the death that cannot die,
And save it even in extremes, began
To vex and plague her. Many a time for hours,
Beside the placid breathings of the King,
In the dead night, grim faces came and went
Before her, or a vague spiritual fear—   70
Like to some doubtful noise of creaking doors,
Heard by the watcher in a haunted house,
That keeps the rust of murder on the walls—
Held her awake: or if she slept, she dream'd
An awful dream; for then she seem'd to stand
On some vast plain before a setting sun,
And from the sun there swiftly made at her
A ghastly something, and its shadow flew
Before it, till it touch'd her, and she turn'd—
When lo! her own, that broadening from her feet,   80
And blackening, swallow'd all the land, and in it
Far cities burnt, and with a cry she woke.
And all this trouble did not pass but grew;
Till ev'n the clear face of the guileless King,
And trustful courtesies of household life,
Became her bane; and at the last she said,
"O Lancelot, get thee hence to thine own land,
For if thou tarry we shall meet again,
And if we meet again, some evil chance
Will make the smouldering scandal break and blaze   90
Before the people, and our lord the King."
And Lancelot ever promised, but remain'd,
And still they met and met. Again she said,
"O Lancelot, if thou love me get thee hence."
And then they were agreed upon a night

(When the good King should not be there) to meet
And part for ever. Vivien, lurking, heard.
She told Sir Modred. Passion-pale they met
And greeted. Hands in hands, and eye to eye,
Low on the border of her couch they sat   100
Stammering and staring. It was their last hour,
A madness of farewells. And Modred brought
His creatures to the basement of the tower
For testimony; and crying with full voice,
"Traitor, come out, ye are trapt at last," aroused
Lancelot, who rushing outward lionlike
Leapt on him, and hurl'd him headlong, and he fell
Stunn'd, and his creatures took and bare him off,
And all was still: then she, "The end is come,
And I am shamed for ever;" and he said,   110
"Mine be the shame; mine was the sin: but rise,
And fly to my strong castle overseas:
There will I hide thee, till my life shall end,
There hold thee with my life against the world."
She answer'd, "Lancelot, wilt thou hold me so?
Nay, friend, for we have taken our farewells.
Would God that thou couldst hide me from myself!
Mine is the shame, for I was wife, and thou
Unwedded: yet rise now, and let us fly,
For I will draw me into sanctuary,   120
And bide my doom." So Lancelot got her horse,
Set her thereon, and mounted on his own,
And then they rode to the divided way,
There kiss'd, and parted weeping: for he past,
Love-loyal to the least wish of the Queen,
Back to his land; but she to Almesbury
Fled all night long by glimmering waste and weald,
And heard the Spirits of the waste and weald
Moan as she fled, or thought she heard them moan:
And in herself she moan'd, "Too late, too late!"   130
Till in the cold wind that foreruns the morn,
A blot in heaven, the Raven, flying high,
Croak'd, and she thought, "He spies a field of death;
For now the Heathen of the Northern Sea,
Lured by the crimes and frailties of the court,
Begin to slay the folk, and spoil the land."

And when she came to Almesbury she spake
There to the nuns, and said, "Mine enemies

Pursue me, but, O peaceful Sisterhood,
Receive, and yield me sanctuary, nor ask   140
Her name to whom ye yield it, till her time
To tell you:" and her beauty, grace and power,
Wrought as a charm upon them, and they spared
To ask it.

        So the stately Queen abode
For many a week, unknown, among the nuns;
Nor with them mix'd, nor told her name, nor sought,
Wrapt in her grief, for housel or for shrift,
But communed only with the little maid,
Who pleased her with a babbling heedlessness
Which often lured her from herself; but now,   150
This night, a rumour wildly blown about
Came, that Sir Modred had usurp'd the realm,
And leagued him with the heathen, while the King
Was waging war on Lancelot: then she thought,
"With what a hate the people and the King
Must hate me," and bow'd down upon her hands
Silent, until the little maid, who brook'd
No silence, brake it, uttering, "Late! so late!
What hour, I wonder, now?" and when she drew
No answer, by and by began to hum   160
An air the nuns had taught her; "Late, so late!"
Which when she heard, the Queen look'd up, and said,
"O maiden, if indeed ye list to sing,
Sing, and unbind my heart that I may weep."
Whereat full willingly sang the little maid.

   "Late, late, so late! and dark the night and chill!
Late, late, so late! but we can enter still.
Too late, too late! ye cannot enter now.

   "No light had we: for that we do repent;
And learning this, the bridegroom will relent.   170
Too late, too late! ye cannot enter now.

   "No light: so late! and dark and chill the night!
O let us in, that we may find the light!
Too late, too late: ye cannot enter now.

   "Have we not heard the bridegroom is so sweet?
O let us in, tho' late, to kiss his feet!

No, no, too late! ye cannot enter now."

So sang the novice, while full passionately,
Her head upon her hands, remembering
Her thought when first she came, wept the sad Queen.   180
Then said the little novice prattling to her,

"O pray you, noble lady, weep no more;
But let my words, the words of one so small,
Who knowing nothing knows but to obey,
And if I do not there is penance given—
Comfort your sorrows; for they do not flow
From evil done; right sure am I of that,
Who see your tender grace and stateliness.
But weigh your sorrows with our lord the King's,
And weighing find them less; for gone is he   190
To wage grim war against Sir Lancelot there,
Round that strong castle where he holds the Queen;
And Modred whom he left in charge of all,
The traitor—Ah sweet lady, the King's grief
For his own self, and his own Queen, and realm,
Must needs be thrice as great as any of ours.
For me, I thank the saints, I am not great.
For if there ever come a grief to me
I cry my cry in silence, and have done.
None knows it, and my tears have brought me good: 200
But even were the griefs of little ones
As great as those of great ones, yet this grief
Is added to the griefs the great must bear,
That howsoever much they may desire
Silence, they cannot weep behind a cloud:
As even here they talk at Almesbury
About the good King and his wicked Queen,
And were I such a King with such a Queen,
Well might I wish to veil her wickedness,
But were I such a King, it could not be."   210

Then to her own sad heart mutter'd the Queen,
"Will the child kill me with her innocent talk?"
But openly she answer'd, "Must not I,
If this false traitor have displaced his lord,
Grieve with the common grief of all the realm?"

"Yea," said the maid, "this is all woman's grief,
That *she* is woman, whose disloyal life
Hath wrought confusion in the Table Round

Which good King Arthur founded, years ago,
With signs and miracles and wonders, there   220
At Camelot, ere the coming of the Queen."

    Then thought the Queen within herself again,
"Will the child kill me with her foolish prate?"
But openly she spake and said to her,
"O little maid, shut in by nunnery walls,
What canst thou know of Kings and Tables Round,
Or what of signs and wonders, but the signs
And simple miracles of thy nunnery?"

    To whom the little novice garrulously,
"Yea, but I know: the land was full of signs   230
And wonders ere the coming of the Queen.
So said my father, and himself was knight
Of the great Table—at the founding of it;
And rode thereto from Lyonnesse, and he said
That as he rode, an hour or maybe twain
After the sunset, down the coast, he heard
Strange music, and he paused, and turning—there,
All down the lonely coast of Lyonnesse,
Each with a beacon-star upon his head,
And with a wild sea-light about his feet,   240
He saw them—headland after headland flame
Far on into the rich heart of the west:
And in the light the white mermaiden swam,
And strong man-breasted things stood from the sea,
And sent a deep sea-voice thro' all the land,
To which the little elves of chasm and cleft
Made answer, sounding like a distant horn.
So said my father—yea, and furthermore,
Next morning, while he past the dim-lit woods,
Himself beheld three spirits mad with joy   250
Come dashing down on a tall wayside flower,
That shook beneath them, as the thistle shakes
When three gray linnets wrangle for the seed:
And still at evenings on before his horse
The flickering fairy-circle wheel'd and broke
Flying, and link'd again, and wheel'd and broke
Flying, for all the land was full of life.
And when at last he came to Camelot,
A wreath of airy dancers hand-in-hand
Swung round the lighted lantern of the hall;   260

And in the hall itself was such a feast
As never man had dream'd; for every knight
Had whatsoever meat he long'd for served
By hands unseen; and even as he said
Down in the cellars merry bloated things
Shoulder'd the spigot, straddling on the butts
While the wine ran: so glad were spirits and men
Before the coming of the sinful Queen."

Then spake the Queen and somewhat bitterly,
"Were they so glad? ill prophets were they all,   270
Spirits and men: could none of them foresee,
Not even thy wise father with his signs
And wonders, what has fall'n upon the realm?"

To whom the novice garrulously again,
"Yea, one, a bard; of whom my father said,
Full many a noble war-song had he sung,
Ev'n in the presence of an enemy's fleet,
Between the steep cliff and the coming wave;
And many a mystic lay of life and death
Had chanted on the smoky mountain-tops,   280
When round him bent the spirits of the hills
With all their dewy hair blown back like flame:
So said my father—and that night the bard
Sang Arthur's glorious wars, and sang the King
As wellnigh more than man, and rail'd at those
Who call'd him the false son of Gorloïs:
For there was no man knew from whence he came:
But after tempest, when the long wave broke
All down the thundering shores of Bude and Bos,
There came a day as still as heaven, and then   290
They found a naked child upon the sands
Of dark Tintagil by the Cornish sea;
And that was Arthur; and they foster'd him
Till he by miracle was approven King:
And that his grave should be a mystery
From all men, like his birth; and could he find
A woman in her womanhood as great
As he was in his manhood, then, he sang,
The twain together well might change the world.
But even in the middle of his song   300
He falter'd, and his hand fell from the harp,
And pale he turn'd, and reel'd, and would have fall'n,

But that they stay'd him up; nor would he tell
His vision; but what doubt that he foresaw
This evil work of Lancelot and the Queen?"

Then thought the Queen, "Lo! they have set her on,
Our simple-seeming Abbess and her nuns,
To play upon me," and bow'd her head nor spake.
Whereat the novice crying, with clasp'd hands,
Shame on her own garrulity garrulously,   310
Said the good nuns would check her gadding tongue
Full often, "and, sweet lady, if I seem
To vex an ear too sad to listen to me,
Unmannerly, with prattling and the tales
Which my good father told me, check me too
Nor let me shame my father's memory, one
Of noblest manners, tho' himself would say
Sir Lancelot had the noblest; and he died,
Kill'd in a tilt, come next, five summers back,
And left me; but of others who remain,   320
And of the two first-famed for courtesy—
And pray you check me if I ask amiss—
But pray you, which had noblest, while you moved
Among them, Lancelot or our lord the King?"

Then the pale Queen look'd up and answer'd her,
"Sir Lancelot, as became a noble knight,
Was gracious to all ladies, and the same
In open battle or the tilting-field
Forbore his own advantage, and the King
In open battle or the tilting-field   330
Forbore his own advantage, and these two
Were the most nobly-manner'd men of all;
For manners are not idle, but the fruit
Of loyal nature, and of noble mind."

"Yea," said the maid, "be manners such fair fruit?
Then Lancelot's needs must be a thousand-fold
Less noble, being, as all rumour runs,
The most disloyal friend in all the world."

To which a mournful answer made the Queen:
"O closed about by narrowing nunnery-walls,   340
What knowest thou of the world, and all its lights
And shadows, all the wealth and all the woe?

If ever Lancelot, that most noble knight,
Were for one hour less noble than himself,
Pray for him that he scape the doom of fire,
And weep for her who drew him to his doom."

"Yea," said the little novice, "I pray for both;
But I should all as soon believe that his,
Sir Lancelot's, were as noble as the King's,
As I could think, sweet lady, yours would be   350
Such as they are, were you the sinful Queen."

So she, like many another babbler, hurt
Whom she would soothe, and harm'd where she would
    heal;
For here a sudden flush of wrathful heat
Fired all the pale face of the Queen, who cried,
"Such as thou art be never maiden more
For ever! thou their tool, set on to plague
And play upon, and harry me, petty spy
And traitress." When that storm of anger brake
From Guinevere, aghast the maiden rose,   360
White as her veil, and stood before the Queen
As tremulously as foam upon the beach
Stands in a wind, ready to break and fly,
And when the Queen had added, "Get thee hence,"
Fled frighted. Then that other left alone
Sigh'd, and began to gather heart again,
Saying in herself, "The simple, fearful child
Meant nothing, but my own too-fearful guilt,
Simpler than any child, betrays itself.
But help me, heaven, for surely I repent.   370
For what is true repentance but in thought—
Not ev'n in inmost thought to think again
The sins that made the past so pleasant to us:
And I have sworn never to see him more,
To see him more."

                And ev'n in saying this,
Her memory from old habit of the mind
Went slipping back upon the golden days
In which she saw him first, when Lancelot came,
Reputed the best knight and goodliest man,
Ambassador, to lead her to his lord   380
Arthur, and led her forth, and far ahead

Of his and her retinue moving, they,
Rapt in sweet talk or lively, all on love
And sport and tilts and pleasure, (for the time
Was maytime, and as yet no sin was dream'd,)
Rode under groves that look'd a paradise
Of blossom, over sheets of hyacinth
That seem'd the heavens upbreaking thro' the earth,
And on from hill to hill, and every day
Beheld at noon in some delicious dale   390
The silk pavilions of King Arthur raised
For brief repast or afternoon repose
By couriers gone before; and on again,
Till yet once more ere set of sun they saw
The Dragon of the great Pendragonship,
That crown'd the state pavilion of the King,
Blaze by the rushing brook or silent well.

But when the Queen immersed in such a trance,
And moving thro' the past unconsciously,
Came to that point where first she saw the King   400
Ride toward her from the city, sigh'd to find
Her journey done, glanced at him, thought him cold,
High, self-contain'd, and passionless, not like him,
"Not like my Lancelot"—while she brooded thus
And grew half-guilty in her thoughts again,
There rode an armed warrior to the doors.
A murmuring whisper thro' the nunnery ran,
Then on a sudden a cry, "The King." She sat
Stiff-stricken, listening; but when armed feet
Thro' the long gallery from the outer doors   410
Rang coming, prone from off her seat she fell,
And grovell'd with her face against the floor:
There with her milkwhite arms and shadowy hair
She made her face a darkness from the King:
And in the darkness heard his armed feet
Pause by her; then came silence, then a voice,
Monotonous and hollow like a Ghost's
Denouncing judgment, but tho' changed, the King's:

"Liest thou here so low, the child of one
I honour'd, happy, dead before thy shame?   420
Well is it that no child is born of thee.
The children born of thee are sword and fire,
Red ruin, and the breaking up of laws,

The craft of kindred and the Godless hosts
Of heathen swarming o'er the Northern Sea;
Whom I, while yet Sir Lancelot, my right arm,
The mightiest of my knights, abode with me,
Have everywhere about this land of Christ
In twelve great battles ruining overthrown.
And knowest thou now from whence I come—from
    him,   430
From waging bitter war with him: and he,
That did not shun to smite me in worse way,
Had yet that grace of courtesy in him left,
He spared to lift his hand against the King
Who made him knight: but many a knight was slain;
And many more, and all his kith and kin
Clave to him, and abode in his own land.
And many more when Modred raised revolt,
Forgetful of their troth and fealty, clave
To Modred, and a remnant stays with me.   440
And of this remnant will I leave a part,
True men who love me still, for whom I live,
To guard thee in the wild hour coming on,
Lest but a hair of this low head be harm'd.
Fear not: thou shalt be guarded till my death.
Howbeit I know, if ancient prophecies
Have err'd not, that I march to meet my doom.
Thou hast not made my life so sweet to me,
That I the King should greatly care to live;
For thou hast spoilt the purpose of my life.   450
Bear with me for the last time while I show,
Ev'n for thy sake, the sin which thou hast sinn'd.
For when the Roman left us, and their law
Relax'd its hold upon us, and the ways
Were fill'd with rapine, here and there a deed
Of prowess done redress'd a random wrong.
But I was first of all the kings who drew
The knighthood-errant of this realm and all
The realms together under me, their Head,
In that fair Order of my Table Round,   460
A glorious company, the flower of men,
To serve as model for the mighty world,
And be the fair beginning of a time.
I made them lay their hands in mine and swear
To reverence the King, as if he were
Their conscience, and their conscience as their King,

To break the heathen and uphold the Christ,
To ride abroad redressing human wrongs,
To speak no slander, no, nor listen to it,
To honour his own word as if his God's,   470
To lead sweet lives in purest chastity,
To love one maiden only, cleave to her,
And worship her by years of noble deeds,
Until they won her; for indeed I knew
Of no more subtle master under heaven
Than is the maiden passion for a maid,
Not only to keep down the base in man,
But teach high thought, and amiable words
And courtliness, and the desire to fame,
And love of truth, and all that makes a man.   480
And all this throve before I wedded thee,
Believing, 'Lo mine helpmate, one to feel
My purpose and rejoicing in my joy.'
Then came thy shameful sin with Lancelot;
Then came the sin of Tristram and Isolt;
Then others, following these my mightiest knights,
And drawing foul ensample from fair names,
Sinn'd also, till the loathsome opposite
Of all my heart had destined did obtain,
And all thro' thee! so that this life of mine   490
I guard as God's high gift from scathe and wrong,
Not greatly care to lose; but rather think
How sad it were for Arthur, should he live,
To sit once more within his lonely hall,
And miss the wonted number of my knights,
And miss to hear high talk of noble deeds
As in the golden days before thy sin.
For which of us, who might be left, could speak
Of the pure heart, nor seem to glance at thee?
And in thy bowers of Camelot or of Usk   500
Thy shadow still would glide from room to room,
And I should evermore be vext with thee
In hanging robe or vacant ornament,
Or ghostly footfall echoing on the stair.
For think not, tho' thou wouldst not love thy lord,
Thy lord has wholly lost his love for thee.
I am not made of so slight elements.
Yet must I leave thee, woman, to thy shame.
I hold that man the worst of public foes
Who either for his own or children's sake,   510

To save his blood from scandal, lets the wife
Whom he knows false, abide and rule the house:
For being thro' his cowardice allow'd
Her station, taken everywhere for pure,
She like a new disease, unknown to men,
Creeps, nó precaution used, among the crowd,
Makes wicked lightnings of her eyes, and saps
The fealty of our friends, and stirs the pulse
With devil's leaps, and poisons half the young.
Worst of the worst were that man he that reigns!   520
Better the King's waste hearth and aching heart
Than thou reseated in thy place of light,
The mockery of my people, and their bane."

He paused, and in the pause she crept an inch
Nearer, and laid her hands about his feet.
Far off a solitary trumpet blew.
Then waiting by the doors the warhorse neigh'd
As at a friend's voice, and he spake again:

"Yet think not that I come to urge thy crimes,
I did not come to curse thee, Guinevere,   530
I, whose vast pity almost makes me die
To see thee, laying there thy golden head,
My pride in happier summers, at my feet.
The wrath which forced my thoughts on that fierce law,
The doom of treason and the flaming death,
(When first I learnt thee hidden here) is past.
The pang—which while I weigh'd thy heart with one
Too wholly true to dream untruth in thee,
Made my tears burn—is also past—in part.
And all is past, the sin is sinn'd, and I,   540
Lo! I forgive thee, as Eternal God
Forgives: do thou for thine own soul the rest.
But how to take last leave of all I loved?
O golden hair, with which I used to play
Not knowing! O imperial-moulded form,
And beauty such as never woman wore,
Until it came a kingdom's curse with thee—
I cannot touch thy lips, they are not mine,
But Lancelot's: nay, they never were the King's.
I cannot take thy hand; that too is flesh,   550
And in the flesh thou hast sinn'd; and mine own flesh,
Here looking down on thine polluted, cries,

'I loathe thee:' yet not less, O Guinevere,
For I was ever virgin save for thee,
My love thro' flesh hath wrought into my life
So far, that my doom is, I love thee still.
Let no man dream but that I love thee still.
Perchance, and so thou purify thy soul,
And so thou lean on our fair father Christ,
Hereafter in that world where all are pure   560
We two may meet before high God, and thou
Wilt spring to me, and claim me thine, and know
I am thine husband—not a smaller soul,
Nor Lancelot, nor another. Leave me that,
I charge thee, my last hope. Now must I hence.
Thro' the thick night I hear the trumpet blow:
They summon me their King to lead mine hosts
Far down to that great battle in the west,
Where I must strike against the man they call
My sister's son—no kin of mine, who leagues   570
With Lords of the White Horse, heathen, and knights,
Traitors—and strike him dead, and meet myself
Death, or I know not what mysterious doom.
And thou remaining here wilt learn the event;
But hither shall I never come again,
Never lie by thy side; see thee no more—
Farewell!"

          And while she grovell'd at his feet,
She felt the King's breath wander o'er her neck,
And in the darkness o'er her fallen head,
Perceived the waving of his hands that blest.   580

    Then, listening till those armed steps were gone,
Rose the pale Queen, and in her anguish found
The casement: "Peradventure," so she thought,
"If I might see his face, and not be seen."
And lo, he sat on horseback at the door!
And near him the sad nuns with each a light
Stood, and he gave them charge about the Queen,
To guard and foster her for evermore.
And while he spake to these his helm was lower'd,
To which for crest the golden dragon clung   590
Of Britain; so she did not see the face,
Which then was as an angel's, but she saw,
Wet with the mists and smitten by the lights,

The Dragon of the great Pendragonship
Blaze, making all the night a steam of fire.
And even then he turn'd; and more and more
The moony vapour rolling round the King,
Who seem'd the phantom of a Giant in it,
Enwound him fold by fold, and made him gray
And grayer, till himself became as mist   600
Before her, moving ghostlike to his doom.

    Then she stretch'd out her arms and cried aloud,
"Oh Arthur!" there her voice brake suddenly,
Then—as a stream that spouting from a cliff
Fails in mid air, but gathering at the base
Re-makes itself, and flashes down the vale—
Went on in passionate utterance:

                            "Gone—my lord!
Gone thro' my sin to slay and to be slain!
And he forgave me, and I could not speak.
Farewell? I should have answer'd his farewell.   610
His mercy choked me. Gone, my lord the King,
My own true lord! how dare I call him mine?
The shadow of another cleaves to me,
And makes me one pollution: he, the King,
Call'd me polluted: shall I kill myself?
What help in that? I cannot kill my sin,
If soul be soul; nor can I kill my shame;
No, nor by living can I live it down.
The days will grow to weeks, the weeks to months,
The months will add themselves and make the years,   620
The years will roll into the centuries,
And mine will ever be a name of scorn.
I must not dwell on that defeat of fame.
Let the world be; that is but of the world.
What else? what hope? I think there was a hope,
Except he mock'd me when he spake of hope;
His hope he call'd it; but he never mocks,
For mockery is the fume of little hearts.
And blessed be the King, who hath forgiven
My wickedness to him, and left me hope   630
That in mine own heart I can live down sin
And be his mate hereafter in the heavens
Before high God. Ah great and gentle lord,
Who wast, as is the conscience of a saint

Among his warring senses, to thy knights—
To whom my false voluptuous pride, that took
Full easily all impressions from below,
Would not look up, or half-despised the height
To which I would not or I could not climb—
I thought I could not breathe in that fine air,   640
That pure severity of perfect light—
I yearn'd for warmth and colour which I found
In Lancelot—now I see thee what thou art,
Thou art the highest and most human too,
Not Lancelot, nor another. Is there none
Will tell the King I love him tho' so late?
Now—ere he goes to the great Battle? none:
Myself must tell him in that purer life,
But now it were too daring. Ah my God,
What might I not have made of thy fair world,   650
Had I but loved thy highest creature here?
It was my duty to have loved the highest:
It surely was my profit had I known:
It would have been my pleasure had I seen.
We needs must love the highest when we see it,
Not Lancelot, nor another."

                              Here her hand
Grasp'd, made her vail her eyes: she look'd and saw
The novice, weeping, suppliant, and said to her,
"Yea, little maid, for am *I* not forgiven?"
Then glancing up beheld the holy nuns   660
All round her, weeping; and her heart was loosed
Within her, and she wept with these and said,

   "Ye know me then, that wicked one, who broke
The vast design and purpose of the King.
O shut me round with narrowing nunnery-walls,
Meek maidens, from the voices crying 'shame.'
I must not scorn myself: he loves me still.
Let no one dream but that he loves me still.
So let me, if you do not shudder at me,
Nor shun to call me sister, dwell with you;   670
Wear black and white, and be a nun like you,
Fast with your fasts, not feasting with your feasts;
Grieve with your griefs, not grieving at your joys,
But not rejoicing; mingle with your rites;
Pray and be pray'd for; lie before your shrines;

Do each low office of your holy house;
Walk your dim cloister, and distribute dole
To poor sick people, richer in His eyes
Who ransom'd us, and haler too than I;
And treat their loathsome hurts and heal mine own;   680
And so wear out in almsdeed and in prayer
The sombre close of that voluptuous day,
Which wrought the ruin of my lord the King."

She said: they took her to themselves; and she
Still hoping, fearing "is it yet too late?"
Dwelt with them, till in time their Abbess died.
Then she, for her good deeds and her pure life,
And for the power of ministration in her,
And likewise for the high rank she had borne,
Was chosen Abbess, there, an Abbess, lived   690
For three brief years, and there, an Abbess, past
To where beyond these voices there is peace.

End of "The Round Table."

The Passing of Arthur

THAT story which the bold Sir Bedivere,
First made the latest left of all the knights,
Told, when the man was no more than a voice
In the white winter of his age, to those
With whom he dwelt, new faces, other minds.

For on their march to westward, Bedivere,
Who slowly paced among the slumbering host,
Heard in his tent the moanings of the King:

"I found Him in the shining of the stars,
I mark'd Him in the flowering of His fields,   10
But in His ways with men I find Him not.
I waged His wars, and now I pass and die.

O me! for why is all around us here
As if some lesser god had made the world,
But had not force to shape it as he would,
Till the High God behold it from beyond,
And enter it, and make it beautiful?
Or else as if the world were wholly fair,
But that these eyes of men are dense and dim,
And have not power to see it as it is: 20
Perchance, because we see not to the close;—
For I, being simple, thought to work His will,
And have but stricken with the sword in vain;
And all whereon I lean'd in wife and friend
Is traitor to my peace, and all my realm
Reels back into the beast, and is no more.
My God, thou hast forgotten me in my death:
Nay—God my Christ—I pass but shall not die."

Then, ere that last weird battle in the west,
There came on Arthur sleeping, Gawain kill'd   30
In Lancelot's war, the ghost of Gawain blown
Along a wandering wind, and past his ear
Went shrilling, "Hollow, hollow all delight!
Hail, King! to-morrow thou shalt pass away.
Farewell! there is an isle of rest for thee.
And I am blown along a wandering wind,
And hollow, hollow, hollow all delight."
And fainter onward, like wild birds that change
Their season in the night and wail their way
From cloud to cloud, down the long wind the dream   40
Shrill'd; but in going mingled with dim cries
Far in the moonlit haze among the hills,
As of some lonely city sack'd by night,
When all is lost, and wife and child with wail
Pass to new lords; and Arthur woke and call'd,
"Who spake? A dream. O light upon the wind,
Thine, Gawain, was the voice—are these dim cries
Thine? or doth all that haunts the waste and wild
Mourn, knowing it will go along with me?"

This heard the bold Sir Bedivere and spake: 50
"O me, my King, let pass whatever will,
Elves, and the harmless glamour of the field;
But in their stead thy name and glory cling
To all high places like a golden cloud

For ever: but as yet thou shalt not pass.
Light was Gawain in life, and light in death
Is Gawain, for the ghost is as the man;
And care not thou for dreams from him, but rise—
I hear the steps of Modred in the west,
And with him many of thy people, and knights   60
Once thine, whom thou hast loved, but grosser grown
Than heathen, spitting at their vows and thee.
Right well in heart they know thee for the King.
Arise, go forth and conquer as of old."

Then spake King Arthur to Sir Bedivere:
"Far other is this battle in the west
Whereto we move, than when we strove in youth,
And brake the petty kings, and fought with Rome,
Or thrust the heathen from the Roman wall,
And shook him thro' the north. Ill doom is mine   70
To war against my people and my knights.
The king who fights his people fights himself.
And they my knights, who loved me once, the stroke
That strikes them dead is as my death to me.
Yet let us hence, and find or feel a way
Thro' this blind haze, which ever since I saw
One lying in the dust at Almesbury,
Hath folded in the passes of the world."

Then rose the King and moved his host by night,
And ever push'd Sir Modred, league by league,   80
Back to the sunset bound of Lyonnesse—
A land of old upheaven from the abyss
By fire, to sink into the abyss again;
Where fragments of forgotten peoples dwelt,
And the long mountains ended in a coast
Of ever-shifting sand, and far away
The phantom circle of a moaning sea.
There the pursuer could pursue no more,
And he that fled no further fly the King;
And there, that day when the great light of heaven   90
Burn'd at his lowest in the rolling year,
On the waste sand by the waste sea they closed.
Nor ever yet had Arthur fought a fight
Like this last, dim, weird battle of the west.
A deathwhite mist slept over sand and sea:
Whereof the chill, to him who breathed it, drew

Down with his blood, till all his heart was cold
With formless fear; and ev'n on Arthur fell
Confusion, since he saw not whom he fought.
For friend and foe were shadows in the mist,   100
And friend slew friend not knowing whom he slew;
And some had visions out of golden youth,
And some beheld the faces of old ghosts
Look in upon the battle; and in the mist
Was many a noble deed, many a base,
And chance and craft and strength in single fights,
And ever and anon with host to host
Shocks, and the splintering spear, the hard mail hewn,
Shield-breakings, and the clash of brands, the crash
Of battleaxes on shatter'd helms, and shrieks   110
After the Christ, of those who falling down
Look'd up for heaven, and only saw the mist;
And shouts of heathen and the traitor knights,
Oaths, insult, filth, and monstrous blasphemies,
Sweat, writhings, anguish, labouring of the lungs
In that close mist, and cryings for the light,
Moans of the dying, and voices of the dead.

Last, as by some one deathbed after wail
Of suffering, silence follows, or thro' death
Or deathlike swoon, thus over all that shore,   120
Save for some whisper of the seething seas,
A dead hush fell; but when the dolorous day
Grew drearier toward twilight falling, came
A bitter wind, clear from the North, and blew
The mist aside, and with that wind the tide
Rose, and the pale King glanced across the field
Of battle: but no man was moving there;
Nor any cry of Christian heard thereon,
Nor yet of heathen; only the wan wave
Brake in among dead faces, to and fro   130
Swaying the helpless hands, and up and down
Tumbling the hollow helmets of the fallen,
And shiver'd brands that once had fought with Rome,
And rolling far along the gloomy shores
The voice of days of old and days to be.

Then spake King Arthur to Sir Bedivere,
And whiter than the mist that all day long
Had held the field of battle was the King:

"Hearest thou this great voice that shakes the world,
And wastes the narrow realm whereon we move,   140
And beats upon the faces of the dead,
My dead, as tho' they had not died for me?—
O Bedivere, for on my heart hath fall'n
Confusion, till I know not what I am,
Nor whence I am, nor whether I be King.
Behold, I seem but King among the dead."

Then spake the bold Sir Bedivere: "My King,
King everywhere! and so the dead have kings,
There also will I worship thee as King.
Yet still thy life is whole, and still I live   150
Who love thee; but who hates thee, he that brought
The heathen back among us, yonder stands,
Modred, unharm'd, the traitor of thine house."

Then spake the King: "My house hath been my doom.
But call not thou this traitor of my house
Who hath but dwelt beneath one roof with me.
My house are rather they who sware my vows,
Yea, even while they brake them, own'd me King.
And well for thee, saying in my dark hour,
When all the purport of my throne hath fail'd,   160
That quick or dead thou holdest me for King.
King am I, whatsoever be their cry;
And one last act of kinghood shalt thou see
Yet, ere I pass." And uttering this the King
Made at the man: then Modred smote his liege
Hard on that helm which many a heathen sword
Had beaten thin; while Arthur at one blow,
Striking the last stroke with Excalibur,
Slew him, and all but slain himself, he fell.

So all day long the noise of battle roll'd   170
Among the mountains by the winter sea;
Until King Arthur's Table, man by man,
Had fall'n in Lyonnesse about their lord,
King Arthur. Then, because his wound was deep,
The bold Sir Bedivere uplifted him,
And bore him to a chapel nigh the field,
A broken chancel with a broken cross,
That stood on a dark strait of barren land:
On one side lay the Ocean, and on one

Lay a great water, and the moon was full.   180

Then spake King Arthur to Sir Bedivere:
"The sequel of to-day unsolders all
The goodliest fellowship of famous knights
Whereof this world holds record. Such a sleep
They sleep—the men I loved. I think that we
Shall never more, at any future time,
Delight our souls with talk of knightly deeds,
Walking about the gardens and the halls
Of Camelot, as in the days that were.
I perish by this people which I made,—   190
Tho' Merlin sware that I should come again
To rule once more; but, let what will be, be,
I am so deeply smitten thro' the helm
That without help I cannot last till morn.
Thou therefore take my brand Excalibur,
Which was my pride: for thou rememberest how
In those old days, one summer noon, an arm
Rose up from out the bosom of the lake,
Clothed in white samite, mystic, wonderful,
Holding the sword—and how I row'd across   200
And took it, and have worn it, like a king;
And, wheresoever I am sung or told
In aftertime, this also shall be known:
But now delay not; take Excalibur,
And fling him far into the middle mere:
Watch what thou sëest, and lightly bring me word."

To him replied the bold Sir Bedivere:
"It is not meet, Sir King, to leave thee thus,
Aidless, alone, and smitten thro' the helm—
A little thing may harm a wounded man;   210
Yet I thy hest will all perform at full,
Watch what I see, and lightly bring thee word."

So saying, from the ruin'd shrine he stept,
And in the moon athwart the place of tombs,
Where lay the mighty bones of ancient men,
Old knights, and over them the sea-wind sang
Shrill, chill, with flakes of foam. He, stepping down
By zigzig paths, and juts of pointed rock,
Came on the shining levels of the lake.

There drew he forth the brand Excalibur,   220
And o'er him, drawing it, the winter moon,
Brightening the skirts of a long cloud, ran forth
And sparkled keen with frost against the hilt:
For all the haft twinkled with diamond sparks,
Myriads of topaz-lights, and jacinth-work
Of subtlest jewellery. He gazed so long
That both his eyes were dazzled as he stood,
This way and that dividing the swift mind,
In act to throw: but at the last it seem'd
Better to leave Excalibur conceal'd   230
There in the many-knotted waterflags,
That whistled stiff and dry about the marge.
So strode he back slow to the wounded King.

Then spake King Arthur to Sir Bedivere:
"Hast thou perform'd my mission which I gave?
What is it thou hast seen? or what hast heard?"

And answer made the bold Sir Bedivere:
"I heard the ripple washing in the reeds,
And the wild water lapping on the crag."

To whom replied King Arthur, faint and pale: 240
"Thou hast betray'd thy nature and thy name,
Not rendering true answer, as beseem'd
Thy fealty, nor like a noble knight:
For surer sign had follow'd, either hand,
Or voice, or else a motion of the mere.
This is a shameful thing for men to lie.
Yet now, I charge thee, quickly go again,
As thou art lief and dear, and do the thing
I bade thee, watch, and lightly bring me word."

Then went Sir Bedivere the second time   250
Across the ridge, and paced beside the mere,
Counting the dewy pebbles, fix'd in thought;
But when he saw the wonder of the hilt,
How curiously and strangely chased, he smote
His palms together, and he cried aloud:

"And if indeed I cast the brand away,
Surely a precious thing, one worthy note,

Should thus be lost for ever from the earth,
Which might have pleased the eyes of many men.
What good should follow this, if this were done?   260
What harm, undone? Deep harm to disobey,
Seeing obedience is the bond of rule.
Were it well to obey then, if a king demand
An act unprofitable, against himself?
The King is sick, and knows not what he does.
What record, or what relic of my lord
Should be to aftertime, but empty breath
And rumours of a doubt? But were this kept,
Stored in some treasure-house of mighty kings,
Some one might show it at a joust of arms,   270
Saying, 'King Arthur's sword, Excalibur,
Wrought by the lonely maiden of the Lake.
Nine years she wrought it, sitting in the deeps
Upon the hidden bases of the hills.'
So might some old man speak in the aftertime
To all the people, winning reverence.
But now much honour and much fame were lost."

So spake he, clouded with his own conceit,
And hid Excalibur the second time,
And so strode back slow to the wounded King.   280

Then spoke King Arthur, breathing heavily:
"What is it thou hast seen? or what hast heard?"

And answer made the bold Sir Bedivere:
"I heard the water lapping on the crag,
And the long ripple washing in the reeds."

To whom replied King Arthur, much in wrath:
"Ah, miserable and unkind, untrue,
Unknightly, traitor-hearted! Woe is me!
Authority forgets a dying king,
Laid widow'd of the power in his eye   290
That bow'd the will. I see thee what thou art,
For thou, the latest-left of all my knights,
In whom should meet the offices of all,
Thou wouldst betray me for the precious hilt;
Either from lust of gold, or like a girl
Valuing the giddy pleasure of the eyes.
Yet, for a man may fail in duty twice,

And the third time may prosper, get thee hence:
But, if thou spare to fling Excalibur,
I will arise and slay thee with my hands."   300

Then quickly rose Sir Bedivere, and ran,
And, leaping down the ridges lightly, plunged
Among the bulrush beds, and clutch'd the sword,
And strongly wheel'd and threw it. The great brand
Made lightnings in the splendour of the moon,
And flashing round and round, and whirl'd in an arch,
Shot like a streamer of the northern morn,
Seen where the moving isles of winter shock
By night, with noises of the Northern Sea.
So flash'd and fell the brand Excalibur: 310
But ere he dipt the surface, rose an arm
Clothed in white samite, mystic, wonderful,
And caught him by the hilt, and brandish'd him
Three times, and drew him under in the mere.
And lightly went the other to the King.

Then spoke King Arthur, drawing thicker breath:
"Now see I by thine eyes that this is done.
Speak out: what is it thou hast heard, or seen?"

And answer made the bold Sir Bedivere:
'Sir King, I closed mine eyelids, lest the gems   320
Should blind my purpose, for I never saw,
Nor shall see, here or elsewhere, till I die,
Not tho' I live three lives of mortal men,
So great a miracle as yonder hilt.
Then with both hands I flung him, wheeling him;
But when I look'd again, behold an arm,
Clothed in white samite, mystic, wonderful,
That caught him by the hilt, and brandish'd him
Three times, and drew him under in the mere."

And answer made King Arthur, breathing hard: 330
"My end draws nigh; 'tis time that I were gone.
Make broad thy shoulders to receive my weight,
And bear me to the margin; yet I fear
My wound hath taken cold, and I shall die."

So saying, from the pavement he half rose,
Slowly, with pain, reclining on his arm,

And looking wistfully with wide blue eyes
As in a picture. Him Sir Bedivere
Remorsefully regarded thro' his tears,
And would have spoken,—but he found not words;   340
Then took with care, and kneeling on one knee,
O'er both his shoulders drew the languid hands,
And rising bore him thro' the place of tombs.

But, as he walk'd, King Arthur panted hard,
Like one that feels a nightmare on his bed
When all the house is mute. So sigh'd the King,
Muttering and murmuring at his ear, "Quick, quick!
I fear it is too late, and I shall die."
But the other swiftly strode from ride to ridge,
Clothed with his breath, and looking, as he walk'd,   350
Larger than human on the frozen hills.
He heard the deep behind him, and a cry
Before. His own thought drove him like a goad.
Dry clash'd his harness in the icy caves
And barren chasms, and all to left and right
The bare black cliff clang'd round him, as he based
His feet on juts of slippery crag that rang
Sharp-smitten with the dint of armed heels—
And on a sudden, lo! the level lake,
And the long glories of the winter moon.   360

Then saw they how there hove a dusky barge,
Dark as a funeral scarf from stem to stern,
Beneath them; and descending they were ware
That all the decks were dense with stately forms,
Black-stoled, black-hooded, like a dream—by these
Three Queens with crowns of gold: and from them rose
A cry that shiver'd to the tingling stars,
And, as it were one voice, an agony
Of lamentation, like a wind that shrills
All night in a waste land, where no one comes,   370
Or hath come, since the making of the world.

Then murmur'd Arthur, "Place me in the barge."
So to the barge they came. There those three Queens
Put forth their hands, and took the King, and wept.
But she, that rose the tallest of them all
And fairest, laid his head upon her lap,
And loosed the shatter'd casque, and chafed his hands,

And call'd him by his name, complaining loud,
And dropping bitter tears against a brow
Striped with dark blood: for all his face was white   380
And colourless, and like the wither'd moon
Smote by the fresh beam of the springing east;
And all his greaves and cuisses dash'd with drops
Of onset; and the light and lustrous curls—
That made his forehead like a rising sun
High from the daïs-throne—were parch'd with dust;
Or, clotted into points and hanging loose,
Mix'd with the knightly growth that fringed his lips.
So like a shatter'd column lay the King;
Not like that Arthur who, with lance in rest,   390
From spur to plume a star of tournament,
Shot thro' the lists at Camelot, and charged
Before the eyes of ladies and of kings.

Then loudly cried the bold Sir Bedivere:
"Ah! my Lord Arthur, whither shall I go?
Where shall I hide my forehead and my eyes?
For now I see the true old times are dead,
When every morning brought a noble chance,
And every chance brought out a noble knight.
Such times have been not since the light that led   400
The holy Elders with the gift of myrrh.
But now the whole Round Table is dissolved
Which was an image of the mighty world,
And I, the last, go forth companionless,
And the days darken round me, and the years,
Among new men, strange faces, other minds."

And slowly answer'd Arthur from the barge:
"The old order changeth, yielding place to new,
And God fulfils himself in many ways,
Lest one good custom should corrupt the world.   410
Comfort thyself: what comfort is in me?
I have lived my life, and that which I have done
May He within himself make pure! but thou,
If thou shouldst never see my face again,
Pray for my soul. More things are wrought by prayer
Than this world dreams of. Wherefore, let thy voice
Rise like a fountain for me night and day.
For what are men better than sheep or goats
That nourish a blind life within the brain,

If, knowing God, they lift not hands of prayer   420
Both for themselves and those who call them friend?
For so the whole round earth is every way
Bound by gold chains about the feet of God.
But now farewell. I am going a long way
With these thou seëst—if indeed I go
(For all my mind is clouded with a doubt)—
To the island-valley of Avilion;
Where falls not hail, or rain, or any snow,
Nor ever wind blows loudly; but it lies
Deep-meadow'd, happy, fair with orchard lawns   430
And bowery hollows crown'd with summer sea,
Where I will heal me of my grievous wound."

So said he, and the barge with oar and sail
Moved from the brink, like some full-breasted swan
That, fluting a wild carol ere her death,
Ruffles her pure cold plume, and takes the flood
With swarthy webs. Long stood Sir Bedivere
Revolving many memories, till the hull
Look'd one black dot against the verge of dawn,
And on the mere the wailing died away.   440

But when that moan had past for evermore,
The stillness of the dead world's winter dawn
Amazed him, and he groan'd, "The King is gone."
And therewithal came on him the weird rhyme,
"From the great deep to the great deep he goes."

Whereat he slowly turn'd and slowly clomb
The last hard footstep of that iron crag;
Thence mark'd the black hull moving yet, and cried,
"He passes to be King among the dead,
And after healing of his grievous wound   450
He comes again; but—if he come no more—
O me, be yon dark Queens in yon black boat,
Who shriek'd and wail'd, the three whereat we gazed
On that high day, when, clothed with living light,
They stood before his throne in silence, friends
Of Arthur, who should help him at his need?"

Then from the dawn it seem'd there came, but faint
As from beyond the limit of the world,
Like the last echo born of a great cry,

Sounds, as if some fair city were one voice   460
Around a king returning from his wars.

Thereat once more he moved about, and clomb
Ev'n to the highest he could climb, and saw,
Straining his eyes beneath an arch of hand,
Or thought he saw, the speck that bare the King,
Down that long water opening on the deep
Somewhere far off, pass on and on, and go
From less to less and vanish into light.
And the new sun rose bringing the new year.

CAMELOT

Book and Lyrics by A L A N J A Y L E R N E R
Music by F R E D E R I C K L O E W E

CAMELOT *was first presented by the Messrs. Lerner,
Loewe and Hart at the Majestic Theatre, New York City,
on December 3, 1960, with the following cast:*

(*In order of appearance*)

SIR DINADAN, *John Cullum*
SIR LIONEL, *Bruce Yarnell*
MERLYN, *David Hurst*
ARTHUR, *Richard Burton*
GUENEVERE, *Julie Andrews*
NIMUE, *Marjorie Smith*
LANCELOT, *Robert Goulet*
MORDRED, *Roddy McDowall*
A PAGE, *Leland Mayforth*
SQUIRE DAP, *Michael Clarke-Laurence*
PELLINORE, *Robert Coote*
SIR SAGRAMORE, *James Gannon*
CLARIUS, *Richard Kuch*
LADY ANNE, *Christina Gillespie*
LADY SYBIL, *Leesa Troy*
A KNIGHT, *Michael Kermoyan*
A KNIGHT, *Jack Dabdoub*
MORGAN LE FEY, *M'el Dowd*
TOM, *Robin Stewart*
KNIGHTS AND LADIES—*Joan August, Mary Sue Berry,
Marnell Bruce, Judy Hastings, Benita James, Marjorie
Smith, Shelia Swenson, Leesa Troy, Dorothy White,
Frank Bouley, Jack Dabdoub, James Gannon, Murray
Goldkind, Warren Hays, Paul Huddleston, Michael
Kermoyan, Donald Maloof, Larry Mitchell, Paul Rich-
ards, John Taliaferro, Virginia Allen, Judi Allinson,
Laurie Archer, Carlene Carroll, Joan Coddington, Katia
Geleznova, Adriana Keathley, Dawn Mitchell, Claudia
Schroeder, Beti Seay, Jerry Bowers, Peter Deign, Randy
Doney, Richard Englund, Richard Gain, Gene GeBauer,
James Kirby, Richard Kuch, Joe Nelson, John Stark-
weather, Jimmy Tarbutton*

Production staged by Moss Hart
Choreography and musical numbers by Hanya Holm
Scenic production by Oliver Smith
Costumes designed by Adrian *and* Tony Duquette
Lighting by Feder

Musical director: Franz Allers
Orchestrations by Robert Russell Bennett *and* Philip J. Lang
Dance and choral arrangements by Trude Rittman
Hair styles by Ernest Adler
Production stage manager: Robert Downing

MUSICAL SYNOPSIS OF SCENES

ACT ONE

SCENE 1: *A Hilltop near Camelot. A long time ago.*
"I Wonder What the King Is Doing Tonight?," Arthur
"The Simple Joys of Maidenhood," Guenevere
SCENE 2: *Near Camelot. Immediately following.*
"Follow Me," Nimue
SCENE 3: *Arthur's Study. Five years later.*
SCENE 4: *A Countryside near Camelot. A few months later.*
"C'est Moi," Lancelot
SCENE 5: *A Garden near the Castle. Immediately following.*
"The Lusty Month of May," Guenevere and Ensemble
SCENE 6: *A Terrace of the Castle. A few weeks later.*
"How to Handle a Woman," Arthur
SCENE 7: *The Tents outside the Jousting Field. A few days later.*
SCENE 8: *The Jousting Field.*
"The Jousts," Arthur, Guenevere, and Ensemble
SCENE 9: *The Terrace. Early evening of the same day.*
"Before I Gaze at You again," Guenevere
SCENE 10: *A Corridor in the Castle. Immediately following.*
SCENE 11: *The Grand Hall. Immediately following.*

ACT TWO

SCENE 1: *The Main Terrace of the Castle. A few years later.*
"If Ever I Would Leave You," Lancelot
"The Seven Deadly Virtues," Mordred
SCENE 2: *The Terrace of the Castle. A month later.*
"What Do Simple Folk Do?," Guenevere and Arthur
SCENE 3: *A Forest near Camelot. A few days later.*
SCENE 4: *The Forest of Morgan Le Fey. Immediately following.*
"The Persuasion," Mordred and Morgan Le Fey

Act I, SCENE ONE.

Scene: A Hilltop near the Castle at Camelot. There is a large tree with great branches reaching high and out of sight, and a small hillock beyond the tree. A light snow is falling.

Time: Afternoon.

At rise: The Overture has ended. A spotlight discovers Sir Dinadan standing on the hillock, peering through a crude telescope into the distance. Around him can be seen Ladies and Gentlemen of the Court, arranged decoratively.

DINADAN [*a pompous young lord, easily astonished, suddenly quite astonished*]

My Sainted Mother! The carriage has stopped! Someone is getting out. A lady.

LIONEL

Are you sure it's her carriage?

[*Merlyn enters. He is a rococo figure of a man, with a huge pointed hat; flowing, heavily embroidered robes; and the legendary apparel of wisdom—a long white beard.*]

DINADAN

It's pure white. The horses are pure white. It's plainly and obviously a bridal carriage. [*He rushes to Merlyn.*] Merlyn, here's a calamity. Guenevere's carriage has halted below the hill.

MERLYN

I know. I remembered she would.

DINADAN

But it was officially arranged for her to stop here at the top of the hill. Royal brides are always greeted atop the hill. What should we do?

MERLYN

Dunce! Sound the trumpet, assemble the Court and march to the bottom.

DINADAN [*stunned*]

It's wildly untraditional.

MERLYN

I hereby proclaim from this time henceforth that all new queens shall be met at the foot of the hill. There! A brand-new tradition! Does that solve it?

DINADAN [*placated*]

Sound the trumpet! We shall greet Lady Guenevere at the foot of the hill in traditional fashion.

[*The Ladies and Gentlemen assemble formally and, with banners flying, parade across the stage and off. Merlyn pauses before the tree and, without looking at it, speaks.*]

MERLYN

Arthur, come down out of the tree. [*There is no response.*] Your Majesty, I know you're up there. Come down at once. [*There is no response.*] Wart, come down at once! You're perfectly safe. There's no one here.

[*King Arthur peers through the branches.*]

ARTHUR

Why so angry, Merlyn? I know you are because you called me Wart.

MERLYN

Yes, Wart. Your schoolboy's nickname. That's what your behavior warrants. Perched in a tree trying to steal a look at your bride. Will you never learn patience?

[*Arthur jumps down. He is a boyish young man in his mid-twenties.*]

ARTHUR [*imperiously*]

I'm the King. Others must learn patience. [*Then, with sudden nervous enthusiasm:*] How is she, Merlyn? Is she beautiful?

MERLYN

I don't recall.

ARTHUR [*irritably*]

Rubbish. Are you pretending you don't see into the future?

MERLYN

When you live backwards in time as I do, and have the future to remember as well as the past, occasionally you do forget a face.

ARTHUR [*dictatorially*]

Merlyn, as your King, I command you to tell me if she is . . .

MERLYN [*giving up*]

She's beautiful.

ARTHUR [*suddenly almost frightened*]

Quite, or very?

MERLYN

Very.

ARTHUR [*frustrated by his own discomfort*]

Merlyn, why have you never taught me love and marriage?

MERLYN

Don't scramble them together that way. They are two different things. Besides, I did give you a lesson once, but your mind was, as usual, elsewhere. You had better heed me well from now on. I shan't be here long.

ARTHUR

Why not?

MERLYN

I've told you, I'm due to be bewitched by a nymph named Nimue, who will steal my magic powers and lock me in a cave for several centuries.

ARTHUR

Nimue! Fiddlesticks! Whenever you're displeased with me, you threaten with this creature Nimue.

MERLYN

It's not a threat; it will happen.

ARTHUR

When you know she is near, change yourself into a bat. [*At his most youthful and charming.*] Merlyn, do you remember when I was a boy and you changed me into a hawk? What a feeling, sailing through the air! For old times' sake, do it again. Right this minute. One last soar through the sky.

MERLYN

So you can soar through the sky to her carriage and see her through the window? No.

ARTHUR [*furious*]

Merlyn, there are times when I insist that you remember who I am. Make me a hawk, or I'll have your head cut off.

MERLYN

It's you who keep forgetting who you are. Think of the joy you've brought to Camelot. A radiant young princess, never before out of her castle, come by treaty to bring peace between peoples. A royal marriage. A new Queen. And where is the King? Swinging in the trees. Thank heaven History never knew. Thank heaven Mallory and Tennyson never found out. Thank heaven your people are

not aware of your behavior. Now go back to the castle, my
boy. At once. [*He exits.*]

ARTHUR [*rebelliously*]

My people indeed! As if they give a thought to what I'm
doing tonight. [*Shouting his defiance:*] Oh, good and loyal
subjects of the Crown, are you really peering up at the
castle with a question mark in each eye, churning to know
how stands the King on his bridal eve, throbbing with
curiosity about the King's humor on his prenuptial night?
[*Defeatedly.*] Yes, you are. That's precisely what you're
doing. Every last, blessed one of you. [*He sings:*]

I know what my people are thinking tonight,
As home through the shadows they wander.
Ev'ryone smiling in secret delight,
They stare at the castle and ponder.
Whenever the wind blows this way,
You can almost hear ev'ryone say:

I wonder what the King is doing tonight.
What merriment is the King pursuing tonight?
The candles at the Court, they never burn'd as bright.
I wonder what the King is up to tonight.
How goes the final hour
As he sees the bridal bower
Being legally and regally prepared?

[*Angrily.*]

Well, I'll tell you what the King is doing tonight:
He's scared! He's scared!

[*He paces up and down, debating the subject with
himself.*]

You mean that a king who fought a dragon,
Whack'd him in two and fix'd his wagon,
Goes to be wed in terror and distress?

[*Admits angrily:*]
Yes!

A warrior who's so calm in battle
Even his armor doesn't rattle,
Faces a woman petrified with fright?

[*Fairly shouting his rage:*]
Right!

You mean that appalling clamoring

That sounds like a blacksmith hammering
Is merely the banging of his royal knees?

> [*Painfully:*]
> Please!

You wonder what the King is wishing tonight . . .
He's wishing he were in Scotland fishing tonight.
What occupies his time while waiting for the bride?
He's searching high and low for some place to hide.

And oh, the expectation,
The sublime anticipation
He must feel about the wedding night to come!
Well, I'll tell you what the King is feeling tonight:
He's numb!
> He shakes!
He quails! He quakes!
Oh, that's what the King is doing tonight.

[*Something, or someone, offstage catches his eye, and
he scrambles back into his place of hiding in the tree.
Suddenly Guenevere, in a flaming red cloak, flies fearfully across the stage. She stops. She looks behind to
see if she has been followed. She satisfies herself that
she is momentarily safe, and seats herself at the foot
of the tree. She is very, very young and very, very
lovely. She clasps her hands and looks heavenward.*]

> GUENEVERE [*sings*]

St. Genevieve! St. Genevieve!
It's Guenevere. Remember me?
St. Genevieve! St. Genevieve!
I'm over here beneath this tree.
You know how faithful and devout I am.
You must admit I've always been a lamb.
But, Genevieve, St. Genevieve,

> [*With vehement rebellion:*]

I won't obey you any more!
You've gone a bit too far.
I won't be bid and bargain'd for
Like beads at a bazaar.

St. Genevieve, I've run away,
Eluded them and fled;
And from now on I intend to pray
To someone else instead.

[*Suddenly lost, she becomes suddenly plaintive again.*]
Oh, Genevieve, St. Genevieve,
Where were you when my youth was sold?
Dear Genevieve, sweet Genevieve,
Shan't I be young before I'm old?

[*She speaks:*]

Shan't I, St. Genevieve? Why must I suffer this squalid destiny? Just when I reach the golden age of eligibility and wooability. Is my fate determined by love and courtship? Oh, no. [*Bitterly:*] Clause one: fix the border; Clause two: establish trade; Clause three: deliver me; Clause four: stop the war; five, six: pick up sticks. How cruel! How unjust! Am I never to know the joys of maidenhood? The conventional, ordinary, garden variety joys of maidenhood?

[*She sings:*]

Where are the simple joys of maidenhood?
Where are all those adoring, daring boys?
Where's the knight pining so for me
He leaps to death in woe for me?
Oh, where are a maiden's simple joys?

Shan't I have the normal life a maiden should?
Shall I never be rescued in the wood?
Shall two knights never tilt for me
And let their blood be spilt for me?
Oh, where are the simple joys of maidenhood?

Shall I not be on a pedestal,
Worshipped and competed for?
Not be carried off, or betterst'll,
Cause a little war?

Where are the simple joys of maidenhood?
Are those sweet, gentle pleasures gone for good?
Shall a feud not begin for me?
Shall kith not kill their kin for me?
Oh, where are the trivial joys . . . ?
Harmless, convivial joys . . . ?
Where are the simple joys of maidenhood?
    [*She turns dejectedly toward the foot of the tree. A
    branch cracks, and Arthur drops to the floor. Guene-
    vere, startled out of her wits, runs.*]

ARTHUR

A thousand pardons, Milady. Wait! Don't run. [*She stops*

in the corner of the stage and looks at him coweringly.]
Please! I won't harm you.
                          GUENEVERE
You lie! You'll leap at me and throw me to the ground.
                          ARTHUR [*amazed, protesting*]
I won't do any such thing.
   [*He takes a step toward her. She takes a step backwards.
   He stops.*]
                          GUENEVERE
Then you'll twist my arm and tie me to a tree.
                          ARTHUR
But I won't.
                          GUENEVERE
Then you'll sling me over your shoulder and carry me off.
                          ARTHUR
No, no, no! I swear it! By the Sword Excalibur! I swear
I won't touch you.
                          GUENEVERE [*hurt*]
Why not? [*Sudden rage.*] How dare you insult me in this
fashion. Do my looks repel you?
                          ARTHUR
No. You're beautiful.
                          GUENEVERE
Well, then? We're alone. I'm completely defenseless. What
kind of a cad are you? Apologize at once.
                          ARTHUR [*at once*]
I apologize. I'm not certain what I've done, but from the
depths of my heart, I apologize.
                          GUENEVERE [*with sudden wisdom*]
Ah! I think I know. You heard me praying.
                          ARTHUR
I couldn't help it, Milady. You prayed rather loudly.
                          GUENEVERE
And you know who I am.
                          ARTHUR
You're Guenevere.
                          GUENEVERE
Yes, of course. You're afraid because I may be your Queen.
That accounts for your respectful, polite, despicable be-
havior.
                          ARTHUR
Milady, I would never harm you for any reason. And as for
what to do with you, I'm at a loss. I know you are to be
Queen and I should escort you back to your carriage. At

the same time, you're a maiden in genuine distress. It's chivalry versus country. I can't quite determine which call to obey.

GUENEVERE [*looking off toward the foot of the hill*]

You'd better decide quickly. They'll soon reach the carriage and discover I'm gone. Then all of Camelot will be searching for me. At least *that* will be exciting. Unless of course everyone in Camelot is like you and they all go home to deliberate.

ARTHUR [*thrown off balance, enamored, captivated, and overcome by a great sense of inadequacy*]

Oh, why isn't Merlyn here! He usually senses when I need him and appears. Why does he fail me now?

GUENEVERE

Who?

ARTHUR

Merlyn. My teacher. He would know immediately what to do. I'm not accomplished at thinking, so I have Merlyn do it for me. He's the wisest man alive. He lives backwards.

GUENEVERE

I beg your pardon?

ARTHUR

He lives backwards. He doesn't age. He youthens. He can remember the future so he can tell you what you'll be doing in it. Do you understand?

[*She comes toward him. He never takes his eyes off her, as the wonder of her comes nearer.*]

GUENEVERE [*now at ease*]

Of course I don't understand. But if you mean he's some sort of fortune-teller, I'd give a year in Paradise to know mine. I can never return to my own castle, and I absolutely refuse to go on to that one.

ARTHUR [*sadly*]

You refuse to go on—ever?

GUENEVERE

Ever. My only choice is . . . Don't stare. It's rude. Who are you?

ARTHUR [*after a thought*]

Actually, they call me Wart.

GUENEVERE

Wart? What a ridiculous name. Are you sure you heard them properly?

ARTHUR

It's a nickname. It was given to me when I was a boy.

GUENEVERE

You're rather sweet, in spite of your name. And I didn't think I'd like anyone in Camelot. Imagine riding seven hours in a carriage on the verge of hysteria, then seeing that horrible castle rising in the distance, and running away; then having a man plop from a tree like an overripe apple. . . . You must admit for my first day away from home it's quite a plateful. If only I were not alone. Wart, why don't you . . . Is it really Wart?

ARTHUR

Yes.

GUENEVERE

Wart, why don't you run away with me?

[*She is enchanted by the notion.*]

ARTHUR

I? Run away with you?

GUENEVERE

Of course. As my protector. Naturally, I would be brutalized by strangers. I expect that. But it would be dreadful if there were no one to rescue me. Think of it! We can travel the world. France, Scotland, Spain. . . .

ARTHUR

What a dream you spin, and how easily I could be caught up in it. But I can't, Milady. To serve as your protector would satisfy the prayers of the most fanatic cavalier alive. But I must decline.

GUENEVERE [*angrily*]

You force me to stay?

ARTHUR

Not at all.

GUENEVERE

But you know you're the only one I know in Camelot. Whom else can I turn to?

ARTHUR

Milady, if you persist in escaping, I'll find someone trustworthy and brave to accompany you.

GUENEVERE

Then do so immediately. There's not much time.

ARTHUR

Oh, do look around you, Milady. Reconsider. Camelot is unique. We have an enchanted forest where the Fairy Queen, Morgan Le Fey, lives in an invisible castle. Most

unusual. We have a talking owl named Archimedes. Highly
original. We have unicorns with silver feet. The rarest kind.
And we have far and away the most equitable climate in all
the world. Ordained by decree! Extremely uncommon.

                    GUENEVERE

Oh, come now.

                    ARTHUR [*sings*]

It's true! It's true! The crown has made it clear:
The climate must be perfect all the year.

A law was made a distant moon ago here,
July and August cannot be too hot;
And there's a legal limit to the snow here
In Camelot.

The winter is forbidden till December,
And exits March the second on the dot.
By order summer lingers through September
In Camelot.

Camelot! Camelot!
I know it sounds a bit bizarre;
But in Camelot, Camelot
That's how conditions are.

The rain may never fall till after sundown.
By eight the morning fog must disappear.
In short, there's simply not
A more congenial spot
For happ'ly-ever-aftering than here
In Camelot.

                    GUENEVERE [*sarcastically*]

And I suppose the autumn leaves fall in neat little piles.

                    ARTHUR

Oh, no, Milady. They blow away completely. At night,
of course.

                    GUENEVERE

Of course.

[*She moves away from him, as if to leave. He leaps after
her and blocks her way.*]

                    ARTHUR

Camelot! Camelot!
I know it gives a person pause

But in Camelot, Camelot
Those are the legal laws.

The snow may never slush upon the hillside.
By nine P.M. the moonlight must appear.
In short, there's simply not
A more congenial spot
For happ'ly-ever-aftering than here
In Camelot.
[*Dinadan enters suddenly, accompanied by one or two Ladies and Gentlemen of the Court.*]

DINADAN [*to the others*]

There she is!

GUENEVERE [*running to Arthur for protection*]

Wart, please . . .

DINADAN [*to Arthur*]

Your Majesty, forgive me. I did not see you for a moment.
[*He bows. Guenevere looks at Arthur in amazement. Arthur avoids her gaze and steps aside, as the Court parades on in stately fashion. The men bow first to the King, and then to the Queen. The ladies give flowers to Guenevere. The formality over, the Court departs. Guenevere stares at the King, at a loss for words.*]

ARTHUR [*turning away*]

When I was a lad of eighteen, our King died in London and left no one to succeed him; only a sword stuck through an anvil which stood on a stone. Written on it in letters of gold it said: "Whoso pulleth out this sword of this stone and anvil is rightwise King born of all England." Many chaps tried to dislodge it, and none could. Finally a great tournament was proclaimed for New Year's Day, so that all the mightiest knights in England would be assembled at one time to have a go at the sword.

I went to London as squire to my cousin, Sir Kay. The morning of the tournament, Kay discovered he'd left his sword at home and gave me a shilling to ride back to fetch it. On my way through London, I passed a square and saw there a sword rising from a stone. Not thinking very quickly, I thought it was a war memorial. The square was deserted, so I decided to save myself a journey and borrow it. I tried to pull it out. I failed. I tried again. I failed again. Then I closed my eyes and with all my force tried one last time. Lo, it moved in my hand. Then slowly it slid out of the stone. I heard a great roar. When I opened my eyes, the square was filled with people shouting: "Long live the King! Long live the King!" Then I looked at the sword and saw the blade gleaming with letters of gold.

That's how I became King. I never knew I would be. I never wanted to be. And since I am, I have been ill at ease in my crown. Until I dropped from the tree and my eye beheld you. Then suddenly, for the first time, I felt I was King. I was glad to be King. And most astonishing of all, I wanted to be the wisest, most heroic, most splendid King who ever sat on any throne. [*There is a moment of silence.*] If you will come with me, Milady, I will arrange for the carriage to return you to your father. [*He moves across the stage. She doesn't follow. He stops.*] This way.

GUENEVERE [*slowly and tenderly*]
I hear it never rains till after sundown.
By eight the morning fog must disappear.
In short, there's simply not
A more congenial spot
For happ'ly-ever-aftering than here
In Camelot.
[*The music continues. It takes Arthur a moment to realize his stroke of fortune. Then he goes to her and kisses her hand.*]

GUENEVERE
I'm afraid, Your Majesty.

ARTHUR
Afraid?

GUENEVERE
Marriage is rather frightening, isn't it?

ARTHUR [*placing her hand on his offered arm*]
I must confess, Your Ladyship, it did occur to me. But now not marrying seems infinitely more terrifying.
[*They take a step or two, then stop.*]

GUENEVERE
What would have happened if we hadn't? To the treaty?

ARTHUR
It would have been broken. War would have been declared.

GUENEVERE
War? Over me? How simply marvelous!
[*He laughs. Then she begins to laugh. She takes his arm and they exit, still laughing. The lights dim, and before the stage is dark, a light shines on the tree, and Merlyn appears from behind it.*]

MERLYN

At last! At last! He's ambitious at last! How foolish of me not to have realized sooner. He didn't need a lecture. He needed a queen.

[*As he walks downstage, the drop falls discreetly behind him.*]

SCENE TWO.

Scene: Near Camelot.

Time: Immediately following.

At rise: Sir Dinadan and a Lady enter. Merlyn, in front of the drop, continues.

MERLYN [*to Dinadan*]

All his life I've tried to teach him to think.

DINADAN

Who are you talking about, Merlyn?

MERLYN

Arthur. All in vain, of course. Then over the hill comes his fated maiden, and for her he wants to be Caesar and Solomon. I tell you, Dinadan, I have waited years for this moment. And now it begins. What a joy it will be to watch! [*A Knight and two other Ladies enter and listen.*] To see him putting together the pieces of his destiny. It won't go quickly. One year . . . two years . . . what does it matter? I can see a night five years from now . . .

[*Suddenly a distant voice is heard. It is a high feminine voice. Merlyn stops. Suspended.*]

VOICE [*singing*]

Far from day, far from night . . .
Out of time, out of sight . . .

DINADAN

Go on. What about five years from now?

MERLYN

Yes! After the Battle of Bedegraine. That's the night it will happen!

[*The voice is heard again. Again Merlyn is caught by it.*]

VOICE

Follow me . . .

Dry the rain, warm the snow . . .
Where the winds never go . . .

DINADAN

Go on. That's the night *what* will happen?

MERLYN [*his face clouded*]

I can't remember. That voice. Don't you hear it?

DINADAN

What voice?

MERLYN [*in hushed fear*]
Nimue, is that you? Oh, please . . . not yet. I must find out what will happen to him.

VOICE
In a cave by a sapphire shore
We shall walk through an em'rald door.
And for thousands of evermores
to come, my life you shall be.

[*Merlyn's behavior is much too eccentric for Dinadan. He exits, followed by the others.*]

MERLYN

Oh, Nimue! So it's you! Must you steal my magic now? Couldn't you have waited a bit longer? [*The music swells. Merlyn walks forlornly toward the voice. Then he stops.*] Wait! Have I told him everything he should know? Did I tell him of Lancelot? [*A vision of Lancelot is revealed behind him.*] I did. [*Fearfully:*] But Lancelot and Guenevere! Did I warn him of Lancelot and Guenevere? And Mordred? [*A vision of Mordred also appears.*] Mordred! I didn't warn him of Mordred, and I must! [*The visions begin to fade.*] I remember nothing of Lancelot and Guenevere. And Mordred! [*With hopeless resignation:*] It's all gone. My magic is gone.

[*The music swells, and the voice sings clear, and Merlyn walks slowly toward it.*]

VOICE

Only you, only I,
World farewell, world goodbye,
To our home 'neath the sea,
We shall fly,
Follow me . . .

[*Just before he exits, he looks back at Camelot for the last time.*]

MERLYN

Goodbye, Arthur. My memory of the future is gone.

I know no more the sorrows and joys before you. I can only wish for you in ignorance, like everyone else. Reign long and reign happily. Oh, and, Wart! Remember to think!

[*The music swells, and the lights dim slowly, as Merlyn follows the voice to his cavernous destiny.*]

SCENE THREE.

Scene: Arthur's Study.

Time: Early evening. Five years later.

At rise: Guenevere is at a tapestry easel working with needle and thread. Arthur is standing next to her.

ARTHUR [*heatedly*]

You cannot deny the facts! Did I or did I not pledge to you five years ago that I would be the most splendid king who ever sat on any throne?

GUENEVERE

You did.

ARTHUR

And in five years, have I become the most splendid king who ever sat on any throne?

GUENEVERE

You have.

ARTHUR

Rubbish! I have not, and you know it well. I'm nothing of what I pledged to you I would be. I'm a failure, and that's that.

GUENEVERE

Arthur, it's not true. You're the greatest warrior in England.

ARTHUR

But for what purpose? Might isn't always right, Jenny.

GUENEVERE

Nonsense, dear, of course it is. To be right and lose couldn't possibly be right.

ARTHUR [*thinking*]

Yes. Might and right, battle and plunder. That's what keeps plaguing me. Merlyn used to frown on battles, yet he always helped me win them. I'm sure it's a clue. If only I could follow it. I'm always walking down a winding dimly lit road, and in the distance I see the outline of a thought. Like the shadow of a hill. I fumble and stumble, and at last I get there; but when I do, the hill is gone. Not there at all. And I hear a small voice saying: "Go back, Arthur, it's too dark for you to be out thinking."

GUENEVERE

My poor love. Let me see you do it. Walk out loud.

ARTHUR

All right. [*He crosses to the end of the stage.*] Proposition: It's far better to be alive than dead.

GUENEVERE

Far better.

ARTHUR [*taking a step forward*]

If that is so, then why do we have battles, where people can get killed?

GUENEVERE [*chews on it a moment*]

I don't know. Do you?

ARTHUR

Yes. Because somebody attacks.

GUENEVERE [*sincerely*]

Of course. That's very clever of you, Arthur. Why do they attack?

[*Arthur leaves "the road" and comes to her.*]

ARTHUR

Jenny, I must confess something I've never told you before for fear you would not believe me.

GUENEVERE

How silly, Arthur, I would never not believe you.

ARTHUR

You know Merlyn brought me up, taught me everything I know. But do you know how?

GUENEVERE

How?

ARTHUR

By changing me into animals.

GUENEVERE

I don't believe it.

ARTHUR

There, you see? But it's true. I was a fish, a bobolink, a beaver and even an ant. From each animal he wanted me to learn something. Before he made me a hawk, for instance, he told me that while I would be flying through the sky, if I would look down at the earth, I would discover something.

GUENEVERE

What did you discover?

ARTHUR

Nothing. Merlyn was livid. Yet tonight, on my way home, while I was thinking, I suddenly realized that when you're in the sky looking down at the earth, there are no boundaries. No borders. Yet that's what somebody always attacks about. And you win by pushing them back across something that doesn't exist.

GUENEVERE

It *is* odd, isn't it?

ARTHUR

Proposition: We have battles for no reason at all. Then why? Why?

GUENEVERE

Because knights love them. They adore charging in and whacking away. It's splendid fun. You've said so yourself often.

ARTHUR

It *is* splendid fun. [*Steps forward.*] But that doesn't seem reason enough.

[*He steps back.*]

GUENEVERE

I think it is. And from a woman's point of view, it's wonderfully exciting to see your knight in armor riding bravely off to battle. Especially when you know he'll be home safe in one piece for dinner.

ARTHUR

That's it! It's the armor! I missed that before. Of course! Only knights are rich enough to bedeck themselves in armor. They can declare war when it suits them, go clodhopping about the country slicing up peasants and foot soldiers, because peasants and foot soldiers are not equipped with armor. All that can happen to a knight is an occasional dent. [*He takes a long run to the fireplace.*] Proposition: Wrong or right, they have the might, so wrong or right, they're always right—and that's wrong. Right?

GUENEVERE

Absolutely.

ARTHUR [*excitedly*]

Is that the reason Merlyn helped me to win? To take all

this might that's knocking about the world and do something with it. But what?

GUENEVERE

Yes, what?

[*Arthur sighs with resignation.*]

ARTHUR

It's gone. I've thought as hard as I can, and I can walk no further. [*He walks around and sits on the chaise longue.*] You see, Jenny? I'm still not a king. I win every battle and accomplish nothing. When the Greeks won, they made a civilization. I'm not creating any civilization. I'm not even sure I'm civilized. . . .

GUENEVERE [*tenderly*]

Dear Arthur. You mustn't belabor yourself like this. Let us have a quiet dinner, and after, if you like, you can stroll again.

ARTHUR

Bless you. [*He takes her hand, kisses her, rises and moves to exit. Then he stops and turns.*] Jenny, suppose we create a *new* order of chivalry?

GUENEVERE

Pardon?

ARTHUR

A new order, a new order, where might is only used for right, to improve instead of destroy. And we invite all knights, good or bad, to lay down their arms and come and join. Yes! [*Growing more and more excited.*] We'll take one of the large rooms in the castle and put a table in it, and all the knights will gather at the table.

GUENEVERE

And do what?

ARTHUR

Talk! Discuss! Make laws! Plan improvements!

GUENEVERE

Really, Arthur, do you think knights would ever want to do such a peaceful thing?

ARTHUR

We'll make it a great honor, very fashionable, so that everyone will want to be in. And the knights of my order will ride all over the world, still dressed in armor and whacking away. That will give them an outlet for wanting to whack. But they'll whack only for good. Defend virgins, restore what's been done wrong in the past, help the oppressed. Might for right. That's it, Jenny! Not might is right. Might *for* right!

GUENEVERE

It sounds superb.

ARTHUR

Yes. And civilized. [*Calls.*] Page! [*To Guenevere:*] We'll build a whole new generation of chivalry. Young men, not old, burning with zeal and ideals. [*The Page enters.*] Tell the heralds to mount the towers. And to have their trumpets. And assemble the Court in the yard. Send word there is to be a proclamation.

PAGE

Yes, Your Majesty! [*He exits.*]

GUENEVERE

Arthur, it will have to be an awfully large table! And won't there be jealousy? All your knights will be claiming superiority and wanting to sit at the head.

ARTHUR

Then we shall make it a round table so there is no head.

GUENEVERE [*totally won*]

My father has one that would be perfect. It seats a hundred and fifty. It was given to him once for a present, and he never uses it.

ARTHUR [*suddenly doubting*]

Jenny, have I had a thought? Am I at the hill? Or is it only a mirage?

[*The Page enters.*]

PAGE

The heralds await, Your Majesty. Shall I give the signal, Your Majesty?

ARTHUR

No, wait. I may be wrong. The whole idea may be absurd. If only Merlyn were here! He would have known for certain. [*Disparagingly.*] Knights at a table. . . .

GUENEVERE [*correcting him*]

A round table.

ARTHUR [*corrected*]

Round table. Might for right, a new order of chivalry, shining knights gallivanting around the countryside like angels in armor, sword-swinging apostles battling to snuff out evil! Why, it's naïve . . . it's adolescent . . . it's juvenile . . . it's infantile . . . it's folly . . . it's . . . it's . . .

GUENEVERE

It's marvelous.

ARTHUR

Yes, it is. It's marvelous. Absolutely marvelous. [*To the Page:*] Page, give the signal.

PAGE

Yes, Your Majesty. [*He exits.*]

ARTHUR [*sings*]

We'll send the heralds riding through the country;
Tell ev'ry living person far and near . . .

GUENEVERE [*interrupting him*]

That there is simply not
In all the world a spot
Where rules a more resplendent king than here
In Camelot.

[*The heralds appear in the towers and sound their horns. Arthur embraces Guenevere and goes to the window to make his proclamation.*]

Dim Out

SCENE FOUR.

Scene: A Countryside near Camelot.

Time: The First of May. A few months later.

At rise: Lancelot du Lac enters and looks fervently at Camelot in the distance. He is a striking figure of a young man, with a stern jaw and burning eyes. His face is unlined for he has never smiled.

LANCELOT [*sings*]

Camelot! Camelot!
In far off France I heard your call.
Camelot! Camelot!
And here am I to give my all.
I know in my soul what you expect of me;
And all that and more I shall be!

A knight of the Table Round should be invincible;
Succeed where a less fantastic man would fail;
Climb a wall no one else can climb;
Cleave a dragon in record time;
Swim a moat in a coat of heavy iron mail.
No matter the pain he ought to be unwinceable,
Impossible deeds should be his daily fare.
But where in the world
Is there in the world
A man so *extraordinaire?*

C'est moi! C'est moi,
I'm forced to admit!
'Tis I, I humbly reply.
That mortal who
These marvels can do,
C'est moi, c'est moi, 'tis I.
I've never lost
In battle or game.
I'm simply the best by far.
When swords are cross'd
'Tis always the same:
One blow and *au revoir!*
C'est moi! C'est moi,
So admir'bly fit;
A French Prometheus unbound.
And here I stand with valor untold,
Exception'lly brave, amazingly bold,
To serve at the Table Round!

The soul of a knight should be a thing remarkable:
His heart and his mind as pure as morning dew.
With a will and a self-restraint
That's the envy of ev'ry saint,
He could easily work a miracle or two!
To love and desire he ought to be unsparkable.
The ways of the flesh should offer no allure.
But where in the world
Is there in the world
A man so untouch'd and pure?

[*Speaking modestly:*]

C'est moi
C'est moi! C'est moi,
I blush to disclose,
I'm far too noble to lie.

That man in whom
These qualities bloom,
C'est moi, c'est moi, 'tis I!

I've never stray'd
From all I believe.
I'm bless'd with an iron will.
Had I been made
The partner of Eve,
We'd be in Eden still.
C'est moi! C'est moi,
The angels have chose
To fight their battles below.
And here I stand as pure as a pray'r,
Incredibly clean, with virtue to spare,
The godliest man I know . . . !
C'est moi!

> [*Dap, his squire, enters, dragging a fallen Knight.*]

DAP

I cannot bring him to, Lancelot. You gave him a shattering blow. The echo broke several branches in the trees.

> [*He lowers the Knight to the ground.*]

LANCELOT

There's water in the flask. Toss it in his face. And hurry. [*Dap throws water in the Knight's face. Lancelot looks up at Camelot.*] Oh, King Arthur, what caliber of man you must be. To have conceived of the Table! To have created a new order of life. I worship you before knowing you. No harm must befall you. Beware, enemies of Arthur! Do you hear me? Beware! From this moment on, you answer to me.

> [*The fallen Knight lifts his head, removing his vizor. It is King Arthur.*]

ARTHUR

What a blow! What a blow! Magnificent. Simply magnificent.

LANCELOT

Now that you have recovered, Sir, I bid you good day. And the next time you raise a spear at me, remember you challenge the right arm of King Arthur.

> [*He starts to leave.*]

ARTHUR [*rising*]

Wait! I am King Arthur.

> [*Dap falls to his knees.*]

LANCELOT [*stunned*]

The King?

ARTHUR

Almost the late King.

LANCELOT [*grief-stricken*]

I . . . struck *you*? Oh, my God! [*He crashes to his knees before Arthur.*] Your Majesty, I am Lancelot du Lac. I heard of your new Order in France and came to join. Oh, I beg Your Majesty to forgive me. Not because I deserve it, but because by forgiving me, I'll suffer more.

ARTHUR

Really, dear chap, I don't want you to suffer at all. I want to congratulate you. Please rise. And you, too, Squire.
[*Dap rises. Lancelot doesn't.*]

LANCELOT

I can't, Your Majesty. I am too ashamed to lift my head.

ARTHUR

Then I command you. [*Lancelot rises, his head still down.*] I tell you, I've never felt a bash in the chest like it. It was spectacular. Where did you learn to do it?

LANCELOT

My skill comes from training, Your Majesty. My strength from purity.

ARTHUR

Oh. A unique recipe, I must say.

DAP

He's a unique man, Your Majesty. At the age of fourteen he could defeat any jouster in France. His father, King Ban, made me his squire when he was only . . .

ARTHUR

King Ban? Of Benwick? What did you say your name was?

LANCELOT [*still pronouncing it in French*]

Lancelot du Lac, Your Majesty.

ARTHUR [*in French*]

Lancelot? [*In English:*] Lancelot! My word, you're Lancelot. Of course! I was told you were coming.

LANCELOT

You were told, Your Majesty?

ARTHUR

By Merlyn, our court magician. He said to me one day: "Arthur, keep your eye out for Lancelot du Lac from the castle of Joyous Gard. He will come to the Court of Camelot, and he will be . . ." what was it . . . ?

LANCELOT

Your ally, if you'll take me? Your friend, who asks not friendship? Your defender, when you need one? Whose heart is already filled with you? Whose body is your sword to brandish? Did he prophesy that, Your Majesty? For all that, I am.

ARTHUR [*flattered and almost embarrassed by the effusion*]

Really, my dear fellow, it's almost more than one could hope for, more than one should ask.

LANCELOT

Then you'll accept me?

ARTHUR

Oh, yes. Without hesitation. [*Lancelot kneels.*] We must arrange for your knighthood immediately.

LANCELOT [*rising*]

No, Your Majesty. Not immediately. Not till I have proven myself. All you know of me now is words. Invest me because of deeds, Sire. Give me an order.

ARTHUR

Now?

LANCELOT

Yes, now! This moment! Send me on a mission. Let me perform for you. Is there some wrong I can right? Some enemy I can battle? Some peril I can undertake?

ARTHUR

Well, actually, there's not much going on today. This is the First of May, and the Queen and some of the Court have gone a-Maying. I was on my way to surprise her when you surprised me.

LANCELOT

Gone a-Maying, Your Majesty?

ARTHUR [*a little embarrassed and covering it with excessive joviality*]

Why, yes. It's a sort of picnic. You eat grapes and chase girls around trees . . . and . . .

LANCELOT

A picnic, Your Majesty?

ARTHUR

Yes. It's a custom we have here. England, you know. It's the time for flower gathering.

LANCELOT [*stunned*]

Knights gathering flowers, Your Majesty?

ARTHUR

Someone has to do it.

LANCELOT

But with so much to be done?

ARTHUR

Precisely because there is so much to be done.

LANCELOT

Of course, Sire.

ARTHUR

Besides, it's civilized. Civilization should have a few gentle hobbies. And I want you to meet the Queen.

LANCELOT

I should be honored. [*To Dap:*] Dap, take the horses to the castle, feed them and dress them for battle.

ARTHUR [*mildly*]

For battle? But there's no one to fight today.

LANCELOT

One never knows, Your Majesty. Enemies seldom take holidays.

ARTHUR

I suppose not. You know, Merlyn . . . [*He stops himself, for a moment lost in thought.*]

LANCELOT

What is it, Sire? Have I offended you? Did I say something that displeased you?

ARTHUR

No, no, Lancelot. I suddenly remembered what Merlyn said of you. How strange. How wondrous. He said you would be the greatest knight ever to sit at my table. But that was long before I had thought of a table. So, he knew it would exist! I thought he meant a dining table. But he meant this: the Round Table. And I have stumbled on my future. I have done the right thing.

LANCELOT

Did you ever doubt it, Your Majesty?

ARTHUR

Of course. Only fools never doubt. [*He holds out his hand.*] Welcome, Lancelot. Bless you for coming, and welcome to the Table!

[*They clasp arms.*]

Dim Out

SCENE FIVE.

Scene: A garden near the Castle. It is lush with the green of spring, and fountains are playing among the trees.

At rise: The music is heard, and Guenevere and her Knights and Ladies, all in various shades of green, white and gold, are indulging choreographically in spring games.

At the height of the gaiety, the music stops abruptly, and all eyes turn to the Queen.

GUENEVERE [*sings*]
Tra la! It's May!
The lusty month of May!
That lovely month when ev'ryone goes
Blissfully astray.

Tra la! It's here!
That shocking time of year!
When tons of wicked little thoughts
Merrily appear.

It's May! It's May!
That gorgeous holiday;
When ev'ry maiden prays that her lad
Will be a cad!

It's mad! It's Gay!
A libelous display.
Those dreary vows that ev'ryone takes,
Ev'ryone breaks.
Ev'ryone makes divine mistakes
The lusty month of May!

Whence this fragrance wafting through the air?
What sweet feelings does its scent transmute?
Whence this perfume floating ev'rywhere?
Don't you know it's that dear forbidden fruit!
Tra la tra la. That dear forbidden fruit!
Tra la la la la.

KNIGHTS *and* LADIES
Tra la la la la!

GUENEVERE
Tra la la la la!

KNIGHTS *and* LADIES
Tra la la la la!

GUENEVERE
Tra la!

KNIGHTS *and* LADIES
Tra la!

GUENEVERE
Tra la!

KNIGHTS *and* LADIES
Tra la!

GUENEVERE
Tra la la la la la la la la la la la
La la! It's May!
The lusty month of May!
That darling month when ev'ryone throws
Self-control away.

It's time to do
A wretched thing or two.
And try to make each precious day
One you'll always rue.

It's May! It's May!
The month of "yes, you may,"
The time for ev'ry frivolous whim,
Proper or "im."

It's wild! It's gay!
A blot in ev'ry way.
The birds and bees with all of their vast
Amorous past
Gaze at the human race aghast
The lusty month of May!

GUENEVERE, KNIGHTS *and* LADIES
Tra la! It's May!
The lusty month of May!
That lovely month when ev'ryone goes
Blissfully astray.

Tra la! It's here!

That shocking time of year!
When tons of wicked little thoughts
Merrily appear.

It's May! It's May!
The month of great dismay;
When all the world is brimming with fun,
Wholesome or "un."

It's mad! It's gay!
A libelous display.
These dreary vows that ev'ryone takes,
Ev'ryone breaks.
Ev'ryone makes divine mistakes
The lusty month of May!

> [*A man in clanking, rusty armor enters. In one hand
> he carries a lance. In one eye he wears a monocle.
> Trailing beside him is a rather seedy mongrel, named
> Horrid. The Knight's name, as we will discover, is
> King Pellinore.*]

PELLINORE

Forgive the interruption. Anyone here seen a beast with
the head of a serpent, the body of a boar and the tail of
a lion, baying like forty hounds?

DINADAN [*coming forward*]

On your knees, Knight. [*Indicating Guenevere.*] You are
in the presence of Her Majesty Guenevere, Queen of England.

PELLINORE [*to Guenevere*]

Oh, really? Howdyado, Your Majesty. Will have to forego
the bending. Beastly hinges need oiling. Been sleeping out
for eighteen years. Do forgive, what? Know it isn't proper,
but there you are. Stiff as a door, what? [*Removes helmet.*]
Oh, it stopped raining.

GUENEVERE [*amused*]

Who are you, Milord?

PELLINORE

Name of King Pellinore. May have heard of me, what?
What? What? [*He looks around for recognition, which
he does not receive.*] No matter. [*To Guenevere:*] You say
you haven't seen a beast with the head of a serpent, the
body of a boar . . .

GUENEVERE

Please, I beg you, don't describe it again. It sounds much too revolting. We have not seen it.

PELLINORE

Called the Questing Beast, what? The Curse of the Pellinores. Only a Pellinore can catch her; that is, or his next of kin. Family tradition. Train all the Pellinores with that idea in mind. Limited education, what?

GUENEVERE

What?

PELLINORE

What? By the way, where am I now?

GUENEVERE

Don't you know?

PELLINORE

Haven't the foggiest. [*A few members of the Court laugh. Pellinore is now a little angry.*] Oh, very easy to laugh, what? But nothing jocular about it to Yours Truly . . . always mollicking about after that beastly Beast. Nowhere to sleep, never know where you are. Rheumatism in the winter, sunstroke in the summer. All this horrid armor that takes hours to put on. Then sitting up all night polishing the beastly stuff. . . . But I'm a Pellinore, amn't I? It's my fate. Oh, but sometimes I do wish I had a nice house of my own to live in, with beds in it, and real pillows and sheets. Oh, dear, what? Where did you say I was?

GUENEVERE

I didn't, but I will.

PELLINORE

Please do.

GUENEVERE

You're in Camelot.

PELLINORE

Thank you. Camelot? [*Looks at the dog.*] Horrid, we've been through here, haven't we? [*The dog, who is lying down, looks up at him.*] Oh, you wouldn't know. All you can see is hair. But I remember. Spent a lovely day here years ago with a nice young chap named Wart. [*To Guenevere:*] Ever meet him, Milady?

GUENEVERE

Constantly. He's my husband, King Arthur of England.

PELLINORE

By Jove! Is he? Is he, is he? Good for him. Well done!

Yours Fondly thought he was grand. Simply grand. Do say hello to him for me. Won't take any more of your time, M'am. Have to mollock on, what? [*To Horrid:*] Come along, Horrid. [*The dog rises.*] The King of England. By jove. Isn't that well done, Horrid?

GUENEVERE

Milord, I am sure the King would love to see you again. Wouldn't you care to spend the night?

PELLINORE [*thunderstruck*]

Spend the night?

GUENEVERE

Yes.

PELLINORE

In a house?

GUENEVERE

In a bed.

PELLINORE

A bed?

GUENEVERE

A feather bed.

PELLINORE

Would it have pillows?

GUENEVERE

Down pillows.

PELLINORE

Oh, I'd love that. By George, I would. That's wonderly kind of you, M'am. Wonderly. [*Points to the dog.*] But could he sleep somewhere else?

GUENEVERE

Of course. Where would you like him to sleep?

PELLINORE

Oh, anywhere around the castle will do. The moat. I don't really like him very much, you know. No earthly use to me. Oh, he's a bit of company. But he's . . . a dog. Easily do without him.

GUENEVERE

He shall sleep in the stable. Clarius, would you escort our guest to the castle?

CLARIUS [*coming forward*]

With pleasure, Milady.

PELLINORE

This is too nice for words, M'am. Most grateful. Come along, Horrid. [*Horrid rises. Pellinore starts to go.*] What a glorious day! There's even a hint of summer in the air. [*Looks at the dog.*] Or is that you? [*They exit. Every-one starts to laugh uproariously.*]

GUENEVERE [*imitating Pellinore*]

By jove, what a curse, what? Mollicking about after that beastly Beast, what? What? What?

[*There is much laughter. And it is at this frivolous, un-knightly moment that Lancelot and King Arthur enter. The Knights and Ladies, still laughing, immediately bow and curtsey.*]

ARTHUR

What, what, what, what?

GUENEVERE [*laughing*]

What a delightful surprise, Arthur.

ARTHUR [*reacting to the laughter*]

What's happened here? Jenny, I want you to meet the son of . . .

GUENEVERE

Forgive us, Arthur. We have just encountered an absolute cartoon of a man, called King Pellinore.

ARTHUR

Pellinore? Why, I remember him from my boyhood. A delicious fellow. Jenny, this is Lancelot du Lac.

GUENEVERE

Milord.

LANCELOT [*bowing*]

Your Majesty.

ARTHUR

This is the Lancelot Merlyn spoke of. He's come all the way from France to become a Knight of the Round Table.

GUENEVERE

Welcome, Milord. I hope your journey was pleasant.

LANCELOT [*to Guenevere*]

I am honored to be among you, Your Majesty. And allow me to pledge to Her Majesty my eternal dedication to this inspired cause.

GUENEVERE [*slightly startled*]

Thank you, Milord. [*To Arthur:*] How charming of you to join us, Arthur. This afternoon . . .

LANCELOT

This splendid dream *must* be made a universal reality!

GUENEVERE

Oh, absolutely. It really must. Can you stay for lunch, Arthur? We're planning . . .

LANCELOT

I have assured His Majesty that he may call upon me at
any time to perform any deed, no matter the risk.

GUENEVERE

Thank you, Milord. That's most comforting. Arthur, we
have . . .

LANCELOT

I am always on duty.

GUENEVERE

Yes, I can see that. Can you stay, Arthur?

ARTHUR

With pleasure, my love. [*He seats himself.*] I want you to
hear the new plan we've been discussing. Explain it,
Lancelot.

LANCELOT

To Her Majesty, Sire? Would Her Majesty not find the
complicated affairs of chivalry rather tedious?

GUENEVERE [*frosting a bit*]

Not at all, Milord. I have never found chivalry tedious . . .
so far. May I remind you, Milord, that the Round Table
happens to be my husband's idea.

LANCELOT

Any idea, however exalted, could be improved.

GUENEVERE [*miffed*]

Really!

LANCELOT

Yes. I have suggested to His Majesty that we create a
training program for knights.

GUENEVERE [*looking at Arthur*]

!!

ARTHUR

Marvelous idea, isn't it?

GUENEVERE

A training program! ?

ARTHUR

Yes. It's a program for training.

LANCELOT [*to Arthur*]

Yes, Your Majesty. There must be a standard established,
an unattainable goal that, with work, becomes attainable;
not only in arms, but in thought. An indoctrination of
noble Christian principle.

GUENEVERE

Whose abilities would serve as the standard, Milord?

LANCELOT

Certainly not mine, Your Majesty. It would not be fair.

GUENEVERE

Not fair in what way?

LANCELOT

I would never ask anyone to live by my standards, Your Majesty. [*Overcome by his lot in life.*] To dedicate your life to the tortured quest for perfection in body and spirit. Oh, no, I would not ask that of anyone.

GUENEVERE

Nor would I. Have you achieved perfection, Milord?

LANCELOT

Physically, yes, Your Majesty. But the refining of the soul is an endless struggle.

GUENEVERE

I daresay. I do daresay. Do you mean you've never been defeated in battle or in tournament?

LANCELOT

Never, Your Majesty.

GUENEVERE

I see. And I gather you consider it highly unlikely ever to happen in the future?

LANCELOT

Highly, Your Majesty.

ARTHUR [*into the breach*]

How was the Channel? Did you have a rough crossing?

GUENEVERE

Now tell me a little of your struggle for the perfection of the spirit.

ARTHUR [*rising and coming between them*]

But I want you to hear about the training program, Jenny.

GUENEVERE

I'm much more interested in his spirit and his noble Christian principles. Tell me, Milord, have you come to grips with humility lately?

LANCELOT [*not understanding*]

Humility, Your Majesty?

ARTHUR [*quickly*]

I think we had better discuss the training program elsewhere. Not here and not now. [*To Guenevere:*] You look far too beautiful, my dearest, to have anything on your mind but frolic and flowers. [*He kisses her hand.*] Have a lovely day. [*To the others:*] And all of you. Come, Lance. Quickly!   [*Arthur exits.*]

LANCELOT

Good day, Your Majesty.

GUENEVERE

Good day to you, Milord.   [*Lancelot exits.*]

DINADAN [*to Lionel*]

By George, that Frenchman is an unpleasant fellow.

LIONEL

He seems to have the King wrapped around his finger.

LADY SYBIL [*to Dinadan*]

He's so poisonously good.

DINADAN

He probably *walked* across the Channel.

GUENEVERE [*after a moment*]

Sir Dinadan . . .

DINADAN [*coming forward*]

Your Majesty.

GUENEVERE

When is the next tournament?

DINADAN

A week from Saturday, Your Majesty.

GUENEVERE

And who are our three best jousters?

DINADAN

Sir Lionel, Sir Sagramore and, with all "humility," I,
Your Majesty.

LIONEL [*coming forward*]

He shall have my challenge in the morning.

GUENEVERE [*pleased*]

Thank you, Sir Lionel.

SAGRAMORE [*coming forward*]

And mine.

GUENEVERE [*delighted*]

Thank you, Sir Sagramore.

DINADAN

And mine.

GUENEVERE [*ecstatic*]

Tra la! It's May!
The lusty month of May!
That darling month when ev'ryone throws
Self-control away.

GUENEVERE, KNIGHTS *and* LADIES

It's mad! It's gay!
A libelous display.
Those dreary vows that ev'ryone takes,

Ev'ryone breaks.
Ev'ryone makes divine mistakes
The lusty month of May!

[*They dance gaily.*]

Dim Out

SCENE SIX.

Scene: A Terrace of the Castle. There is an entrance to a castle room. On a table are a decanter of port and three glasses.

Time: Sundown. Two weeks later.

At rise: Pellinore and Arthur are playing backgammon. They are both standing eying the board like two field commanders.

Behind the table stands Lancelot, reading from a scroll, paying no attention to the game.

A Page stands at attention off to one side.

ARTHUR

I'm afraid I've got you, Pelly.

PELLINORE

Not yet. Yours Hopefully hasn't given up. [*He throws the dice.*] Oh, fishcakes!

ARTHUR

If you lose, you'll owe me Italy, Spain and Egypt.

PELLINORE

When did I lose Spain?

ARTHUR

Last night.

PELLINORE

So I did. Oh bosh, who wants it anyway? Filthy place, Spain. All that heel-clicking nonsense. [*He flamencoes for a moment.*] Stepping on bugs, that's what they're doing, what?

ARTHUR

Come along, Pelly. Don't try to rattle me with amusement. It's your move. Get on with it.

[*Pellinore steps back to survey the board. The right move comes to him and he moves forward to make it, when—*]

LANCELOT [*exuberantly*]

Bravo, Arthur! [*The brilliant move is startled out of Pellinore's mind and lost forever.*] I agree completely. Let armor fight armor! Let knights fight fairly! It is not chivalry when only peasants get killed. Bravo!

ARTHUR

It's certainly more civilized. Well, Pelly. I'm waiting.
[*Pellinore steps back to survey, finds the move again and steps forward to make it.*]

LANCELOT [*explosively*]

C'est magnifique, Arthur! [*Pellinore is staggered. The move is lost.*] When our knights go abroad through the land, our enemies will know what they will have to face. No more immunity. Death or reformation. *C'est merveilleux!*

ARTHUR

But read on! [*To Pellinore:*] Come on, Pelly. Either play or give up.
[*Pellinore watches Lancelot and moves quickly before he is thrown off again.*]

PELLINORE

There!
[*Arthur quickly throws the dice and removes two markers from the board.*]

ARTHUR

Egypt's mine.

PELLINORE

Oh, bulrushes! How can a chap make the right move with the town crier blasting away in his ear? [*To Lancelot:*] I know this is admirable work you're doing, but couldn't you do it in your own room? What? Your own *chambre de coucher?*

LANCELOT

I'm terribly sorry, Pellinore. I didn't mean to throw you off your game.

PELLINORE

Really, my dear chap! Don't you ever do anything but run around the Round Table? Have you no hobbies? Don't you ever go fishing? Collect things? Catch butterflies? Aren't you interested in astronomy, or making models of things?

LANCELOT [*simply*]

No, Pellinore, I'm not.

PELLINORE

Well, Arthur, if this is the sort of knight you intend to breed, you'll bore History to death. And furthermore, that idea of knights fighting knights is perfectly frightful. God's feet! What's the sense of being a knight if you can get killed like everyone else? I guarantee you, Arthur, the chaps downstairs won't cotton to this at all.

ARTHUR

All new ideas are resisted, Pelly. But they'll get used to it in time.

PELLINORE [*referring to Lancelot*]

But he never gets off it! Why can't he come home in the evening, hang up his spear and shield and frolic about a bit the way other chaps do?

ARTHUR

Be patient, Pelly. He will.

LANCELOT [*gently*]

No, Arthur. I won't. Pellinore is quite right. I am irritating. I always will be. [*To Pellinore:*] All fanatics are bores, Pellinore, and I'm a fanatic. Even when I was a child I irritated the other children. I wanted to play their games, but I knew I could not. Even then I was filled with a sense of divine purpose. I'm not saying I enjoy it. All my life I've locked the world out. And, you know, when you lock the world out, you're locked in.

PELLINORE

I don't know what you're talking about.

ARTHUR

Never mind, Pelly. I do. [*Arthur motions to the Page to remove the backgammon table, which he does. To Lancelot:*] Are you truly satisfied with the proclamation, Lance? Is there anything you would like to add?

LANCELOT

Not at all, Arthur. It's perfect. Of course, there are one or two changes I'd like you to consider.

PELLINORE

Naturally.

[*The Page enters with a rose on a salver.*]
ARTHUR [*taking the rose. There is a note pinned to it. He calls out*]

Jenny, it's for you! [*Indicating the scroll.*] Where, Lance?
LANCELOT [*rolling up the scroll quickly*]

It's not pressing, Arthur. We can do it tomorrow.

ARTHUR

No. I want to hear it now!

LANCELOT

I'd rather not, Arthur. [*Moving to go.*] If you'll excuse me . . .

[*He starts to leave and meets Guenevere entering.*]

GUENEVERE [*haughtily*]

Good evening, Milord.

LANCELOT [*uncomfortably but politely*]

Good evening, Your Majesty.

GUENEVERE

While I was napping, did I miss any improvements in chivalry?

LANCELOT

No, Your Majesty. If you will excuse me . . .

[*He starts to go.*]

GUENEVERE

Milord! [*Lancelot stops.*] When you're arranging things with God tonight, do be sure and give us nice weather tomorrow.

LANCELOT

No one could refuse your wish, Milady. Good night, Sire. Good night, Milord.   [*He exits.*]

PELLINORE

Terrible chap. Doesn't take after his father, I'll tell you that. I knew the old King. Good man. Had a bad attack of liver last time I saw him. Yellow as a buttercup. Horrible!

ARTHUR

Jenny, why do you persist in baiting the boy?

GUENEVERE

Baiting? Not at all. Haven't you heard his latest claim? He says he can perform miracles!

PELLINORE

Miracles, what!

ARTHUR

Oh, come now. Both of you. It's quite obvious it was merely a figure of speech.

GUENEVERE

Nonsense. He announced to the Knights as clear as a bell that his purity gives him miraculous powers.

PELLINORE

Purity, what?

ARTHUR

And I tell you clear as a bell he was referring to his physical prowess, which is vast indeed.

PELLINORE

Well, we shall see about his physical prowess in the tournament tomorrow. Sagramore, Lionel and Dinadan have all challenged him to a joust. Three damn strong men.

[*Arthur gives Guenevere the rose. She reads the note.*]

ARTHUR

He's accepted to fight all three on one and the same day?

PELLINORE

Quite. I tell you, Arthur, in all my travels I've never met anyone like him. Doesn't drink. Has no lady. Talks to no one but you and God. Crammed full of religion. An all around unpleasant fellow.

GUENEVERE

Pelly, please tell the Chamberlain the order of jousts tomorrow will be Dinadan, Sagramore and Lionel.

PELLINORE

The big chap last, what? Splendid arrangement. By jove, what a day. Yours Merrily can hardly wait. Good night, Arthur. Good night, M'am. The big one last, eh? Oh, ho, ho, ho.   [*He exits.*]

GUENEVERE

A note of thanks from Sir Lionel. I'm allowing him to carry my kerchief tomorrow.

ARTHUR

Jenny, I would be grateful if you'd withdraw your permission from Sir Lionel.

GUENEVERE

At this late date, Arthur? It would be rather awkward.

ARTHUR

Then let Lancelot carry your kerchief against Sagramore.

GUENEVERE

I promised it to Sagramore.

ARTHUR

Then against Dinadan.

GUENEVERE

He asked so prettily, I couldn't refuse.

ARTHUR [*angrily*]

What? This is appalling! Jenny there are issues involved here which obviously you've overlooked. It will seem to the Court as if you're rooting for his downfall, championing his defeat.

GUENEVERE

We don't know he'll be defeated. Besides, he knocked you unconscious and you woke up his bosom friend. Perhaps he'll knock them out, too, and they'll all take a house by the sea together.

ARTHUR [*exasperated*]

Jenny, at the risk of disappointing the other knights, I ask you to withdraw your permission from all.

GUENEVERE

Arthur, I believe you're jealous of the Knights and their attentions to me. Are you, my love?

ARTHUR [*fuming*]

Jealous?! Jealous?! What absolute rubbish! You know perfectly well I'm delighted the Court adores you. I'd be astonished if they didn't. And I trust you as I do God above. They've carried your kerchief in tournament a hundred times, and . . . and . . . and . . . Jenny, you've dragged me off the subject and I want to get back on it. Will you withdraw your permission?

GUENEVERE [*quietly and firmly*]

Only if you command me—as King.

ARTHUR [*gently*]

And if I do, will you forgive me?

GUENEVERE

Never.

ARTHUR

If I ask as your husband, will you, as a favor?

GUENEVERE

No. The Knights are against him, and I quite agree with them. I find him just as overbearing and pretentious as they do.

ARTHUR [*at the peak of exasperation*]

That is not the issue. The issue is your kerchief. Can we not stay on the subject?

GUENEVERE [*calmly*]

There is nothing more to be said. If the King wishes me to withdraw permission, let him command me! And Yours Humbly will graciously obey. What? What?

[*She turns and exits.*]

ARTHUR

What!! [*Raging.*] Blast! [*He paces up and down.*] Blast you, Merlyn! This is all your fault! [*He sings:*]

You swore that you had taught me ev'rything from A to Zed,

With nary an omission in between.
Well, I shall tell you what
You obviously forgot:
That's how a ruler rules a Queen!

> [*He continues pacing.*]

And what of teaching me by turning me to animal and
    bird,
From beaver to the smallest bobolink!
I should have had a whirl
At changing to a girl,
To learn the way the creatures think!

> [*He paces again. Then a thought occurs to him.*]

But wasn't there a night, on a summer long gone by,
We pass'd a couple wrangling away;
And did I not say, Merlyn: What if that chap were I?
And did he not give counsel and say . . .

> [*He tries to remember.*]

What was it now? . . . My mind's a wall.
Oh, yes! . . . By jove, now I recall.

How to handle a woman?
There's a way, said the wise old man;
A way known by ev'ry woman
Since the whole rigmarole began.

Do I flatter her? I begged him answer . . .
Do I threaten or cajole or plead?
Do I brood or play the gay romancer?
Said he, smiling: No indeed.

How to handle a woman?
Mark me well, I will tell you, sir:
The way to handle a woman
Is to love her . . . simply love her . . .
Merely love her . . . love her . . . love her.

[*The music continues. Arthur doesn't move from his
position. He ponders a moment, then turns his head and
looks in the direction of Guenevere.*]

What's wrong, Jenny? [*He walks a few steps, then stops
and looks off again.*] Where are you these days? What are
you thinking? [*He walks again and stops again.*] I don't
understand you. [*After a moment.*] But no matter. Merlyn

told me once: Never be too disturbed if you don't understand what a woman is thinking. They don't do it often.
[*He walks again.*] But what do you do while they're doing
it? [*He smiles as he remembers.*]

How to handle a woman?
Mark me well, I will tell you, Sir:
The way to handle a woman . . .
Is to love her . . . simply love her . . .
Merely love her . . . love her . . . love her.

[*He stands quietly, as*]

The Lights Dim Out

SCENE SEVEN.

Scene: The Tents outside the Jousting Field.

Time: The following day.

*At rise: The tents are occupied by the following: Sir
Lionel, Sir Dinadan, Sir Sagramore and Lancelot.*

*A Knight enters and goes to each of the three challengers,
clasping arms with each in a gesture of good luck. He
passes Lancelot by.*

A trumpet sounds. The joust is about to begin.

LANCELOT [*sincerely*]
I wish you success, Milords.
            LIONEL [*with a smile*]
Thank you, Milord. Are you being chivalrous or ironic?
            LANCELOT
Neither. I mean it truly.
            LIONEL
Then save your wishes for your continuing good health.
            DINADAN
Have you prayed, Milord?
            LANCELOT
I have, Sir Dinadan. I have prayed for us all.
            DINADAN
How benevolent. How benevolent. Do you know what I

shall be thinking, Lancelot, when I see you on your
horse? There he is, the Sermon on the Mount.

[*He marches off. They all follow.*]

SCENE EIGHT.

*Scene: The Jousting Field. There is a grandstand in the
rear.*

Time: Immediately following.

*At rise: This stage is filled. Arthur and Guenevere are
standing in the royal box of the grandstand. Two heralds
flank them.*

*The music is playing gaily, as several of the Court Jesters
perform a mock joust. They exit.*

FIRST KNIGHT [*sings*]
Sir Dinadan's in form and feeling in his prime.
ALL
Yah! Yah! Yah! Oh, we'll all have a glorious time!
SECOND KNIGHT
Sir Sagramore is fit, and Sir Li'nel feels sublime.
ALL
Yah! Yah! Yah! Oh, we'll all have a glorious time!
[*Suddenly pointing to the field.*]
Now look you there! Sir Dinadan's astride.
It's obvious he will be the first to ride.
[*Calling:*]
Good fortune, Dinadan! We hail you, Dinadan!
Yah! Yah! Yah! Yah! Yah! Yah! . . .
[*The joust begins, and the crowd gathers together and
watches excitedly*].
Sir Dinadan! Sir Dinadan!
Oh, there he goes with all his might and main.
He's got a steady grip upon the rein.
Sir Dinadan! Sir Dinadan!
Oh, try to gallop by him on the right,
For that's the arm where you have all the might.
By jove, they're coming near!
Sir Dinadan is raising up his spear!

Oh, charge him, Dinadan!
You have him now, so charge him, Dinadan!
Here comes the blow! Here comes the blow!

> > > > > > > > > > *[Catastrophe!]*

Oh, no!

> > > > > > > > *[They shuffle about in disgust.]*

FIRST KNIGHT

'Twas luck, that's all it was; pure luck and nothing more.

A LADY

Sagramore will even up the score.

SECOND KNIGHT

The Frenchman struck him first, but the blow was not
that great.

SECOND LADY

Sagramore will open up his pate.

> > > > > *[They suddenly see Sagramore on the field.]*

A GROUP

Sir Sagramore! He's riding on the field!

SECOND KNIGHT

Oh, there's the black and crimson of his shield.

> > > > > > > > > *[The joust begins.]*

There he goes! There he goes!
He's bending low and spurring on his steed.
He's charging him at record breaking speed.
Sagramore! Oh, make his armor crack and split in
two . . .
A mighty whack as only you can do.
Now, look you through the dust!
Sir Sagramore is ready for the thrust!
And now they're circling 'round!
Sir Sagramore will drive him to the ground!
Here comes . . . the blow! Here comes . . . the blow!

> > > > > > > > > > *[Disaster.]*

Oh, no!

> > > > > > > > > *[Gloom descends.]*

ARTHUR *[pointedly]*

He did that rather well, don't you think, dear?

GUENEVERE *[tightly]*

That horse of Sagramore's is too old.

ARTHUR

But felling Dinadan with one blow, dear . . .

GUENEVERE

Sir Dinadan, I am told, has a nasty cold.

[*The third joust begins, and the crowd becomes electric. And desperate.*]

ALL

Sir Lionel! Sir Lionel!
Oh, charge at him and throw him off his horse!
Oh, show him what we mean by English force!
Sir Lionel! Sir Lionel!
I've never seen him ever ride as fast!
That Frenchman will be hopelessly outclass'd!
His spear is in the air!
I tell you Lancelot hasn't got a pray'r!
His shield is much too low!
A good hard thrust and downward he will go!
And here's the blow! Here comes . . . the blow!

[*Horror.*]

Oh, no! Oh, no!

[*They are aghast.*]

Sir Lionel is down!
Dear God, it isn't true!
Sir Lionel is dead!
The spear has run him through!

[*Two Knights run from the scene. A moment later they return, carrying the fallen body of Sir Lionel on a litter. Arthur descends from the grandstand and comes to Lionel. He kneels down beside him and pulls the blanket over his face. The crowd is in shocked silence. Guenevere, who has descended from the stand, stands to one side, grief-stricken.*

Lancelot enters. The crowd falls back to let him pass, eying him with disapproval.

Seemingly oblivious to them all, he walks to Lionel and kneels beside him. He takes his limp hand in his and bows his head in prayer, pressing Lionel's hand against him, as if trying to force his own life into the lifeless man before him.

Suddenly a finger twitches. Lionel's hand moves! Then his arm! Then an eyelid flickers! And Sir Lionel slowly, painfully, dazedly, lifts himself to one elbow.

The crowd gasps.

Lancelot rises. It seems as if he has poured so much of his own life into Lionel that for a moment he is drained. Without a word, he slowly crosses the stage. As he passes each Knight and Lady, each bows and curtsies low and humble before him.]

*The last person he passes is Guenevere. He stops
before her and bows. He rises, and their eyes look
deep into each other's. She curtsies before him, with
her hand to her heart. They stand transfixed by each
other's eyes. Arthur watches with fearful sadness.*

The music swells as]

The Lights Fade

SCENE NINE.

Scene: The Terrace.

Time: Early evening of the same day.

*At rise: Arthur is seated on a bench in troubled thought.
Pellinore is standing near him.*

PELLINORE

A miracle, Arthur! A miracle! By jove! Absolutely miraculous, what? Imagine restoring that chap to life. And that's a big chap, Arthur. An enormous, big chap. I mean, however the boy did it, it took an awful lot of whatever it is he uses, what? [*An idea.*] I say! Do you think he could help my rheumatism? Or does he only go in for bigger things? I mean, from sleeping out all those years, I have a pain that starts about here . . . [*He reaches around to his back.*]

ARTHUR [*impatiently*]

I don't know, Pellinore. I don't know. The boy is in the hall. Go down and ask him. The walk will do you good, and the quiet will do me good.

PELLINORE

I say! That's a bit snappy, Arthur. Very well, I shall.
[*He starts to exit.*]

ARTHUR

Wait, Pelly. It was a bit "snappy." I apologize.

PELLINORE

Of course. Unimportant. [*He goes to the decanter.*] Have a spot, what?

ARTHUR

No, thank you. You've never been in love, have you, Pelly?

PELLINORE

No time, old man. Been too busy chasing the Beast. Now I'm not young enough. Or old enough.

ARTHUR [*almost to himself*]

And I'm too young and too old. Too old not to be uncertain of fears that may be phantom, and too young not to be tormented by them.

PELLINORE

How's that, Arthur? [*Guenevere enters. Arthur stares at her. She avoids his glance and finds a chair.*] Well, M'am, it was quite a day, what?

GUENEVERE

Yes, it was, Pelly.

PELLINORE

I must say, you were very generous with the boy, M'am. When he stood there looking at you and you stood there looking at him, it was very touching. Didn't you think so, Arthur?

ARTHUR [*subdued*]

Pelly, summon the Chamberlain. Alert the Court there are to be festivities this evening.

PELLINORE [*starting to go*]

Right.

ARTHUR

Have him come to my study. And bring the names of those awaiting knighthood.

PELLINORE

Right. [*Stops.*] Festivities, eh? By jove, I'd better skip over to the blacksmith's and pick up my formal togs. [*He exits.*]

ARTHUR [*after watching Guenevere for a moment*]

You seem tired, Jenny.

GUENEVERE

I am, rather.

ARTHUR

I'm sorry to have to put you through a formal affair tonight, but I thought Lance should be invested immediately.

GUENEVERE

Oh, I agree. I shall be all right.

[*Arthur goes to her.*]

ARTHUR

Jenny, tomorrow why don't you take Lady Anne and go to

the lodge for a few days? She always amuses you with her gossip of the Court. I'll join you for the weekend. It might do you good to get away from Round Tables and chivalry for a little while. Don't you think? [*Guenevere doesn't answer.*] Don't you think? [*She still doesn't answer. He turns and exits. The music begins. Guenevere covers her face with her hands.*]

GUENEVERE [*desperately*]

Oh, Lance, go away. Go away and don't come back. [*She sings:*]

Before I gaze at you again
I'll need a time for tears.
Before I gaze at you again
Let hours turn to years.
I have so much
Forgetting to do
Before I try to gaze again at you.

Stay away until you cross my mind
Barely once a day.
Till the moment I awake and find
I can smile and say

That I can gaze at you again
Without a blush or qualm,
My eyes a-shine like new again,
My manner poised and calm.
Stay far away!
My love, far away!
Till I forget I gazed at you today . . . today.

[*Lancelot enters. Guenevere doesn't see him at first.*]

LANCELOT

Forgive me, Milady. I didn't mean to disturb you, but I was told that Arthur wanted to see me.

GUENEVERE [*as casually as possible*]

I believe he does. And you're not disturbing me at all. You are to be knighted.

LANCELOT [*troubled*]

When, Milady?

GUENEVERE

This evening.

LANCELOT

I wish he would not.

GUENEVERE

Why?

LANCELOT

I'm not worthy of it, Milady. I don't deserve it.

GUENEVERE

Not deserve it, Lancelot! What greater wonder could you ever perform? Oh, no, I'm sure Arthur will insist. Now, if you'll excuse me. I must change for dinner. [*She starts to leave.*] Do wait here. Arthur will be . . .

LANCELOT [*quietly*]

Jenny, don't go. [*She pauses, hearing him say her name for the first time, almost knowing what he is about to say.*] Jenny, I love you. God forgive me, but I do.

GUENEVERE

God forgive us both, Lance.

LANCELOT

I have known it since the first afternoon. Not when we met; but when I walked away. When . . .

[*Guenevere turns to him. Arthur enters. She turns away.*]

ARTHUR

Lance! What a stunning achievement, my boy! And the Court! You could almost hear everyone's heart break open to you. [*Good-humoredly.*] Surely I may arrange for your knighthood now. Unfortunately, sainthood is not in my power.

LANCELOT

I shall be honored, Arthur.

ARTHUR

You both must hurry and dress. But before you do, I think we three should have a quiet drink together. If you'll make an exception, Lance. [*He turns to the decanter and starts to pour the first glass.*] Do you have any idea the impact the miracle will have on the country? [*Lancelot and Guenevere turn slowly toward each other as he pours, until their eyes meet. They take an involuntary step toward each other. Arthur turns back with one glass filled, and sees their look. He continues talking, looking from one to the other, feverishly—painfully.*] When this is known, they'll be flocking to the Round Table from one end of England to the other . . . from Scotland . . . Wales . . . and all those quests we've been planning for the Knights may not even be necessary . . . I mean, when people hear . . . what has happened at Camelot . . . they may lay down their arms

and come of their own free will . . . it's quite possible no
one will bear arms at all any more . . . and that there will
really be peace . . . all borders will disappear . . . and all
the things I dreamed . . . I dreamed . . . I dreamed . . .

[*His voice trails off in utter defeat, and he stands motion-
less in an abject trance. The sound of the March to the
Grand Hall is heard in the orchestra, as*]

The Lights Dim Out Slowly

SCENE TEN.

Scene: A Corridor in the Castle.

Time: Immediately following.

*The Knights of the Court parade to the Grand Hall with
Banners aflying in ceremonial drill.*

SCENE ELEVEN.

*Scene: The Grand Hall. Two thrones dominate the scene.
Looking down on the hall and surrounding it, is a balcony.*

Time: Immediately following.

*At rise: Ladies and Gentlemen of the Court are filing in
to appropriate music in choreographed pattern.*

*Arthur and Guenevere enter in full regal splendor, and
take their places before the thrones.*

*Pellinore stands next to Arthur, holding Excalibur.
Lancelot stands off to the side of Pellinore. Dinadan stands
next to Guenevere, holding a scroll.*

The music continues under.

ARTHUR
Excalibur!

[*He takes the sword from Pellinore.*]

DINADAN

To be invested Knights of the Round Table of England: of Brackley, Colgrevance. [*Colgrevance comes forward, kneels before the King and is touched on each shoulder with the Sword Excalibur. As he does, his banner swoops down from the balcony and hangs over the hall. He rises, bows again before Guenevere, and returns to his place.*] Of Winchester, Bliant. [*The same.*] Of Wales, Guilliam. [*The same.*] Of Cornwall, Castor. [*The same.*] Of Joyous Gard, Lancelot du Lac.

[*Lancelot comes forward and bows. Arthur pauses, then very slowly, knights him. Lancelot rises and returns to his place. The music swells. The Court files out. Guenevere descends from the throne and exits. Dinadan and Pellinore await the King. Arthur descends from the throne slowly, then stops and stands lost in his own thoughts, Pellinore senses the King wishes to be alone and makes a brief sign to Dinadan. They exit. Arthur slowly looks up.*]

ARTHUR

Proposition: If I could choose, from every man who breathes on this earth, the face I would most love, the smile, the touch, the voice, the heart, the laugh, the soul itself, every detail and feature to the smallest strand of hair—they would all be Jenny's.

Proposition: If I could choose from every man who breathes on this earth a man for my brother and a man for my son, a man for my friend, they would all be Lance.

[*His bitterness mounts.*]

Yes, I love them. I love them, and they answer me with pain and torment. Be it sin or not sin, they betray me in their hearts, and that's far sin enough. I see it in their eyes and feel it when they speak, and they must pay for it and be punished. I shan't be wounded and not return it in kind. I'm done with feeble hoping. I demand a man's vengeance!

[*He moves violently, then tries to control himself.*]

Proposition: I'm a king, not a man. And a civilized king. Could it possibly be civilized to destroy what I love? Could it possibly be civilized to love myself above all? What of their pain and their torment? Did they ask for this calamity? Can passion be selected?

[*His voice rising.*]

Is there any doubt of their devotion . . . to me, or to our Table?

[*He raises high the sword in his hand.*]

By God, Excalibur, I shall be a King! This is the time of
King Arthur, and we reach for the stars! This is the time
of King Arthur, and violence is not strength and compassion is not weakness. We are civilized! Resolved: We
shall live through this together, Excalibur: They, you and
I! And God have mercy on us all.

[*The decision made, he becomes almost relaxed, almost
at peace.*]

They're waiting for us at the table. [*He starts to walk off.*]
Let's not delay the celebration.

[*The music swells, as*]

The Curtain Falls

Act II, SCENE ONE.

Scene: The Main Terrace of the Castle. Beyond the flower-covered walls at the rear can be seen the green rolling hills of the English countryside. Far in the distance is the tree in which Arthur first hid so many years ago.

Time: Afternoon. Several years later.

At rise: Guenevere is seated at a table, Lancelot at a small bench a distance away. He has a scroll, which he now unrolls to read. The music is playing. Just as he is about to read, a few couples move by across the rear of the stage. He looks over his shoulder and waits for them to pass. When they do, he reads and sings.

> LANCELOT
> Toujours j'ai fait le même voeux,
> Sur terre une déesse, au ciel un Dieu.
>
> Un homme désire pour etre heureux
> Sur terre une déesse, au ciel un Dieu.
>
> Years may come; years may go;
> This, I know, will e'er be so:
>
> The reason to live is only to love
> A goddess on earth and a God above.
> [*The music continues.*]

> GUENEVERE
> Did you write that, Lance?
> LANCELOT
> Yes.
> GUENEVERE
> Why do you always write about you? Why don't you ever write about me?

LANCELOT

I can't write about you. I love you too much. [*Desperately.*]
Jenny, I should leave you and never come back. I've said it
to myself day after day, year after year. But how can I?
Look at you. *When* would I? [*He sings:*]

    If ever I would leave you
    It wouldn't be in summer;
    Seeing you in summer, I never would go.
    Your hair streaked with sunlight . . .
    Your lips red as flame . . .
    Your face with a luster
    That puts gold to shame.

    But if I'd ever leave you,
    It couldn't be in autumn.
    How I'd leave in autumn, I never would know.
    I've seen how you sparkle
    When fall nips the air.
    I know you in autumn
    And I must be there.

And could I leave you running merrily through the
    snow?
Or on a wintry evening when you catch the fire's glow?

    If ever I would leave you,
    How could it be in springtime,
    Knowing how in spring I'm bewitch'd by you so?
    Oh, no, not in springtime!
    Summer, winter or fall!
    No, never could I leave you at all.
        [*He walks to her. She raises her hand to stop him and,
        with a look, reminds him that he must not draw too
        near. He walks away, but turns to her again.*]
    If ever I would leave you,
    How could it be in springtime,
    Knowing how in spring I'm bewitch'd by you so?
    Oh, no, not in springtime!
    Summer, winter or fall!
    No, never could I leave you at all.
                    [*She gazes at him tenderly.*]

LANCELOT

Jenny, do you think Arthur knows?

GUENEVERE

Don't speak of it, Lance. Of course he doesn't. If he ever

did, I wouldn't want to live. And neither would you.

LANCELOT

No, he couldn't know. As much as he loves us, not even
Arthur could . . .

[*A few Ladies, led by Lady Anne, enter. Guenevere rises
immediately, interrupting Lancelot.*]

GUENEVERE [*lightly*]

It is time to go, Lady Anne?

LADY ANNE [*approaching*]

Yes, Milady.

[*The Ladies come to Guenevere and put her cloak
around her.*]

GUENEVERE [*to Lancelot, easily*]

I have a thrilling engagement this afternoon, Lancelot. I'm
giving the prizes at the cattle show. [*To Lady Anne:*] I can't
wait to see who wins.

LADY ANNE

I have the list of winners for you, Milady.

[*She hands her a card.*]

GUENEVERE [*taking it*]

Oh, lovely! The Aberdeen Angus for a change. [*To Lancelot:*] I'm so pleased for him. He's been trying so hard, and
he's been losing to the Short Horns for years. Thank you
for waiting with me, Lancelot.

LANCELOT

Thank you for allowing me, Milady.

[*Guenevere exits with the Ladies. Lancelot looks after
her and exits. A young man enters from behind a column.
His attire is foppish, his eyes mischievous, his smile
wicked. His name is Mordred. He casts a glance in the
direction of Guenevere, and one in the direction of
Lancelot.*]

MORDRED

Ah, Camelot. Where the King gives freedom and the
Queen takes liberties. You poor things. Perhaps we can
arrange a little rendezvous for you.

[*Arthur's voice is heard. Mordred drops back and out
of sight as Arthur enters.*]

ARTHUR [*entering*]

Lance! I have it solved . . . [*Pellinore follows him. Arthur
turns to him. He does not see Mordred.*] Oh, I thought
Lance was here, Pelly.

MORDRED [*coming forward, innocently*]

He just left, Your Majesty. He was here with the Queen.

PELLINORE [*outraged*]

You're not a member of this Court. How dare you enter these grounds unannounced!

MORDRED [*genially*]

But I was announced, Milord. Did the Chamberlain not say that there was a young man from Scotland who came with royal greetings?

PELLINORE

And were you not informed all visitors were to return tomorrow afternoon?

MORDRED

I shall be busy tomorrow afternoon.

PELLINORE

By Jove, what impertinence! He shall be taught a lesson.
   [*He reaches for his sword and takes a step in Mordred's direction.*]

MORDRED [*shrinking away in fear*]

Keep away! Don't touch me! I'm unarmed!

ARTHUR

Call the guard, Pelly, and have this young ass thrown out.

MORDRED [*regaining his composure*]

That's not a very kind way to treat the son of Queen Morgause.
   [*Arthur is stunned to the roots. He slowly turns and, almost fearfully, looks at Mordred.*]

MORDRED [*delighted at the reaction*]

Yes, Your Majesty. I am Mordred.

ARTHUR [*shaken*]

Wait, Pelly. Mordred?

MORDRED [*bowing low*]

Your Majesty.

ARTHUR

Leave us, Pellinore.

PELLINORE

I shall be waiting nearby, if you need me, Arthur.

[*He exits.*]

MORDRED [*cheerfully*]

I bring you greetings, Your Majesty, from Queen Morgause and King Lot.

ARTHUR

I trust your mother is well, Mordred.

MORDRED

The Queen is splendid, thank you. As witchy as ever. Still beautiful, which of course she would be, with all her

magic and sorcery. I've been wandering about the castle. I
hope you don't mind. It's quite grand, really. I love the way
you've mixed English with French. Very tasteful.

ARTHUR

And King Lot?

MORDRED

The King? Never happier. He was so delighted I left.
He's always hated me, you know. Do you know what he did
to me once? Mother had a youth potion that took off ten
years. When I was nine, he gave it to me to make me minus
one. I kept asking Mother why he disliked me so, and . . .

ARTHUR [*acidly*]

What brings you to Camelot, Mordred?

MORDRED

A desire of blood, Your Majesty. I have quite a family
here, you know. My dear aunt, Morgan Le Fey, whom I've
never seen.

ARTHUR [*pressing him*]

Nor has anyone else. The castle where she and her court
live is quite invisible. It hardly seems reason for making
this long journey.

MORDRED [*looking him square in the eye*]

And there's you, Your Majesty. As I was saying, I kept
asking Mother why King Lot despised me so, and one day
not long ago, she told me the marvelous news: he's not my
father. How once, when she was visiting England, she met
an attractive lad named Arthur, invited him to her room,
and bewitched him for the night. Is that the way the story
goes, Your Majesty?

ARTHUR

Yes. That's the way the story goes, Mordred.

MORDRED

You can imagine her surprise when later he became the
King of all England.

ARTHUR [*sternly*]

Very well, Mordred. Now you are here. What are your
plans?

MORDRED

That's for you to decide, Your Majesty.

ARTHUR

Very well. Then I shall tell you what I suggest, what I
offer, what I wish. That you stay here and become a Knight
of the Round Table. You have youth, brains and a proper
heritage. Much could be done, if you apply yourself.

MORDRED

How generous of you, Your Majesty! I can think of
nothing that would please me more than to win your con-
fidence.

ARTHUR

I'm certain of that. And I shall be watching carefully, very
carefully, to see if you deserve it. [*In full command.*] Tonight you will have dinner with the Queen and me, and we
will try to get to know each other better. Tomorrow your
training will begin. But I must warn you, Mordred, no
favoritism will be shown. You must earn the right to
knighthood by virtue and proper deeds.

MORDRED

I shall try, Your Majesty.

ARTHUR

The adage, "Blood is thicker than water," was invented
by undeserving relatives.

[*Arthur exits. Mordred looks after him and sticks out
his tongue.*]

MORDRED [*sings*]

Virtue and proper deeds, Your Majesty?
Like what?
Courage, Milord?
Purity and Humility, my liege?
Diligence? Charity? Honesty? Fidelity?
The seven deadly virtues?
No, thank you, Your Majesty.

The seven deadly virtues,
Those ghastly little traps,
Oh, no, Milord, they weren't meant for me.
Those seven deadly virtues,
They're made for other chaps,
Who love a life of failure and ennui.

Take Courage! Now there's a sport—
An invitation to the state of rigor mort!

And Purity! A noble yen!
And very restful ev'ry now and then.

I find Humility means to be hurt;
It's not the earth the meek inherit, it's the dirt.

Honesty is fatal and should be taboo.
Diligence? A fate I would hate.
If Charity means giving, I give it to you,
And Fidelity is only for your mate.

You'll never find a virtue
Unstatusing my quo,
Or making my Be-elzebubble burst.
Let others take the high road,
I will take the low;
I cannot wait to rush in
Where angels fear to go.
With all those seven deadly virtues,
Free and happy little me has not been cursed.
  [*He folds his arms and chuckles to himself.*]

Dim Out

SCENE TWO.

Scene: The Terrace of the Castle.

Time: Late afternoon, a month later.

At rise: Arthur is standing in thought. Guenevere is seated, doing her embroidery, which she holds on her lap.

ARTHUR [*suddenly*]
Jenny, I feel old.
        GUENEVERE
Nonsense, dear.
        ARTHUR
It's true. I was thinking of it this morning. I walked briskly as ever to my study and arrived much later than I expected to. The days seem longer; the nights seem shorter; and my horse seems higher.
        GUENEVERE
You don't get enough fresh air, Arthur. You spend far too much time in your precious civil court.
        ARTHUR
I can't help it. I only mean to stay for a moment, but I become absolutely transfixed. Not because I'm proud of it,

which I am. But it's so exciting. Before, when disputes were settled by physical combat, I always knew the outcome, because I could tell at a glance which was the better swordsman. But now, with a jury and a judge, you never know till you hear the verdict. It's positively riveting.

GUENEVERE

I know it is. But I do worry about the jury, Arthur. They don't know the parties involved. They don't really care who wins. Are you sure it's wise to trust decisions to people so impartial?

ARTHUR

But that's the point . . .

[*Pellinore enters in high dudgeon.*]

PELLINORE

Arthur . . . ! [*To Guenevere:*] Good evening, M'am.

GUENEVERE

Good evening, Pelly.

PELLINORE

Damn it, Arthur. [*To Guenevere:*] Forgive me, damn it . . . [*To Arthur:*] But, damn it! I've just left the chaps downstairs, and I can't stand it any longer. Yours Miserably has got to speak up.

ARTHUR

About what, Pelly?

PELLINORE

About what? Not about "what." About who, what? Mordred. That's what.

GUENEVERE

Oh, please, Pelly. Let's not talk about Mordred. This is the first night in a month he's not coming for dinner, and I feel as if I were going to a party.

PELLINORE

I'm sorry, M'am, but I must. Arthur, you have to face it: you have sired a snake! And to top it all, you've set him loose to poison your own Court. Do you have any idea what foul things he's saying and doing?

ARTHUR [*troubled, but calm*]

Yes, I do.

PELLINORE [*with indignant sarcasm*]

Oh, you do, do you? Are you aware of the snaky way he's stirring up the Knights?

ARTHUR

Yes. He's preying on their provincialism and trying to make them yearn for their own lands.

PELLINORE [*surprised*]

Oh, you know that. [*Ominously.*] But, when he disappears every afternoon, do you have any idea what he's up to?

ARTHUR

He's searching the forest for his aunt, Morgan Le Fey.

PELLINORE [*taken aback*]

Oh, you know that too? But I'll wager you don't know what he's saying about chivalry?

ARTHUR

Yes. He's mocking it with vulgar limericks.

PELLINORE

He's mocking it with vulgar . . . You know all that?!

ARTHUR

Yes. And I know why. To destroy me and those I love—and make his inheritance come faster.

PELLINORE

Then why, in the holy name of heaven, don't you stop him, Arthur? Arthur, you've simply got to stop thinking thoughts and think of something.

GUENEVERE [*gravely*]

Is this true, Arthur?

ARTHUR

Yes, it is. [*Firmly.*] But we practice civil law now, and we cannot take the law back into our own hands. Talking is not a crime, nor is walking in the woods. When he violates the law, the law shall deal with him.

PELLINORE

Do you mean to say, Arthur, a chap has to wait till he's killed before he can attack?

ARTHUR [*after a moment*]

Pelly, I'm afraid I have no answer to that.

PELLINORE

Well, I never thought I'd hear myself say it, but, Arthur, what you need is a new idea.

GUENEVERE [*actually reassuring Arthur*]

And one will be found, Pelly. You shall see.

PELLINORE

I hope so, M'am. I hope so. I'm very worried. You know, M'am, in many ways chasing the Beast is much easier than living with people. It's true, when you're questing, the winter chills you and the summer scorches; the wind slaps you about a bit and the rain drenches you. But it's orderly. You can count on it. And they never all get together and do it to you at the same time. But people . . . ? [*Shudders.*]

I'm not referring to you, M'am. Or to you, Arthur.
You're . . . special people. That's why I stay on, I suppose.

ARTHUR

I'll tell you, Pelly, I could do with some fresh air. Let's
get away from people tomorrow and go partridge shooting.

PELLINORE

I'd love that, Arthur. [*To Guenevere:*] Well, goodnight,
M'am. Goodnight, Arthur.

[*He exits happily.*]

GUENEVERE

Arthur, I hope you suffer no guilt about Mordred. I feel
nothing about him, and neither should you. [*Lightly, to
ease him.*] God knows you're not the first king to have one
of those things running around.

ARTHUR

No. I do feel nothing for him. And there's no escaping
the fact he's an appalling specimen.

GUENEVERE

Amen. The one thing I can say for him is that he's bound
to marry well. Everybody is above him.

ARTHUR

Yet, there he is, Jenny. And even if he were banished,
he would remain a constant menace to the throne. And to
us. Jenny, don't you wish you'd never been born a queen?

GUENEVERE

Oh, occasionally. It's never being alone that bothers me
most. Do you know, I have never been without someone
around me in my entire life? Neither at Camilliard, or
Camelot. I mean, completely, totally, solitarily alone?
Sometimes I wish the castle were empty, everyone gone,
no one here but me. Do you know what I would do? I
would bolt every door, lock every window, take off all my
clothes and run stark naked from room to room. I would
go to the kitchen, naked; prepare my own meals, naked;
do some embroidery, naked; and put on my crown, naked.
And when I passed a mirror, I would stop and say: [*With
a broad cockney accent.*] " 'Ello, Jenny old thing! Nice to
see you!" [*Arthur laughs.*] But I must say, on the whole,
being a queen can be . . .   [*She pauses.*]

ARTHUR

Can be what?

GUENEVERE [*with sudden dejection*]

A weary load. That dreadful boy. One more added burden
we could quite well do without.

ARTHUR

Yes, but a burden we can't escape.

GUENEVERE

Royalty never can. Why is that, Arthur? Other people do.
They seem to have ways and means of finding respite.
What do they do? Farmers, cooks, blacksmiths . . .
[*She sings:*]

　What do the simple folk do
　To help them escape when they're blue?
　The shepherd who is ailing,
　The milkmaid who is glum,
　The cobbler who is wailing
　From nailing
　　　　　His thumb?

　When they're beset and besieged,
　The folk not noblessely obliged . . .
　However do they manage
　To shed their weary lot?
　Oh, what do simple folk do
　We do not?

ARTHUR [*seriously*]

　I have been informed
　By those who know them well,
　They find relief in quite a clever way.
　When they're sorely pressed,
　They whistle for a spell;
　And whistling seems to brighten up their day.
　And that's what simple folk do;
　So they say.

GUENEVERE

They whistle?

ARTHUR

So they say.

[*Guenevere hopefully begins to whistle. Arthur, at first
surprised, joins in. They whistle away for a moment.
Finding small comfort, he stops and looks at her hopelessly. She, too, stops and sighs.*]

GUENEVERE

　What else do the simple folk do
　To perk up the heart and get through?
　The wee folk and the grown folk
　Who wander to and fro
　Have ways known to their own folk

We throne folk
                    Don't know.

When all the doldrums begin,
What keeps each of them in his skin?
What ancient native custom
Provides the needed glow?
Oh, what do simple folk do?
Do you know?
                    ARTHUR
Once along the road
I came upon a lad
Singing in a voice three times his size.
When I asked him why,
He told me he was sad,
And singing always made his spirits rise.
So that's what simple folk do,
I surmise.
                    GUENEVERE
They sing?
                    ARTHUR
I surmise.
          [*They throw themselves into happy song.*]
                GUENEVERE *and* ARTHUR
Arise, my love! Arise, my love!
Apollo's lighting the skies, my love.
The meadows shine
With columbine
And daffodils blossom away.

Hear Venus call
To one and all:
Come taste delight while you may.
The world is bright,
And all is right,
And life is merry and gay . . . !
          [*Guenevere stops short and turns to him with frus-
          trated disgust.*]
                    GUENEVERE
What else do the simple folk do?
They must have a system or two.
They obviously outshine us
At turning tears to mirth;

Have tricks a royal highness
Is minus
      From birth.

What then I wonder do they
To chase all the goblins away?
They have some tribal sorc'ry
You haven't mentioned yet;
Oh, what do simple folk do
To forget?

      ARTHUR

Often I am told
They dance a fiery dance,
And whirl til they're completely uncontrolled.
Soon the mind is blank,
And all are in a trance,
A vi'lent trance astounding to behold.
And that's what simple folk do,
So I'm told.
    [*They burst into a surprisingly wild hornpipe together.*
    It proves hardly a cure.]

      GUENEVERE

What else do the simple folk do
To help them escape when they're blue?

      ARTHUR

They sit around and wonder
What royal folk would do.
And that's what simple folk do.

      GUENEVERE [*sadly*]

Really?!

      ARTHUR

I have it on the best authority.

      GUENEVERE *and* ARTHUR

Yes, that's what simple folk do.
        [*They look at each other forlornly.*]

      Dim Out

SCENE THREE.

Scene: A Forest near Camelot. At this moment, it is shrouded and obscure, and the scene is played before a transparent curtain.

Time: Late afternoon the following day.

At rise: Mordred is discovered with two large baskets of candy. As he calls into the forest, he darts from side to side, listening for an answer.

MORDRED

Morgan Le Fey? . . . Morgan Le Fey? . . . Sister of my mother, it's I, Mordred, who comes to visit you . . . Can you hear me, dear Aunt? . . . Am I near your invisible castle? . . . Am I, dear Morgan? . . . dear sweet Aunt Morgan? . . . dear sweet Queen Aunt Morgan? Can you not hear me?

MORGAN LE FEY [*her drawling, cooing voice is heard in the distance*]

Go away, Mordred. Go away! You were a nasty little boy, and I'm told you've become a nastier little man.

MORDRED

I beseech you, Your Majesty. Give me a moment of your time.

MORGAN LE FEY [*lazily irritated*]

Not now, Mordred. I am eating my dinner and shan't be finished till tomorrow.

MORDRED

What a pity! I have chocolates.

MORGAN LE FEY [*a touch of excitement in her voice*]

Chocolates? You say you have chocolates?

MORDRED

Hard candies and caramels! Cherry creams—with soft centers?

MORGAN LE FEY [*feverishly*]

Cherry creams with soft centers? Don't move, my darling nephew! Your darling aunt is on her way. Court!

[*The music swells and a forest begins to rise before his eyes. He disappears with the candy to hide it, as the lights come up behind him.*]

SCENE FOUR.

Scene: The Forest of Morgan Le Fey. It is a labyrinth of tanglewood.

Time: Immediately following.

At rise: Mordred appears. Before his eyes, weird and startling figures, half human, half animal, all members of Morgan Le Fey's Court, appear in choreographic pantomime. Finally the way is paved for the entrance of Morgan Le Fey herself.

She seems in her late twenties, quite wild and quite beautiful, her hair flowing, her gown flimsy. Mordred kneels at her feet.

MORDRED

Your Majesty.

MORGAN LE FEY [*waving the Courtiers off with her hand*]

Arise, Mordred. And give me the candy.

MORDRED [*rising*]

I have your candy, dear Aunt. Baskets and baskets, in sugary profusion. But first let us discuss what you shall do for me.

MORGAN LE FEY

I shall do nothing for you, nothing at all. Why should I do anything for anyone? I have all I want of life: passionate afternoons, gluttonous nights, and slovenly mornings.

MORDRED

Very well, then.

MORGAN LE FEY

Give me my candy, or I shall go home and continue eating my dining room.

MORDRED

Eating your dining room?

MORGAN LE FEY

And why not? My chairs are made of vegetables; my table's made of cheese, and my doors are gingerbread.

MORDRED

And the floor?

MORGAN LE FEY

Roast beef, wall to wall. But, candy I never get, so I desire it most of all.

MORDRED

Then why should you be denied it, when all I ask is to play a prank on King Arthur?

MORGAN LE FEY

King Arthur? Oh, Wart! I used to watch him from my invisible window out walking with Merlyn. He was a dear little boy. No. I don't wish to harm him.

MORDRED

No harm.

MORGAN LE FEY

You're the son of a wicked mother, Mordred, and I know you're up to mischief.

MORDRED

No mischief at all. Just a delicious little game that will amuse you. Arthur is out hunting. Lure him to your forest, and detain him for the night.

MORGAN LE FEY

Detain him for the night? No. Such games are for the afternoon. At night, I eat. And I'm more ravenous every minute.

MORDRED

Please, dear Aunt? Make him drowsy and build a wall around him? The invisible kind you do so well.

MORGAN LE FEY

How do you know I build invisible walls?

MORDRED

Mummy told me. Please, dear Aunt?

MORGAN LE FEY

No! I will not harm little Wart. [*She calls.*] Court! [*The music begins.*] Farewell, nasty Mordred!

[*The Court reappears, as Morgan prepares to depart.*]

MORDRED [*sings*]

Enough candy I'll bring
To furnish a new wing.

[*Morgan Le Fey hesitates, tempted. Then, with courageous resolve, she continues her departure.*]

Masses and masses
Of gummy molasses.
  [*The thought of it bewitches her. She finds it difficult
  to leave.*]
Fudge by the van!

                              [*She's sorely tempted.*]
Fresh marzipan!
  [*Her defenses crumble, and she reaches for his out-
  stretched hand.*]
All yours it will be
If you'll build me a wee
Little wall.

                      [*They begin to dance together.*]
            MORGAN LE FEY
Do you promise, you devil,
It's all on the level?
            MORDRED
I solemnly swear
It's a harmless affair.
            MORGAN LE FEY
On your honor, dear lad?
            MORDRED
Honor? You're mad!
            MORGAN LE FEY
Ye gods, but you're low!
My answer is "No,"
And that's all!

                          [*She turns away from him.*]

            MORDRED
A basket or two
Of marshmallow goo . . . !

                              [*She stops.*]

A licorice stick
That takes two years to lick . . . !
            MORGAN LE FAY [*she can stand it no longer*]
Where's the King?

Bring the King!

I shall build him a wall
Three and seven feet tall!
I'll hurry and mix
Some invisible bricks.

MORDRED

Oh, Queen! You're a joy!

MORGAN LE FEY

Be gone, nasty boy!

[*Mordred exits gleefully. A strange, birdlike creature is summoned by Morgan Le Fey. The creature leaps onto the stage. An arrow flies towards him. He catches it and disappears. Morgan Le Fey darts behind the tree, as Arthur and Pellinore enter.*]

PELLINORE

Where's the bird, Arthur? Where's the bird? You hit it. I saw it. Where did it go?

ARTHUR [*looking around, puzzled*]

Strange, Pelly. I've never seen this forest before. I used to play in this valley when I was a boy. But it was like a meadow. There were no trees.

PELLINORE

Nature, old boy. Things pop up, you know. Where's the bird?

ARTHUR

Sh-h-h. It's awfully quiet around here, isn't it? [*Morgan Le Fey appears from behind the tree and listens.*] Not a leaf rustling, not a whisper in the woods. It makes one rather drowsy. Would you care to rest a bit?

PELLINORE

No thank you, old man. I want to find that bird, what? I mean, if you hit a bird with an arrow, it ought to fall down like a gentleman.

[*He exits. Arthur sighs drowsily and seats himself before a tree stump.*]

ARTHUR [*sleepily*]

Merlyn, do you remember how often we walked this valley when I was a boy? [*He yawns.*] Do you know what I miss of those days? Not my youth. My innocence. My innocence . . .

[*He closes his eyes and sleeps. Morgan Le Fey and her Court appear from the woods, carrying imaginary bricks. In balletic pantomime, flying back and forth across the stage with more and more bricks, they construct a high invisible wall around the sleeping King. When it is complete, Morgan Le Fey "pats it" all around, to make certain it is perfect. Finding it to her pleasure, she disappears, followed by her Court. Pellinore enters.*]

PELLINORE

Arthur? [*Arthur awakens.*] The bird's hopeless, Arthur. Let's push on.

ARTHUR

Where am I? What's happened? How long have I been asleep? Pelly, we must get back to the castle. I have strange feelings.

PELLINORE

Righto. If you want.

[*He starts to walk away. Arthur tries to follow and collides with the invisible wall.*]

ARTHUR

Good God! [*He feels his way around the wall.*]

PELLINORE

Well, old man, are you coming or aren't you?

ARTHUR

I'm trapped!

PELLINORE [*coming to him*]

I say, Arthur. Who are you waving at? What's wrong with you? [*He runs into the wall.*] I say! What is this? It feels like a wall! But I don't see it.

ARTHUR [*with tragic awareness*]

It is a wall.

PELLINORE

Where did it come from? How did it get here?

ARTHUR

Morgan Le Fey! Morgan Le Fey! Is this your sorcery? [*To Pellinore, desperately:*] Pelly, get back to the castle. Find Lance. Find Jenny. Warn them to be careful.

PELLINORE [*stunned*]

You know, Arthur?

ARTHUR

Do as I say, Pelly! [*Pellinore exits.*] Morgan Le Fey! Morgan Le Fey! Morgan Le Fey!

Dim Out

SCENE FIVE.

Scene: The Corridor to the Queen's bedchamber.

Time: Later than night.

At rise: Lady Anne and Lady Sybil bow onto the stage, addressing the Queen, who is offstage.

LADY ANNE
Good night, Milady.

LADY SYBIL
Good night, Your Majesty.

LADY ANNE
Sleep well, Your Majesty.

[*They cross the stage to exit. Lancelot walks quietly on behind them. He watches until they are out of sight. He takes one quick look around and exits in the direction of the Queen's chamber. Mordred appears at the other end of the corridor. He moves furtively across the stage and looks off after Lancelot. He snaps his fingers. Five Knights enter, their swords strapped tight. He goes to them. Before he can speak, Pellinore enters behind him.*]

PELLINORE
You, there!

MORDRED
The name is Mordred. And if I were you, I'd remember it.

PELLINORE
Well, I'm not you, and I intend to forget it. Where's Lancelot?

MORDRED [*insinuatingly*]
Lancelot? Now, where would you expect to find Lancelot at this hour?

PELLINORE
I looked in the chapel. He's not there. Has the Queen retired for the night?

MORDRED
That, Milord, is an iffy question.

PELLINORE
Look here, whatever-your-name-is. I don't know what slushes through that swampy little mind of yours, but while the King is away, I am in charge of this palace. And I'm not a believer in all this civil law nonsense. You make one false move, and you'll face the jury in two sections, what? Carry the head in myself. Gladly. [*He starts to exit.*] Oh, wouldn't I love that!   [*He exits.*]

MORDRED
Pellinore, in a little while, I shall be in charge of this castle. And shortly after that, gentlemen, the kingdom.

[*He draws a sword from one of the men and beckons them to follow.*]

Dim Out

SCENE SIX.

Scene: The Queen's Bedchamber. It is a large, beautiful room. The moonlight streams in through the window.

Time: Immediately following.

At rise: Guenevere, in a white loosely flowing gown, is seated at her dressing table, slowly brushing her long hair. The music of "If Ever I Would Leave You" is playing softly.

Lancelot enters quietly. He wears no armor and has only a dagger in his belt. He looks around the bedroom as he enters, as if seeing it for the first time, which in truth he is. He pauses a few feet from Guenevere.

LANCELOT [*hushed; tremulously, fearfully*]
Jenny . . . ? [*Guenevere rises quickly and looks at him in astonishment. He goes to her.*] Jenny, I was in the yard . . . I couldn't sleep . . . I saw the light in your window . . . I knew you were alone . . . I tried to stay away . . . I tried, but I . . . Jenny, I . . . [*He takes her in his arms and they embrace passionately. Suddenly she withdraws in fear.*]

GUENEVERE
Did anyone see you?

LANCELOT
No one. The castle is dark. I was careful. Jenny, don't be afraid.

GUENEVERE
But I am afraid.

LANCELOT
I swear we're alone. No one saw me enter. Jenny, there's nothing to fear. Arthur won't be back until . . . [*He stops himself, ashamed.*] Forgive me, Jenny.

GUENEVERE [*sadly*]
We're not alone, are we, Lance? [*He takes her in his arms tenderly.*]

LANCELOT [*fervently*]
We are, we are.

GUENEVERE

We're not. Here you are, with your arms around me, and
the first thing we think of is him.

[*She leaves him.*]

LANCELOT [*pleadingly*]

But you love me, Jenny.

GUENEVERE

Of course, I do. And I always shall. Night after night I've
thought of you here and wished for it with all my being.
And suddenly, we're less alone than ever.

LANCELOT

But why?

GUENEVERE

Now that the people are gone, can't you see the shadow
between us? It's wider than the sea. It fills the room. Perhaps it would have been better if we had never said a word
to each other at all. [*She sings:*]

    I loved you once in silence,
    And mis'ry was all I knew.
    Trying so to keep my love from showing,
    All the while not knowing
    You loved me too.

    Yes, loved me in lonesome silence;
    Your heart filled with dark despair . . .
    Thinking love would flame in you forever,
    And I'd never, never
    Know the flame was there.

    Then one day we cast away our secret longing;
    The raging tide we held inside would hold no more.
    The silence at last was broken!
    We flung wide our prison door.
    Ev'ry joyous word of love was spoken . . . !

    And now there's twice as much grief,
    Twice the strain for us;
    Twice the despair,
    Twice the pain for us
    As we had known before.

LANCELOT [*desperately*]

Jenny, it's because we're here, here in Camelot that
everything is so wretched.

GUENEVERE

No, Lance.

LANCELOT

Jenny, come away with me. To Joyous Gard. Let us have it open and above board at last.

GUENEVERE

Lance, I've told you a thousand times I shall never leave Arthur. Ever. Now, let us say no more about it.

LANCELOT [*raging*]

But this agonizing torment! Day after day, year after year. Would God I had your talent for acceptance, your invincible English calm!

GUENEVERE [*turning on him*]

Oh, the insensitivity of sensitive men! Always suffering so much they can suffer nothing for others. You think you're the only one in torment. I'm just as tortured, just as anguished as you. But what would you have us do to this man we both love? Run away! Leave him! Make him publicly miserable! Force him to declare war on you, where either one of you, if not both, would be killed, as well as hundreds of others. What sort of heartbreaking solution is that?

[*For a moment they are silent.*]

LANCELOT [*with quiet resignation*]

Forgive me, Jenny. I shall never mention it again. I swear. Nor shall I come to you again. I swear that, too.

[*He moves to leave.*]

GUENEVERE

Lance? [*He stops.*] Have we no more tender words to say to each other? [*She sings:*]

The silence at last was broken!
We flung wide our prison door.
Ev'ry joyous word of love was spoken . . .
And after all had been said,
Here we are, my love,
Silent once more
And not far, my love . . .
From where we were be . . .

[*He puts his arm around her tenderly. Five Knights and Mordred tiptoe silently into the room.*]

MORDRED [*quietly*]

Lancelot . . . Don't touch your dagger. [*Lancelot whirls around. Guenevere turns, horror-stricken.*] I accuse you of treason, and order you both to stand trial for your crime. Surrender in the name of the King.

[*Lancelot walks toward Mordred to surrender. Then*

*suddenly he leaps forward and snatches the sword from
Mordred's hand. For a second the Knights are too
startled to move. Mordred shrinks away in terror. Lancelot backs up, his sword held high menacingly, and with
his free hand, reaches for the outstretched hand of the
Queen. The Knights spread out slowly to surround him,
waiting for him to make the first move.]*

LANCELOT [*to Guenevere, without taking his
eyes off the Knights*]

If I escape, I shall come and rescue you. If I am killed,
send word to Joyous Gard. Someone will come.

[*Then he jumps at the Knights. They all freeze into a
tableau as*]

The Lights Dim Out Slowly

SCENE SEVEN.

*Scene: Camelot. Two towers rise into the air. The rest is
an endless blue.*

*At rise: A hooded figure appears. He sings. As he does,
the stage fills with similarly garbed figures, who slowly
move into one group beside the singer.*

THE SINGER

Out of the room, down the hall,
Through the yard, to the wall;
Slashing fiercely, left and right,
Lance escaped them and took flight.

On a day, dark and drear,
Came to trial Guenevere.
Ruled the jury for her shame
She be sentenced to the flame.

As the dawn filled the sky,
On the day she would die,
There was wonder far and near;
Would the King burn Guenevere?

[*Arthur enters forlornly and stands alone.*]

THE CHORUS

Would the King let her die?
Would the King let her die?
There was wonder far and near:
Would the King burn Guenevere?

[Mordred enters.]

MORDRED *[with wicked joy]*

Arthur! What a magnificent dilemma! Let her die, your
life is over; let her live, your life's a fraud. Which will
it be, Arthur? Do you kill the Queen or kill the law?

ARTHUR *[defiantly, resolutely, tragically]*

Treason has been committed! The jury has ruled! Let
justice be done.

[Mordred disappears.]

THE CHORUS

She must burn. She must burn.
Spoke the King: She must burn.
And the moment now was here
For the end of Guenevere.

*[Guenevere enters. She is accompanied by a priest,
carrying a cross, and two soldiers to guard her. She
approaches Arthur. She pauses and looks up at him.
He slowly turns and looks at her. Their eyes hold a
moment. She continues. She exits. But Arthur has
crumbled inside.]*

THE CHORUS

Slow her walk, bowed her head,
To the stake she was led . . .

[A Herald mounts the tower.]

THE HERALD

The Queen is at the stake, Your Majesty. Shall I signal
the torch? *[Arthur cannot answer. The Herald calls fran-
tically:]* Your Majesty . . . ! Your Majesty . . . ! *[But the
King has no answer.]*

THE CHORUS

In his grief, so alone
From the King came a moan . . .

[Mordred appears.]

ARTHUR

I can't! I can't! I can't let her die!

MORDRED

Well, you're human after all, aren't you, Arthur? Human
and helpless.

A SINGER

Then suddenly earth and sky were dazed by a pounding
  roar.
And suddenly through the dawn an army began to pour.
And lo! Ahead the army, holding aloft his spear,
Came Lancelot to save his dear
Guenevere!

ARTHUR [*crying out*]

Lance! Lance! Come save her.

HERALD [*desperately*]

Shall I signal the torch, Your Majesty?

DINADAN [*rushing in*]

Arthur, an army from Joyous Gard is storming the gate.
Shall I double the guard? [*Arthur shakes his head dazedly.*]
Arthur, you're inviting a massacre!

[*Dinadan rushes off.*]

ARTHUR

Save her, Lance! Save her!

THE CHORUS

  By the score fell the dead,
  As the yard turned to red.
  Countless numbers felt his spear
  As he rescued Guenevere.

MORDRED

Sweet heaven, what a sight! Can you see it from there,
Arthur? Can you see your goodly Lancelot murdering your
goodly Knights? Your table is cracking, Arthur. Can you
hear the timbers split?

ARTHUR [*in anguish*]

Merlyn! Merlyn, make me a hawk. Let me fly away from
here!

MORDRED [*with mad glee*]

What a failure you are, Arthur! How did you think you
could survive without being as ruthless as I?

ARTHUR

Merlyn! . . . Merlyn! . . .

THE CHORUS

  In that dawn, in that gloom,
  More than love met its doom.
  In the dying candles' gleam
  Came the sundown of a dream.

DINADAN [*entering*]

Most of the guard is killed, Arthur, and over eighty
Knights. They're heading for the Channel. I'll make ready

the army to follow. Arthur, we want revenge!
     [*Dinadan turns to leave. His face runs with blood.*]
                    ARTHUR [*broken*]
Oh, God, is it all to start again? Is my almighty fling at
peace to be over so soon? Am I back where I began? Am
I? Am I? [*Mordred screams with laughter and exits. Five
soldiers enter with the King's armor and sword. He stands
like a prisoner being shackled while they fasten his armor
to him.*]

                    THE CHORUS
     Guenevere, Guenevere!
     In that dim, mournful year,
     Saw the men she held most dear
     Go to war for Guenevere.

     Guenevere! Guenevere!
     Guenevere! Guenevere!
     Saw the men she held most dear
     Go to war for Guenevere!
     Guenevere! Guenevere! Guenevere!
          [*The sky turns red. More soldiers enter.*]

                The Lights Dim

          SCENE EIGHT.

     *Scene: A Battlefield outside Joyous Gard. Tents can be
seen in the distance, and there is one large tent downstage.*

     Time: Early dawn. A week later.

     *At rise: Arthur stands alone on the battlefield. Lancelot
appears in the shadows.*

                    LANCELOT
Jenny. He's here!
     [*Guenevere enters. She goes to Arthur. He turns to her.*]
                    ARTHUR
Was either of you injured in the escape?
                    LANCELOT
Untouched, Arthur.
                    GUENEVERE
Arthur, we want to return with you to England. No mat-

ter the cost, we must try to put things right.

LANCELOT

This war will do horrible harm to the Table, Arthur. We must stop it before it grows.

GUENEVERE

Let us pay for what we have done.

ARTHUR

At the stake? No! I won't take you back. I shan't let you return. For what end! Justice? They've forgotten justice. They want revenge! Revenge! That most worthless of causes. It's too late, Lance. The Table is dead. It exists no more.

GUENEVERE

What?

ARTHUR

Over half the Knights were killed in the yard. Mordred has fled to Orkney, taking some with him. I suppose to organize an army against me. The rest are waiting in their tents, itching for dawn, cheerful to be at war. It's the old uncivilized days come back again. Those dreadful days we all tried to put to sleep forever.

LANCELOT [*unbelievingly*]

It's your wish, Arthur, that this dread battle go on?

ARTHUR

No, it's not my wish, Lance. But I can think no longer what to do but ride the tide of events. Oh, what a blight thinking is. How I wish I'd never tried to think at all. All we've been through, for nothing but an idea! Something you cannot taste or touch, smell or feel; without substance, life, reality or memory. [*Trumpets sound in the distance.*] The charade begins soon. You must go back to Joyous Gard.

LANCELOT

Jenny is not at Joyous Gard, Arthur. She stays with the holy sisters. Is there nothing to be done?

ARTHUR

Nothing, but play out the game and leave the decisions to God. Now go. [*Lancelot goes to Arthur. They quietly and solemnly clasp arms. Lancelot pauses for a moment, and looks at Guenevere. Then, without a word, exits quickly.*] You must go, too, Jenny.

GUENEVERE

I know. So often in the past, Arthur, I would look up in your eyes, and there I would find forgiveness. Perhaps one

day in the future it shall be there again. But I won't be
with you. I won't know it. [*He holds out his arms. She goes
into them. As she withdraws, she looks up into his face.*]
Oh, Arthur, Arthur, I see what I wanted to see.

ARTHUR

Goodbye, my love . . . [*Guenevere exits, taking a different
path from Lancelot.*] . . . My dearest love. [*He stands for a
moment in silence. A rustling is heard behind the tent.*]
Who's there? Who's there? Come out, I say!

[*A young lad, about fourteen, appears from behind the
tent. His name is Tom.*]

TOM [*frightened*]

Forgive me, Your Majesty. I was searching for the Ser-
geant of Arms and got lost. I didn't wish to disturb you.

ARTHUR

Who are you, boy? Where did you come from? You
ought to be in bed. Are you a page?

TOM

I stowed away on one of the boats, Your Majesty. I came
to fight for the Round Table. I'm very good with the bow.

ARTHUR

And do you think you will kill people with this bow of
yours?

TOM

Oh yes, Milord. A great many, I hope.

ARTHUR

Suppose they kill you?

TOM

Then I shall be dead, Milord. But I don't intend to be
dead. I intend to be a Knight.

ARTHUR

A Knight . . . ?

TOM

Yes, Milord. Of the Round Table.

ARTHUR

When did you decide upon this nonexistent career? Was
your village protected by Knights when you were a small
boy? Was your mother saved by a Knight? Did your father
serve a Knight?

TOM

Oh, no, Milord. I had never seen a Knight until I stowed
away. I only know *of* them. The stories people tell.

ARTHUR

From the stories people tell you wish to be a Knight?

[*A strange light comes into his eyes.*] What do you think you know of the Knights and the Round Table?

TOM

I know everything, Milord. Might for right! Right for right! Justice for all! A Round Table where all Knights would sit. Everything!

[*Arthur walks away. Then suddenly he turns to the boy with a trembling inner excitement.*]

ARTHUR

Come here, my boy. Tell me your name.

TOM

It is Tom, Milord,

ARTHUR

Where is your home?

TOM

In Warwick, Milord.

ARTHUR

Then listen to me, Tom of Warwick. You will not fight in the battle, do you hear?

TOM [*disappointed*]

Yes, Milord.

ARTHUR

You will run behind the lines and hide in a tent till it is over. Then you will return to your home in England. Alive. To grow up and grow old. Do you understand?

TOM

Yes, Milord.

ARTHUR

And for as long as you live you will remember what I, the King, tell you; and you will do as I command.

TOM [*no longer disappointed*]

Yes, Milord.

ARTHUR [*sings:*]

Each evening from December to December
Before you drift to sleep upon your cot,
Think back on all the tales that you remember
Of Camelot.

Ask ev'ry person if he's heard the story;
And tell it strong and clear if he has not:
That once there was a fleeting wisp of glory
Called Camelot.

Camelot! Camelot!
Now say it out with love and joy!

TOM [*bursting with it*]

Camelot! Camelot!

ARTHUR [*his arm around the boy's shoulder*]

Yes, Camelot, my boy . . .

Where once it never rained till after sundown;

By eight A.M. the morning fog had flown . . .

Don't let it be forgot

That once there was a spot

For one brief shining moment that was known

As Camelot . . .

[*Pellinore enters carrying the Sword Excalibur.*]

PELLINORE

Arthur . . . ?

ARTHUR [*feverishly*]

Give me the sword.

PELLINORE [*handing it to him*]

Here.

ARTHUR

Kneel, Tom. Kneel. [*The boy does.*] With this sword, Excalibur, I knight you Sir Tom of Warwick. [*He touches the boy on each shoulder.*] And I command you to return home and carry out my orders.

TOM [*rising*]

Yes, Milord.

PELLINORE

What are you doing, Arthur? You have a battle to fight.

ARTHUR

Battle? I've won my battle, Pelly. Here's my victory! [*The music swells behind him.*] What we did will be remembered. You'll see, Pelly. Now, run, Sir Tom! Behind the lines!

TOM [*radiantly*]

Yes, Milord.   [*He runs off.*]

ARTHUR [*his eyes following the boy*]

Run, Sir Tom! Run boy! Through the lines!

PELLINORE

Who is that, Arthur?

ARTHUR

One of what we all are, Pelly. Less than a drop in the great blue motion of the sunlit sea. [*He smiles. There is jubilance in his voice.*] But it seems some of the drops sparkle, Pelly. Some of them do sparkle! Run, boy!

[*The music swells. He takes a firm grip on his sword and moves to exit, as*]

The Curtain Falls

Notes on "Idylls of the King"

THE COMING OF ARTHUR

1. *Cameliard:* legendary realm.

9. *harried:* pillaged.

13. *Aurelius:* ancestor of the last Roman emperor of Britain.

14. *King Uther:* Uther Pendragon, Arthur's father.

17. *puissance:* power. *Table Round:* King Arthur's celebrated board around which he and his knights discussed affairs of state. The table was so shaped to prevent quarrels over precedence. The actual size of the board is indefinite, but the one at the castle of Winchester in England, reputed to have been King Arthur's, is 18 feet in diameter. One legend has it that the Round Table was built by Joseph of Arimathaea, who brought the Holy Grail to Britain (see "The Holy Grail," ll. 46–53), and was later acquired by Uther, Arthur's father. According to another legend, the table was fashioned by Merlin, Arthur's great teacher.

35. *Caesar's eagle:* symbol of the Roman armies.

36. *Urien:* King of North Wales.

50. *golden symbol:* dragon.

96. *pavilions:* tents.

124–5. *warrior whom he loved/And honour'd most:* Lancelot.

130. *warded:* protected.

141. *holp:* helped.

169. *Gorloïs:* First husband of Arthur's mother, Ygerne.

170. *Anton:* Arthur's foster father who raised him from infancy; he is also known as Sir Ector.

189. *Orkney:* kingdom in northern Scotland. *Bellicent:* Arthur's half sister; also known as Morgause. She is variously depicted in Arthurian literature as both good and evil.

In Malory, Arthur unknowingly sires Modred with her—a rather disastrous mistake.

212. *postern-gate:* back gate.

243. *Modred:* Arthur's chief nemesis.

252. *enow:* enough.

273. *casement:* window.

274. *vert and azure:* green and blue.

279. *Mage:* magician.

284. *samite:* heavy, rich silk fabric.

288. *minster:* church.

294. *Excalibur:* Arthur's miraculous sword given him by the mysterious Lady of the Lake. It is sometimes identified with the sword Arthur pulled from the stone to prove his royal blood and claim to the throne of Britain.

298. *elfin Urim, on the hilt:* oracular ornaments on the handle of his sword. The Jewish priests of Biblical times wore such ornaments on their breastplates.

307. *brand:* sword.

362. *changeling:* a child secretly exchanged for another in infancy. The act was often thought to be the practice of witches.

386. *strand:* shore.

400. *wont:* habit, custom.

432. *rick:* a pile of grain or hay.

450–1. *and return'd/Among the flowers:* The Queen revealingly relates her feelings of her first encounter with Lancelot in "Guinevere," ll. 375–404.

MERLIN AND VIVIEN

2. *Broceliande:* legendary forest in Brittany, region in northwest France.

5. *Vivien:* also known as Nimue.

7. *Mark:* King of Cornwall, region in southwest England. Mark is the husband of Isolt and the uncle of Tristram, the two famous lovers of medieval romance.

9. *Caerleon:* village of Monmouthshire on the river Usk. It is one of the places where Arthur is said to have held court. Sometimes it is identified with Camelot. Tennyson resided here for a time while writing the *Idylls.*

10. *Tintagil:* town in Cornwall.

42. *father:* King Pellinore. In *Camelot* he is the loyal and amusing knight who spends his time chasing about after the Questing Beast.

73. *Lyonnesse:* region west of Cornwall, now under the sea.

117. *lubber:* clumsy.

123. *seeling:* blinding a hawk, done by sewing the eyelids closed. *jesses:* short straps secured about the legs of a hawk.

125. *rake:* fly after game.

133. *quarry:* prey.

139. *Leaven'd:* changed.

200. *Breton sands:* shore of Brittany.

223. *sallows:* willows.

248. *arras:* tapestry.

374. *rood:* crucifix.

376. *bided tryst:* awaited a secret meeting with her love. *stile:* steps for passing over a fence or wall.

424. *roundel:* lyric.

474. *dexter:* the right side.

477. *graff:* a ditch.

485. *prurient:* restlessly craving.

552. *guerdon:* reward.

558. *peep:* first appearance.

567. *impaled:* tortured on a sharp stake.

605. *Wroth:* indignant.

636. *cairn'd:* rocky.

654. *whelm:* crush.

707. *reckling:* one to be cared for.

748. *wether:* a castrated ram.

751. *Hic Jacets:* Latin, "Here lies . . .", used in epitaphs.

792. *leal:* loyal.

796. *poach'd:* trampled.

821. *tithes:* tenths.

822. *backbiter:* slanderer.

899. *cageling:* bird confined in a cage.

934. *furrowing:* cutting through. *javelining:* spearing.

LANCELOT AND ELAINE

2. *Astolat:* region, perhaps in Surrey.

7. *soilure:* stain.

9. *blazon'd:* depicted.

10. *tinct:* tint.

31. *jousts:* tournaments.

36. *tarn:* small mountain lake.

37. *clave:* clung.

44. *lichen'd:* covered with fungus.

53. *shingly scaur:* coarse, rocky hillside.

76. *this world's hugest:* London.

106. *mead:* meadow.

118. *devoir:* duty.

162. *downs:* hills.

196. *wot:* knows.

243. *lineaments:* lines and features of the face.

279. *Badon hill:* said to be the scene of Arthur's last great battle against the heathens.

293. *cuirass:* armor. *Lady's Head:* head of the Virgin Mary.

297. *white Horse:* insignia worn by the Saxon invaders.

298. *parapet:* protective wall.

338. *rathe:* early in the day.

410. *wending:* traveling.

446. *crescent:* young and growing.

518. *stanch'd:* stopped the flow of blood.

643. *sallying:* lively.

739. *wormwood:* bitter herb.

766. *wit:* know.

767. *fain:* glad.

787. *caper and curvet:* prance and leap.

800. *casque:* helmet.

953. *realm beyond the seas:* territory in France. In *Camelot* Lancelot's castle is referred to as Joyous Gard.

1093. *shrive:* make confession.

1135. *Pall'd:* clothed.

1170. *oriel:* large bay window.

1178. *cygnet:* young swan.

1253. *girt:* surrounded.

1324. *obsequies:* burial ceremonies.

1346. *affiance:* faith.

1400. *dusky mere:* marsh or gloomy lake.

THE HOLY GRAIL

5. *cowl:* monk's hood.

21. *pale:* enclosure of the cloister.

31. *Holy Grail:* The Grail was the cup from which Christ drank at the Last Supper. According to other sources, it was the vessel which received the blood of

Christ at the Crucifixion. It has been variously described as a cup, a platter, a stone, a sword, and a lance. Several scholars have traced the Grail legend back to ancient fertility and nature cults.

32. *vainglories:* excessive pride.

48. *Aromat:* Arimathaea.

50. *Moriah:* name for Biblical hill of eastern Jerusalem, the site of Solomon's temple.

51. *Arimathaean Joseph:* It is said that he founded England's first Christian Church at Glastonbury.

52. *Glastonbury:* town in Somersetshire.

54. *bode:* remained.

61. *Arviragus:* legendary king of Britain.

63. *wattles:* twigs.

144. *a son of Lancelot:* According to Malory, Galahad is Lancelot's son by Elaine, the daughter of King Pelles.

172. *'The Siege perilous':* the dangerous seat.

211. *Red-rent:* scratched and bloody.

233. *gird:* encircled.

300. *Taliessin:* one of the great books of Welsh poetry said to have been written in the sixth century by the bard, Taliessin.

350. *wyvern:* mythological two-legged winged creature, having the head of a dragon. *griffin:* mythological monster which is half lion and half eagle.

427. *clomb:* climbed.

453. *gray-hair'd wisdom of the east:* the three wise men who came to adore the baby Jesus.

462. *sacring of the mass:* consecration at Holy Mass.

545. *breviary:* prayer book.

547. *thorpe:* village.

548. *martin's nest:* swallow's nest.

558. *Chafferings:* bargainings.

569. *eft:* lizard.

570. *burdock:* type of prickly plant.

661. *Paynim:* heathens.

679. *scud:* clouds.

715. *basilisks:* mythological reptiles whose breath was fatal. *cockatrices:* mythological serpents with a deadly glance; similar to the basilisks.

716. *talbots:* hunting hounds of ancient times.

750. *Athwart:* across.

759. *Cana:* ancient town of Galilee where Jesus performed his first miracle by turning water into wine.

767. *welter:* bathe.

808. *shingle:* coarse gravel found on a beach. *surge:* waves.

809. *shock:* hit hard against.

810. *Carbonek:* enchanted castle which housed the Grail.

892. *My greatest:* Lancelot.

893. *Another hath beheld it afar off:* Percivale.

896. *one hath had the vision face to face:* Galahad.

902. *hind:* farmhand.

PELLEAS AND ETTARRE

11. *circlet:* crown.

48. *hoary boles:* aged tree trunks.

53. *trapt:* adorned.

54. *bracken:* fern.

61. *damsels-errant:* wandering ladies.

90. *marge:* shore.

113. *peradventure:* possibly.

157. *Usk:* river in Wales and England.

188. *papmeat:* soft food for infants.

196. *hest:* command.

207. *priory:* monastery.

227. *minion:* dependent.

234. *donjon:* chief tower in ancient castles.

258. *fulsome:* offensive.

261. *reck:* care.

272. *caitiffs:* base, despicable people.

283. *craven:* coward.

293. *liefer:* more willingly.

309. *lazar's rag:* leper's clothing.

328. *thrall:* enslave.

333. *troth:* faith.

341. *prime to vespers:* morning to evening prayers.

421. *lurdane:* lazy and stupid.

437. *dishallow:* violate.

462. *dung and nettles:* prickly, stinging plants.

476. *rowel:* spur.

566. *disedge:* blunt, dull.

585. *unfrowardly:* compliantly.

590. *quail'd:* shrank back.

GUINEVERE

4. *novice:* a nun who has not yet taken the vows.

11. *couchant:* lying down, but with the head raised.

15. *Lords of the White Horse:* Saxons who remained in Britain.

16. *Hengist:* the Saxon leader.

32. *colewort:* cabbage.

126. *Almesbury:* Amesbury, town in Wiltshire; site of a nunnery and of Stonehenge.

127. *weald:* woodland.

147. *housel:* receiving Holy Communion. *shrift:* confession.

163. *list:* incline.

239. *beacon-star:* warning signal.

241. *headland:* high point of land projecting into the sea.

266. *spigot:* peg used to stop the vent in a cask. *butts:* wine casks.

279. *lay:* song.

289. *Bude and Bos:* places along the coast of Cornwall.

311. *gadding:* rambling.

421. *no child is born of thee:* Little mention is ever made of Guinevere's barrenness, a fact which must have given her additional cause for despair. In Tennyson's idyll, "The Last Tournament," she is presented by Arthur with a foundling. At first she holds back her affection, but gradually she comes to love the child with a great deal of tenderness, only to have the baby die in infancy.

485. *Tristram and Isolt:* There are several versions of this very popular story. Tristram, the nephew of King Mark of Cornwall, and Isolt, Mark's wife, fall hopelessly in love with each other through the effects of a potion they unwittingly swallow. The course of their tragic affair is stormy and strife-ridden, full of secret meetings, estrangements, and ending with the death of the lovers. In Tennyson, Mark, upon finding the lovers together, sneaks up behind Tristram and cleaves open his head.

487. *ensample:* example.

535. *the flaming death:* penalty for a wife's infidelity in the Middle Ages.

554. *I was ever virgin:* Tennyson is one of the few

writers of Arthurian legend who represent Arthur so chastely.

570. *My sister's son:* Modred.

677. *dole:* alms.

688. *ministration:* preaching of God's worship.

THE PASSING OF ARTHUR

26. *Reels back into the beast:* See "The Coming of Arthur," ll. 5–33.

77. *One lying in the dust at Almesbury:* Guinevere.

78. *folded in the passes:* concealed the passages and roads.

82. *upheaven:* thrown up.

107. *host to host:* army to army.

108. *hard mail:* fabric of interwoven metal rings used as protective armor. *hewn:* cut through.

109. *brands:* swords.

177. *chancel:* part of the church reserved for the use of the clergy.

182. *unsolders:* breaks apart.

224. *haft:* handle.

225. *jacinth:* a precious sapphire-like stone.

231. *waterflags:* leafy plants.

272. *lonely maiden of the Lake:* mysterious Lady of the Lake. See "The Coming of Arthur," ll. 282–93.

303. *bulrush beds:* beds of reeds.

313. *brandish'd:* waved.

353. *goad:* rod used to urge on an animal.

354. *harness:* armor.

358. *dint:* force.

361. *hove:* stood.

366. *Three Queens:* See "The Coming of Arthur," ll. 275–8.

383–4. *his greaves and cuisses dash'd with drops/Of onset:* his knee armor and thigh armor covered with blood from the battle.

400–1. *Such times have been not since the light that led/The holy Elders:* Such times have not been since the birth of Christ, when the three Wise Men came from the East, guided by the star of Bethlehem.

401. *myrrh:* aromatic herb.

427. *Avilion:* legendary island, sometimes called "Island of the Blessed"; also spelled "Avalon."

434. *brink:* edge.